AF538547

AGRICULTURE AND ENVIRONMENTAL BIOTECHNOLOGY

AGRICULTURE
AND
ENVIRONMENTAL BIOTECHNOLOGY

Edited by

Dr. Pawan Kumar 'Bharti'
Centre for Agro-Rural Technologies (CART-India)
20, Jamaalpur Man, Raja Ka Tajpur
Bijnore (UP) - 246 735 (India)
E-mail: gurupawanbharti@rediffmail.com

&

Dr. Avnish Chauhan
Department of Applied Science
Phonics Group of Institutions
Roorkee, Haridwar (Uttarakhand)
(India)

Associate Editor

Mr. Jaswant Ray
Department of Zoology
Mewar University
Chittorgarh - 312 901 (Rajasthan)
(India)

DISCOVERY PUBLISHING HOUSE PVT. LTD.
NEW DELHI-110 002

Published by:
Tilak Wasan
DISCOVERY PUBLISHING HOUSE PVT. LTD.
4383/4B, Ansari Road, Darya Ganj
New Delhi-110 002 (India)
Phone : +91-11-23279245, 43596064-65
Fax : +91-11-23253475
E-mail : discoverypublishinghouse@gmail.com
sales@discoverypublishinggroup.com
parul.wasan@gmail.com
web : www.discoverypublishinggroup.com

First Edition: **2014**

ISBN: 978-93-5056-479-0

Agriculture and Environmental Biotechnology

Printed at:
Aditi Fine Art Press
Delhi

Preface

Present day we are facing excessive pollution caused by industrialized agriculture where variety of chemical fertilizers and pesticides belongs to diverse chemical class are being used. Hence, these chemical fertilizers and pesticides have emerged as indispensible tool in modern agriculture. Their residue is contaminating the environment, hampers the balance of the eco-system and pesticides also destroy predator and parasites of the target organisms, leading to the reduction of beneficial species. They contaminate the ground water by leaching. Pesticides enter the food chain and lead to bio-magnification as their residues are found on fruits and vegetables.

Because of intensive crop production practices with excessive use of agrochemicals, agricultural lands worldwide have become vulnerable to degradative processes. Chemical-based, conventional agricultural has created many sources of pollution that can contribute to degradation of the environment and destruction of our natural resource base directly or indirectly. Problems such as soil erosion, nutrient depletion and loss of organic matter, decline in soil productivity, contamination of surface and ground water, non target effect on natural enemies & beneficial microbes are associated with agrochemicals. Moreover, their residue when enter in food chain through fruits and vegetables leads to bio-magnification of residue. Consequently, there has been a growing public concern about adverse impacts of agrochemicals on agriculture, environment and on the safety and quality of food.

Strategies for increasing diversified agricultural productivity on sustainable basis have become imperative because of its role in poverty scale-up and economic development. Agriculture is expected to continue to be the engine of economic growth and other numerous ancillary benefits, by being increasingly more productive and more efficient to meet the needs of an increasing population but has often been plagued by climate, ecological, and socio-economic problems; weak institutional policy reforms and poor infrastructure for crop production, handling, and marketing, thus causing fluctuations in food availability, hunger as well as adverse effect on economies.

Water resources are not distributed evenly in space or time around the world. Global circulation patterns create wet and dry climate zones, and in some regions seasonal or multi-annual climate cycles generate distinct wet and dry phases. Although developed nations generally have more water available than many countries in Africa and the Middle East, some areas with good water endowments still are subject to 'water stress' because they are withdrawing water from available supplies at extremely high rates. High-intensity water uses in industrialized nations include agricultural production and electric power generation, which requires large quantities of water for cooling. In the United States electric power production accounts for 39% of freshwater withdrawals, although almost all of this water is immediately returned to the rivers from which it is withdrawn. Agriculture requires much more water because irrigation increases transpiration to the atmosphere.

This book provides comprehensive coverage of the fundamental principles and current practices and trends in the field of agriculture ecology and environmental biotechnology.

This book updates the subject matter, illustrations and problems to incorporate new concepts and issues related to agriculture, ecology, environment and biotechnology.

Particularly thanks are due to all contributors from Egypt, Nigeria, India; and publisher also for their contribution and assistance.

I hope this book will be of benefit to both present and future colleagues, who teach, study and working in the field of environment, ecology, environmental pollution, agriculture and biotechnology.

Dr. Pawan Kumar 'Bharti'
(*gurupawanbharti@rediffmail.com*)

Contents

Tree as Bio-Indicator of Automobile Pollution in Dehradun City
A Case Study

Avnish Chauhan

ABSTRACT

The plant species selected for the study were *Ficus religiosa*, *Mangifera indica*, *Polyalthia longifolia*, *Delonix regia*. Reduction in chlorophyll *'a'*, chlorophyll *'b'*, total chlorophyll content, ascorbic acid, carotenoid, pH, relative water content and APTI was recorded in the leaf samples of all selected trees collected from polluted site when compared with samples from control area. The data obtained were further analyzed by using two-way ANOVA and also obtained significant changes in all these parameters was found in the leaf samples collected from polluted site trees, exposed to automobile exhaust in comparison to control site.

There was maximum (43.36%) reduction of chlorophyll *'a'* content in the leaves of *Ficus religiosa* and minimum (26.57%) reduction was in the *Mangifera indica*, while maximum (30.99%) carotenoid was depleted in *Polyalthia longifolia* and minimum (18.42%) depleted in *Mangifera indica* at polluted site as compared to control site. The maximum (44.67%) reduction of ascorbic acid was observed in the leaves of *Delonix regia* and minimum (22.93%) reduction was observed in the leaves of *Polyalthia longifolia*.

Keywords: Air Quality Index, Bioindicator, Chlorophyll, APTI, Automobile pollution.

Department of Applied Science, Phonics Group of Institutions, Roorkee, Haridwar (Uttarakhand), India.

INTRODUCTION

Changes in the gaseous composition of earth's atmosphere have become a prime concern for today's world due to human activities. Urban air pollution poses a significant threat to animal, plants and human health, is receiving attention as a growing share of the world's population is now living in urban centers and demanding a clearance urban environment. India and other developing countries have experienced a progressive degradation in air quality due to industrialization, urbanization, lack of awareness, number of motor vehicles, use of fuels with poor environmental performance, badly maintained poor roads and ineffective environmental regulations [11]. Most of the cities located in Northern India are afflicted with the presence of unusually high concentration of air pollutants viz. SO_2, NO_x, SPM and RSPM. Studies on the impact of automobile pollution on plant response have attracted much interest. Urban vegetation can directly and indirectly affect local and regional air quality by altering the urban atmosphere. Trees remove gaseous air pollution by leaf stomata and particles by intercepting.

Urban air pollution has become a serious environmental problem to trees and crops [4]. Motor vehicles account for 60-70% of the pollution found in urban environment [1], followed by industries (20-30 %) in India. Trees experience the greatest exposure and influenced greatly by pollutant concentration due to their perennial habit [21]. Regional impact of air pollution on local plant species is one of the major ecological issues. The climate conditions, the physico-chemical properties of air pollutants and their residence time in the atmosphere have the impact on surrounding plants and animals [28]. Presence of trees in the urban environment can thus improve air quality through enhancing the upper of gases and particles [16, 31]. Trees act as a sink of air pollutants and this reduce their concentrations in the air [19].

Chlorophyll itself is actually not a single molecule but a family of related molecules, designated chlorophyll *'a'*, *'b'*, *'c'*, and *'d'*. Chlorophyll *'a'* is the molecule found in all plant cells and therefore its concentration is what is reported during chlorophyll analysis. Accessory pigments absorb energy that chlorophyll *'a'* does not absorb. Accessory pigments include chlorophyll *'b'*, xanthophylls and carotenoid [11].The present investigation has been carried out to determine the effects of automobile exhaust on photosynthetic pigments such as chlorophyll *'a'*, *'b'*, total chlorophyll, carotenoid, ascorbic acid, relatively humidity, pH and APTI (Air pollution tolerance index) trees grown at the famous Clock Tower of Dehradun and also plants from pollution free atmosphere. All these parameters at polluted site were compared with control site.

MATERIALS AND METHODS

Study Sites

Polluted site was located at roundabout of famous Clock Tower in Dehradun which is the most busy roundabout in Dehradun city and traffic jam condition prevalent here throughout the day, posses a high number of two wheelers, three wheelers and four wheelers. While the control site was located at Tarla Nagal village, Sahastradhara Road, Dehradun. The control site was situated about 11 kms away from polluted site where pollution level is almost very low, posse's very dense forest and vegetations covers.

Air pollutants (SO_2, NO_x, SPM and RSPM) monitoring data at polluted site was obtained from State Pollution Control Board, Dehradun. However at the control site the concentration of air pollutants was measured with the help of RDS APM 460 by sucking air into appropriate reagent for 24 hours at every 30 days and after air monitoring it procured into lab and analysis for the concentration level. The SPM and RSPM were analyzed using Respirable Dust Sampler (RDS) APM 460 and operated at an average flow rate of 1.0-1.5 $m^3\ min^{-1}$. Preweighed glass fiber filters (GF/A) of Whatman were used as per standard methods. SO_2 and NO_x were collected by bubbling the sample in a specific absorbing (sodium tetrachloromercuate of SO_2 and sodium hydroxide for NO_x) solution at an average flow rate of 0.2-0.5 min^{-1}.

The impinger samples were put in ice boxes immediately after sampling and transferred to a refrigerator until analyzed. The concentration of NO_x was measured with standard method of Modified Jacobs- Hochheiser method [10], SO_2 was measured by Modified West and Geake method [30], SPM and RSPM using filter paper methods. The apparatus was kept at a height of 2 m from the surface of the ground. Using air pollutants data the air quality index was calculated. Leaves samples collected from both polluted and control sites. All the plants were matured and well aged. The fresh leaf samples collected from trees (about 5-8 feet height from ground level).

The chlorophyll *'a'*, chlorophyll *'b'* and total chlorophyll were measured as per standard method of Maclachlan and Zalik [17]. Carotenoid was determined by the method of Duxbury and Yentsch [8]. Ascorbic acid was determined by the method of Sadashivam and Manikam [23]. Ten samples of each of the tree species were analyzed on each sampling date. Similarly replicate samples and analytical blank were also analyzed to check the reliability of data. Relative moisture content by Weatherly [29] and Air pollution tolerance index (APTI) was estimated using the method of Singh and Rao [24]. Leaf samples of selected trees were collected fortnightly during the study period from the Clock Tower (Polluted site) and 11 km far away from the control site. These were weighed in a single pan electric balance (0.01mg accuracy) for measuring the dust content and then thoroughly washed with double distilled water for further analysis. AQI (air quality index) is then calculated with the concentration values using the following equation [22].

$$AQI = 1/3\ [(SO_2)/Sso_2 + (NO_x)/S_{NOX} + SPM/S_{SPM}] \times 100$$

The assessment studies were conducted on *Ficus religiosa, Mangifera indica, Polyalthia longifolia* and *Delonix regia* during 2008-2009.

RESULTS

Concentrations of Primary Pollutants

The concentration of primary pollutants recorded has been presented in table 1.1. Concentration of NO_x at polluted site was 26.68, 27.02 and 27.92 μgm^{-3} during winter, monsoon and summer, respectively, At control site it was reported as 1.69, 1.60 and 1.93 μgm^{-3} during winter, monsoon and summer, respectively, whereas the standard limit prescribed by Central Pollution Control Board, New Delhi (CPCB) is 80 μgm^{-3} for residential and rural areas. SO_2 recorded at polluted site was 25.29, 25.14 and 26.61 μgm^{-3} during winter, monsoon and summer, respectively, while at the control site it was reported as 2.29, 1.98 and 2.16 μgm^{-3} during the same period. Whereas the standard limit prescribed by CPCB, New Delhi of India is 80 μgm^{-3} for residential area.

The highest concentration (285.47 μgm^{-3}) of SPM was recorded during summer reason at polluted site, while the lowest concentration (199.04 μgm^{-3}) was recorded during the monsoon. The highest concentration (137.50 μgm^{-3}) of RSPM was recorded during summer season at polluted site while the lowest concentration (89.93 μgm^{-3}) was recorded during monsoon season at polluted site. The standard limits for SPM and RSPM was 200 and 100 μgm^{-3}, respectively. It is clear from above results that concentration of gaseous pollutants (SO_2 and NO_x) remained under standard limit of CPCB, however, SPM and RSPM were higher than the standard limits of CPCB, New Delhi. Using the table 1.1 the Air Quality Index (AQI) values were calculated, presented in table 1.2.

The high value (70.30) of AQI observed during summer at polluted site, whereas the lowest concentration (54.91) was recorded during the monsoon at polluted site. Polluted site was termed under the categories "Moderate Air Pollution" (MAP), while the control site was termed under the categories of "Clean Air" (CA). Polluted site is very very busy road which bears high number of scooters, motor cycles, three wheelers, cars, buses. As polluted site bears very high traffic volumes and there is traffic jams condition because roads are narrow at two side of Clock Tower roundabout. The higher concentrations of SO_2, NO_x, SPM and RSPM were observed during the study period at polluted site in Haridwar, it may be due to plying of petrol and diesel vehicles [3].

It has been reported that heavy diesel vehicles emitted 24 times (empirically) more fine particulates than light duty gasoline powered vehicles [13]. Chauhan and Joshi [5] found that the concentration of SO_2 and NO_x was under the standard limit of CPCB while the concentration of SPM was higher than the standard limit of CPCB, New Delhi in urban and industrial areas of Haridwar.

Table 1.1: Primary Air Pollutants Recorded from Control and Polluted Sites during the Study Period

Site	NO_x μgm^{-3}			SO_2 μgm^{-3}			SPM μgm^{-3}			RSPM μgm^{-3}			Air Quality Index (AQI)		
	W	M	S	W	M	S	W	M	S	W	M	S	W	M	S
P	26.68	27.02	27.92	25.29	25.14	26.61	276.11	199.04	285.47	128.02	89.93	137.50	67.80	54.91	70.30
C	1.69	1.60	1.93	1.69	1.60	1.93	92.23	82.14	76.19	34.41	35.80	36.04	17.03	15.18	14.40
	80.00 $\mu g\ m^{-3}$			80.00 $\mu g\ m^{-3}$			200.00 $\mu g\ m^{-3}$			100.00 $\mu g\ m^{-3}$			CPCB standard(24 hr)		

Where: SPM = Suspended particulate matte, RSPM = Respirable suspended particulate matter, W= Winter, M= Monsoon, S= Summer, CPCB= Central Pollution Control Board, New Delhi, India.

Table 1.2: Rating Scale of AQI Values at Polluted and Control Sites

Index Value	Remarks	Polluted Site			Control Site		
0-25	Clean air (CA)	Winter	Monsoon	Summer	Winter	Monsoon	Summer
26-50	Light air pollution (LAP)	MAP	MAP	MAP	CA	CA	CA
51-75	Moderate air pollution (MAP)						
76-100	Heavy air pollution (HAP)						
>100	Severe air pollution (SAP)						

Where: W= Winter, M= Monsoon, S= Summer

Chlorophyll Pigments

Variations in physiological characteristics of the selected tree species exposed to ambient air pollutants are given in table 1.3.

Chlorophyll *a* and *b* contents in the leaf samples of *Ficus religiosa* were reported as 1.43±0.08 and 1.13±0.05 mg gm^{-1} at control site whereas these were 0.81±0.06 and 0.61±0.05 mg gm^{-1} respectively, at polluted sites. A decrease of 43.36% in chlorophyll *a* and 46.02% in chlorophyll *b* was recorded at polluted site in comparison to control site. Total chlorophyll content recorded for *Ficus religiosa* was 2.56±0.48 and 1.42±0.09 mg gm^{-1} at control and polluted sites, respectively.

Chlorophyll *a* and *b* contents of *Mangifera indica* were reported as 2.71±0.07 and 2.03±0.09 mg gm^{-1} at control site and 1.99±0.05 and 1.63±0.12 mg gm^{-1} at polluted sites, respectively. A decrease of 26.57% and 19.70% was thus recorded in chlorophyll *a* and *b* contents at polluted site, respectively. Total chlorophyll content recorded at control and polluted sites was 4.74±1.22 and 3.62±0.58 mg gm^{-1}, respectively. There was a reduction of 23.63% in the total chlorophyll content in the leaf samples from the polluted site as compared to control site.

Chlorophyll *a* and *b* contents of *Polyalthia longifolia* were reported as 1.33±0.17 and 0.84±0.12 mg gm^{-1} at control and 0.96±0.44 and 0.59±0.06 mg gm^{-1} at polluted site, respectively. A decrease of 36.84% and 38.54% was recorded in chlorophyll *a* and *b* at polluted site, respectively. Total chlorophyll content recorded at polluted site for *Polyalthia longifolia* was 2.17±0.22 and it was 1.55±0.28 mg gm^{-1} at control site, a reduction of 28.57% in the total chlorophyll content of plant samples from polluted site as compared to control site was recorded.

Chlorophyll *a* and *b* contents of *Delonix regia* were reported as 1.64±0.11 and 1.01± 0.15 mg gm^{-1} at control site and 1.04±0.11 and 0.76±0.14 mg gm^{-1} at polluted sites, respectively, with a decrease of 38.41% and 26.92% in chlorophyll *a* and *b*, respectively. Total chlorophyll content recorded at control site was 2.65±0.14 mg gm^{-1} which was 1.81±0.12 mg gm^{-1} at polluted site, thus in this case there was reduction of 31.70% at the polluted site as compared to control site.

Carotenoid and Ascorbic Acid

Carotenoid contents of *Ficus religiosa* recorded at control and polluted site were 1.49±0.14 and 1.03±0.07 mg per gm, respectively. A decrease of 30.87% was thus recorded in the amount of carotenoid in the polluted site as compared to control site. Ascorbic acid content recorded was 1.50±0.11 and 0.83±0.07 mg per 100 gm at control and polluted sites, respectively. In this case there was a reduction of 44.67% in ascorbic acid content of samples collected from polluted site as compared to control site.

Table 1.3: Changes in the Physical and Bio-chemical Characteristics of Tree Species due to Auto Exhaust Emission

Parameters	*Ficus religiosa*		*Mangifera indica*		*Polyalthia longifolia*		*Delonix regia*	
	Control Site	Polluted Site	Control Site	Polluted Site	Control Site	Polluted Site	Control Site	Polluted Site
Chlorophyll *a* (mg/g)	1.43 ± 0.08	0.81 ± 0.06***	2.71 ± 0.07	1.99 ± 0.05***	1.33 ± 0.17	0.96 ± 0.44***	1.64 ± 0.11	1.04 ± 0.11***
Chlorophyll *b* (mg/g)	1.13 ± 0.05	0.61 ± 0.05***	2.03 ± 0.09	1.63 ± 0.12***	0.84 ± 0.12	0.59 ± 0.06***	1.01 ± 0.15	0.76 ± 0.14***
Total Chlorophyll (mg/g)	2.56 ± 0.48	1.42 ± 0.09***	4.74 ± 1.22	3.62 ± 0.58***	2.17 ± 0.22	1.55 ± 0.28***	2.65 ± 0.14	1.81 ± 0.12***
Carotenoid (mg/gm)	1.49 ± 0.14	1.03 ± 0.06***	2.66 ± 0.12	2.17 ± 0.19***	1.42 ± 0.14	0.98 ± 0.16***	1.30 ± 0.08	0.90 ± 0.06***
Ascorbic Acid (mg/100gm)	1.50 ± 0.11	0.83 ± 0.07***	2.10 ± 0.11	1.57 ± 0.11***	1.34 ± 0.09	1.04 ± 0.09***	1.49 ± 0.09	0.91 ± 0.10***
Relative moisture content (%)	68.97 ± 4.33	55.98 ± 4.61***	66.99 ± 3.17	52.03 ± 3.99***	58.50 ± 2.86	48.12 ± 3.77***	70.56 ± 4.15	59.12 ± 4.16***
Dust deposited (mg/leaf)	0.10 ± 0.02	0.46 ± 0.02**	0.09 ± 0.02	0.53 ± 0.02***	0.08 ± 0.02	0.43 ± 0.05**	0.08 ± 0.04	0.39 ± 0.06*
pH	7.59 ± 0.13	6.43 ± 0.21***	6.93 ± 0.22	6.01 ± 0.23***	6.47 ± 0.13	5.73 ± 0.22***	6.92 ± 0.37	5.64 ± 0.29***
APTI	8.39 ± 0.17	6.25 ± 0.18***	9.15 ± 0.11	6.71 ± 0.14***	7.01 ± 0.13	5.57 ± 0.18***	8.48 ± 0.17	6.59 ± 0.28***

Significant at: $^{*}p < 0.05$, $^{**}p<0.01$, $^{***}p<0.001$, APTI= Air Pollution Tolerance Index

Carotenoid of *Mangifera indica* recorded at control and polluted sites were 2.66±0.12 and 2.17±0.19 mg per gm, respectively. A decrease of 18.42% was thus recorded in the amount of carotenoid in the polluted site as compared to control. Ascorbic acid content recorded was 2.10±0.11 and 1.57±0.11 mg per 100 gm at control and polluted sites, respectively. In this case there was a reduction of 25.24% in ascorbic acid content of samples collected from polluted site as compared to control.

Carotenoid of *Polyalthia longifolia* recorded at control site was 1.42±0.14 and 0.98±0.16 mg per gm at polluted site. A decrease of 30.99% was thus recorded in the amount of carotenoid in the polluted site as compared to control. Ascorbic acid content recorded was 1.34±0.09 and 1.04±0.09 mg per 100 gm at control and polluted sites, respectively. In this case there was a reduction of 22.39% in ascorbic acid content of samples collected from polluted site as compared to control site.

Carotenoid of *Delonix regia* was recorded at control and polluted sites were 1.30±0.08 and 0.90±0.06 mg per gm, respectively. A decrease of 30.78% was thus recorded in the amount of carotenoid in the polluted site as compared to control site. Ascorbic acid content recorded was 1.49±0.09 and 0.91±0.10 mg per 100 gm at control and polluted sites, respectively. In this case there was a reduction of 38.93% in ascorbic acid content of samples collected from polluted site as compared to control site.

Relative Moisture Content, Dust Content, pH and APTI

Relative moisture content of *Ficus religiosa* leaves collected from control site was 68.97±4.33% while it was 55.98±4.61% at polluted site. Thus there was a reduction of 18.83% in relative moisture content of samples collected from polluted site as compared to control. Amount of dust deposited on leaves was higher (0.46±0.02 mg per leaf) in polluted site in comparison to control site (0.10±0.02 mg per leaf). pH of leaves of control site was recorded as 7.59±0.13, where as pH of leaves sampled form polluted site was recorded as 6.43±0.21. Thus a change of 15.28% toward the acidic side was recorded in the samples collected from polluted site. Air pollution tolerance index of *Ficus religiosa* was determined as 8.39±0.17 and 6.25±0.18 at control and polluted sites, respectively.

Relative moisture content of *Mangifera indica* leaves was higher (22.33%) in the plant samples collected from control site as compared to samples collected from polluted site. Amount of dust deposited on leaves was higher (0.53±0.02 mg per leaf) in polluted site in comparison to control site (0.09±0.01 mg per leaf). pH of leaves of control site was recorded as 6.93±0.22, where as pH of leaves sampled form polluted site was recorded as 6.01±0.23. Thus a change of 13.28% toward the acidic side was recorded in the samples collected from polluted site. Air pollution tolerance index of *Mangifera indica* was determined as 9.15±0.11 and 6.71±0.14 polluted site.

Relative moisture content *Polyalthia longifolia* was higher by 17.74% in the plant samples collected from control site. The amount of dust deposited on leaves was higher (0.43±0.05 mg per leaf) in polluted site in comparison to control site (0.08±0.02 mg per leaf). pH of leaf of control site was recorded as 6.47±0.13, where as pH of leaf sampled from polluted site was recorded as 5.73±0.22. Thus a change of 11.44% towards the acidic side was recorded in the samples collected from polluted site. Air pollution tolerance index of *Polyalthia longifolia* was determined as 7.01±0.13 and 5.57±0.18 at control and polluted sites, respectively.

Relative moisture of *Delonix regia* was recorded at control site was 70.56±4.15% whereas it was 59.12±4.16% at polluted site. Thus there was a reduction of 16.21% in relative moisture content of samples collected from polluted site as compared to control site. Amount of dust deposited on leaves was higher (0.39±0.06 mg per leaf) in polluted site in comparison to control site (0.08±0.04 mg per leaf). pH of leaves collected from control site was recorded as 6.92±0.37, where as pH of leaves sampled form polluted site was recorded as 5.64±0.29. Thus a change of 18.50% toward the acidic side was recorded in the samples collected from polluted site. Air pollution tolerance index of *Delonix regia* was determined as 8.48±0.17 and 6.59±0.28 at control and polluted sites, respectively.

DISCUSSION

Highest decrease in chlorophyll *'a'* content of the samples collected from polluted site in comparison with control sites was thus recorded in *Ficus religiosa* (43.36%) whereas lowest was for *Mangifera indica* (26.57%). Two-way ANOVA shows that reduction in chlorophyll *'a'*, chlorophyll *'b'* and total chlorophyll contents of *Ficus religiosa, Mangifera indica, Polyalthia longifolia* and *Delonix regia* were significant at 0.001% level. The concentrations of chlorophyll *'a'*, *'b'*, total chlorophyll, carotenoid, ascorbic acid, relative moisture content, pH and APTI were always found to be lower at polluted site as compared to control site leaves of the same age Chauhan [4]. Rao and Leblanc [20] have also reported reduction in chlorophyll content brought by acidic pollutants like SO_2 which causes phaeophytin formation by acidification of chlorophyll. Reductions in chlorophyll content of a variety of crop plants due to NO_2, SO_2 and O_3 exposure have also been reported by Agrawal et al., [2]. Lerman [15] has suggested that continuous application of cement dust clog the stomata, so interfering with gaseous exchange.

Highest decreases in carotenoid content was reported for *Polyalthia longifolia* (30.99%) while lowest decreases in *Mangifera indica* (18.47%). Two-way ANOVA shows significant reductions in all selected tree species were significant at 0.001 % level. Carotenoid protects chlorophyll from photoxidative destruction [25]. The carotenoid contents of some crop plants were found to decrease in response to SO_2 [18, 24, 33]. Joshi and Swami, [11] also reported significant reduction in carotenoid content of different plants grown at polluted sites.

Two-way ANOVA shows the decline in ascorbic acid content in all four plant species were significant at 0.001% level. Highest reduction in ascorbic acid content was observed for *Ficus religiosa* (44.67%) and lowest reduction for *Polyalthia longifolia* (22.93%). Ascorbic acid, a natural antioxidant in plants plays significant role in pollution tolerance [6]. Ascorbic acid is concentrated mainly in chloroplasts [9].

Relative moisture content of all four tree species was significant at 0.001 % level using two-way ANOVA. A high water content with a plant body may help to maintain its physiological balance under air pollution stress condition. High relative water content favors resistance in plants [7]. *Ficus religiosa* and *Polyalthia longifolia* were significant at 0.01 % level and *Mangifera indica* and *Delonix regia* were significant at 0.001% and 0.05% level, respectively.

The change in pH in the leaf sample collected from polluted site was significant at 0.001% level in four tree species. All the plant samples collected from polluted site exhibited a pH towards acidic side, which may be due to the presence of SO_2 and NO_x in the ambient air causing a change in pH of the leaf sap towards acidic site [27]. Highest change in dust content was found in *Ficus religiosa* which was significant at 0.001% level. High traffic load contributes high dust fall on the plant leaves this also depends upon the condition of roads [14] and size and structure of leaves [12]. Two-way ANOVA show that reduction in APTI of all four tree species was significant at 0.001 % level. Air pollution tolerant index is an index denotes capability of a plant to combat against air pollution. Plants which have higher index value are tolerant to air pollution and can be caused as sink to mitigate pollution, while plants with low index value show less tolerance and can be used to indicate levels of air pollution [24].

REFERENCES

1. Agrawal, M.: Plant Factors as Indicator of SO_2 and O_3 Pollutants. *Proc. International Symposium on Biological Monitoring of the State Environment (Bio- indicator)'*, pp. 225-231. Indian National Science Academy, New Delhi (1985).
2. Agrawal, M., B. Singh, M. Rajput, F. Marshall, and J.N.B. Bell: Effect of Air Pollution of Periurban Agriculture: A Case Study. Environmental Pollution, 126 (2003), 323-329.
3. Chauhan, A.: Effect of Automobile and Industrial Air Pollutants on Some Selected Trees Grown at the Edge of Road Side in Haridwar. Journal of Natural & Physical Science, 22 (1-2) (2008), 37-47.
4. Chauhan A. and P.C. Joshi: Effect of Ambient Air Pollution on Photosynthetic Pigments on Some Selected Trees in Urban Area. Ecology Environment and Conservations, 14(4) (2008), 23-27.

5. Chauhan A. and P.C. Joshi: Air Quality Index and its Variations in Haridwar. Journal of Environment and Bio-Science, 22(2) (2008), 171-176.
6. Chen, Y.M., P.W. Lucas and A.R. Wellburn: Relative Relationship Between Foliar Injury and Change in Antioxidants Levels in Red and Norway Spruce Exposed to Acidic Mists. Environmental Pollution, 69(1990), 1-15.
7. Dedio, W.: Water Relations in Wheat Leaves as Screening Test for Drought Resistance. Canadian Journal of Plant Science, 55(1975), 369-378.
8. Duxbury, A.C. and C.S. Yentsch : Plankton Pigment Monographs. J. Marine Res. 15 (1956), 91-101.
9. Franke, W. and U. Heber: Über die Quantitative Verteilund der Ascorbinsäure innerhalb der Pflanzenzelle. Zeitschrift Naturf, 196(1964), 1146-1149.
10. Jacob, M.B. and S. Hochheiser: Continuous Sampling and Ultra-micro Determination of Nitrogen Dioxide in Air. Analytical Chemistry, 32(1958), 426.
11. Joshi, P.C. and A. Chauhan: Performance of Locally Grown Rice Plants (*Oryza sativa* L.) Exposed to Air Pollutants in a Rapidly Growing Industrial Area of District Haridwar, Uttarakhand, India. Life Science Journal, 5(3) (2008), 41-45.
12. Joshi, P.C. and A. Swami: Physiological Responses of Some Tree Species Under Roadside Automobile Pollution Stress Around City of Haridwar, India. Environmentalist, 27(2007), 365-374.
13. Krichstetter, T.W., R.A. Harly, N.M. Kreisberg, M.R. Stolzenburg and S.V. Hering: On Road Measurement of the Find Particles and Nitrogen Oxide Emissions from Light and Heavy Duty Motor Vehicles. Atmospheric Environment, 33 (1999), 2955-2968.
14. Lone, P.M., A.A. Khan and S.A. Shah: Study of Dust Pollution Caused by Traffic in Aligarh City. Indian Journal of Environmental Health, 47(4) (2005), 33-36.
15. Lerman, S.: Cement-kiln Dust and the Bean Plant (*Phaseolus vulgaris* L. Black Valentine Var.); indepth Investigations into Plant Morphology, Physiology and Pathology. Ph.D. Dissertation, University of California, Riverside, 1972.
16. Mc Pherson, E.G., D.J. Nowak and R.E. Rowntree: Chicago's Urban Forest Ecosystem: Results of the Chicago Urban Forest Climate Project USDA General Technical Rep; NE-186. USDA, Washington, DC, 1994.
17. Maclachlan, C. and S. Zalik: Plastid Structure, Chlorophyll Concentration and Free Amino Acid Composition of a Chlorophyll Mutant of Barley. Canadian Journal of Botany, 41 (1963), 1053-1062.
18. Pandey, S.N.: *Effects of Coal Smoke and Sulphur Dioxide Pollution on Plants*. Ph.D. Thesis, Banaras Hindu University, Varansi, India, 1978.
19. Prajapati, S.K. and B.D. Tripathi: Seasonal Variation of Leaf Dust Accumulation and Pigment Content in Plant Species Exposed to Urban Particulates Pollution. Journal of Environmental Quality, 37(2008), 865-870.
20. Rao, D.N. and F. Leblanc: Effects of SO_2 on the lichens alga with Special Reference to Chlorophyll. Bryologist, 69(1966), 69-75.
21. Raina, A.K. and A. Sharma: Effects of Vehicular Pollution on the Leaf Micro-morphology, Anatomy and Chlorophyll Contents of *Syzygium cumini* L. Indian Journal of Environmental Protection, 23(8) (2003), 897-902.
22. Rao, M.N. and H.N.V. Rao: Air Pollution. Tata McGraw Hill Publishing Company Limited, New Delhi, 1998.
23. Sadasivam, S. and A. Manikam: In: Biochemical Methods for Agriculture Science. Wiley Eastern Ltd., New Delhi, India, 1991.

24. Singh, S.K. and D.N. Rao: Evaluation of Plants for Their Tolerance to Air Pollution. *Proceedings of Symposium on Air Pollution Control*. Vol. 1., Indian Assoc. for Air Pollution Control, New Delhi, 1983.
25. Sifermann-Harms, D.: The Light Harvesting and Protective Functions of Carotenoids in Photosynthetic Membranes. Physiol. Plant., 69 (1987), 561-568.
26. Singh, N.: *Responses of Certain Leguminous Plants to Sulphur Dioxide Pollution*. Ph.D. Thesis, Banaras Hindu University, Varansi, India, 1981.
27. Swami, A., D. Bhatt and P.C. Joshi: Effects of Automobile Pollution on sal (*Shorea robusta*) and rohini (*Mallotus phillipinensis*) at Asarori, Dehradun. Himalayan Journal of Environment and Zoology, 18 (1) (2004), 57-61.
28. Wagh, N.D., P.V. Shukla, S.B. Tambe, and S.T. Ingle: Biological Monitoring of Roadside Plants Exposed to Vehicular Pollution in Jalgaon City. J. Environ. Biol., 27(2) (2006), 419-421.
29. Weatherly, P.E.: The State and Movement of Water in the lea. Symposium of the Society of Experimental Biology, 19(1965), 157-184.
30. West, P.W. and G.C. Gaeke: Fixation of Sulphur Dioxide as Sufitomercurate III and Subsequent Colorimetric Determination. Analytical Chemistry, 28 (1956), 1816.
31. Ziegler, I.: Effects of SO_2 on the Activity of Ribulose 1, 5- diphosphate Carboxylase in Isolated Spinach Chloroplasts. Planta, 103 (1992), 155-163.
32. Smith, W.H.: Lead Contamination of Road Side White Pine. Forest Science, 17(1971), 195-198.
33. Nandi, P.K.: *Phytotoxicity of Sulphur Dioxide air Pollution and its Control*. Ph.D. Thesis, Banaras Hindu University, Varansi, India, 1984.

2

Effect of Sugar Mill Effluent on Cereal Crops at Germination and Growth Stage *Physico-Biochemical Analysis*

Avadhesh Kumar Koshal

ABSTRACT

Sugar industry in India is an old rural agro-based seasonal industry and is playing an important role in socio-economic development of rural and urban India. Meerut district has higher production of sugarcane also called "green land of U. P." The Daurala Sugar Works established in 1932. It is largest sugar factory in Western Uttar Pradesh. The experimental material for the present study consists of two-cereal crops wheat (*Triticum aestivum* var. PBW 373) & Barley (*Hordeum vulgare* var. Manjula).

After seedling were sampled at 2, 4 & 6 day of germination dissected out in to different parts & subjected to length & weight measurements observation were analyzed statistically for arithmetic mean & standard deviation of ten seedlings. The experiments were performed in 0%, 25%, 50% & 100% concentration of sugar mill effluents incase of cereals. The plant growth stunted, leaves are yellow, and plant yield reduced germination percentage inhibits. Root length decreases, chlorophyll content less pH of root & leaf range between 5 to 8 so in to growth improper manner and yield percentage decrease. The presented data clearly demonstrate that sugar mill effluent water cause considerable

Research Associate (GIS), NICRA Project Project Directorate for Farming Systems Research Meerut, (U.P.) PIN - 250 110.

reduction in different growth parameters & the experiment of seedling growth analysis, all the dry weight fraction measured were found to be significantly decreased with regard to chlorophyll it was seen that the reduction in *chlorophyll a* was almost more as comparison to reduction in chlorophyll b.

These data evidence that *chlorophyll a* is more sensitive that *chlorophyll b.* At the germination time fresh weight and dry weight lesser then normal plants. Plants are not much healthy not resistant to better to environment, flowering later than normal plant. It has been observed in our experiment that sugar mill effluents in general, inhibit the seed germination growth, yield and biochemical parameters in wheat var.PBW-373 & Barley var. Manjula which has been taken in this study.

Keywords: Effluent, Seedling growth, Seedling germination & Growth parameters.

INTRODUCTION

Pollution is an undesirable change in the physical-chemical characteristics of air, land & water that may or will harmfully affect human life or that of desirable species, living conditions & cultural assets; or that may or will waste or deteriorate our raw material resources (Sharma, 1995). Pollution increases not only because as people multiply & the space available to each person becomes smaller, but also because the demands per person are continuously increasing.

Water resources have been the most exploited natural resource, since man stride on the earth. Pollution of water bodies is increasing steadily due to rapid population growth, industrial proliferation, urbanization, increasing living standards and wide spheres of human activities. Fresh water constitutes only a small fraction (2%) of the earth's total water supply. Nearly all of this about 1.98% of the total is locked in the masses of polar ice caps glaciers and clouds. The remaining fraction 0.0192% is found in the lake, wells and underground reserves is the world's which mankind for various uses taps.

Sugar industry in India is an old rural agro-based seasonal industry and is playing an important role in socio-economic development of rural and urban India. It has grown in size, resulting in increase of sugar production from 1.2 tons in 1930 to 120 lac tons in 1990-1991 i.e, 100 times increase. Water pollution is vital concern from the waste effluent released from the industries (Manivasakam, 1987). As per factory data, the crushing capacity of Daurala sugar works in 1932 was 500 tons sugar cane per day, which has crossed 9688.05 thousand metric tons in a year (1998-1999). It produces molasses of 452.7 thousand liter in a season of 174 days and the factory produce large quantity of effluents or sludge per day. This effluent water is used to irrigate agricultural crops. Irrigation of crop plants is one of the highly beneficial propositions of waste disposal. The wastewater (effluents) is produced from sugar mills continuously and hence it could cater the need of irrigation of crops. It is not only prevent the waste from being an environmental hazard, but also serve as an additional potential source of fertilizers for agriculture use (Swaminathan & Vaidheeswaran 1991).

Meerut district has higher production of sugarcane also called "green land of U. P. (Koshal, 2010)." Daurala Sugar Works was established in the year 1932 at Daurala, a small village near Meerut on New Delhi – Haridwar National Highway No.56. It is largest sugar factory in Western Uttar Pradesh. It is a first plant in India to manufacture double-refined sugar of international quality. The present study was carried out to study the effect of effluent water of Daurala Sugar Works on growth and yield of wheat and barley crops.

Study Area

Daurala Sugar Works (Fig. 2.1) located at Daurala, on 14 Km. away from Meerut City (U.P.). Meerut district has semi arid climate with air temperature ranging between 5.5 °C (minimum) and 45 °C (maximum). The average annual rainfall is 804 mm. mostly received in July to September. The soils are dominantly sandy loam to loam in texture and soil reaction (pH) is neutral. Sugarcane, potato and wheat are major crops grown in the area. Wheat and Barley are rabi season crops sown in November-December and harvested in last March or April.

MATERIALS AND METHODS

The experimental material for the present study consists of two cereal crops wheat (*Triticum aestivum* var. PBW 373) & Barley (*Hordeum vulgare* var. Manjula). The seeds of these plants were procured from G.B. Pant Agriculture Technology University, western campus, Modipuram, Meerut. U.P. Soil samples were collected from campus of Botany Department of University. The sugar mill effluent was collected directly from the point of discharge of effluent of the Daurala Sugar works, Daurala, Meerut U.P. in 20 liters plastic cans (Fig. 2.1a & 2.1b). Approximately 2 kgs. of soil were filled in fifty polythene bags. Seeds of uniform shape & size were selected & sown in the polythene bags containing soils. Five sets were designed for experiment at all critical growth stages irrigated with sugar mill effluent in concentrations of control 0%, 25%, 50% & 100%.

Germination Parameters, Growth, Yield Parameters & Biochemical Parameters

The experiment was carried out in laboratory conditions. At the vegetative stage, length & fresh weight of root and shoot length was measured.

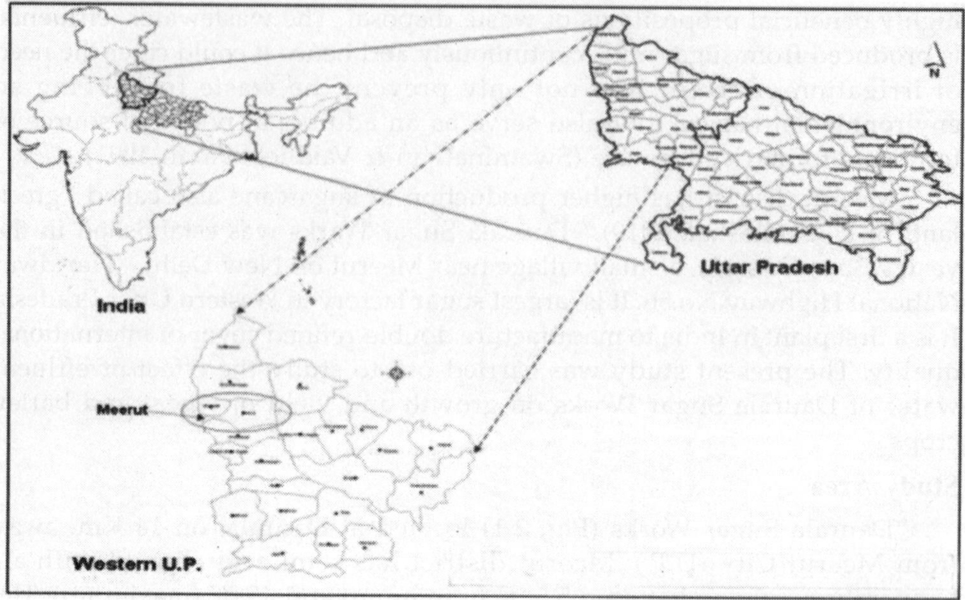

Fig. 2.1: **Study Area of Western U.P. – Meerut**

Fig. 2.1 (a): **Front View of Daurala Sugar Mill**

Fig. 2.1 (b): **Effluent Water**

Dry weight of vegetative stage parts i.e. roots & shoot was recorded after proper drying of plant parts. After seedling were sampled at 2, 4 & 6 day of germination dissected out in to different parts & subjected to length & weight measurements observation were analyzed statistically for arithmetic mean & standard deviation of ten seedlings. Results of the studies are given in tables' germination & seedling for seedling growth studies experiments were performed in 0%, 25%, 50% & 100% concentration of sugar mill effluents incase of cereals. The effluents of sugar mill was collected & sterilized. It was then diluted with distilled water to get different concentration viz. 0%, 25% 50% & 100%. The distilled water alone as such served as control. Seeds were selected for uniformity (criteria beings the size & colour of seeds) & then these seeds were surface sterilized with 0.1% $HgCl_2$ for two minutes & washed thoroughly with distilled water. Incase of cereals these seeds were transferred on moist filter paper in petriplates containing above-mentioned concentration of sterilized effluent. Simultaneously a control is run in distilled water.

These seedlings were dissected out in to root & shoot cotyledon parts in cereals. Root Length (cm.), Leaf Length (cm.), Total Length (cm.), Length fresh weight & dry weight of these seedling parts were recorded in case of residual cotyledon only the fresh & dry weight was recorded. The yield parameters were recorded on 120 days of wheat and barley crops.

The biochemical analysis pH & chlorophyll estimation of different stages (30, 60, 90 & 120 days) of cereal crops at different treatment level.

Chlorophyll Content

10 mg. Fresh leaves were homogenized with 80% acetone & a pinch of sodium bi carbonate. Then the homogenate was centrifuged at 4000 rpm for 5 minutes. The final volume of the supernatant was made to 1oml by adding acetone. The optical density of the extract was read at 645nm & 663nm by sprectronic-21 spectrometer. The amount of chlorophyll a, chlorophyll b & total chlorophyll was calculated. According to the Aaron's formula (1949):

Chlorophyll a (mg/ml) = 12.72A 663-2.58 A664-

Chlorophyll b (mg/ml) = 22.87A664-4.67A 663-

Total chlorophyll (mg/ml) = 8.05A664-20.29A663

When V = Volume & W = Weight of leaves.

pH (Reaction)

pH of plants, leaves, roots & residues were analyzed. 5-mg plant materials crushed with 10 ml-distilled water centrifuged at 500 rpm/second homogenize solution taken to observe pH reading. pH Reading taken by pH meter.

RESULTS AND DISCUSSION

After detail analysis of two cereal crops are wheat (*Triticum aestivum* var. PBW-373.) and barley (*Hordeum vulgare* var. Manjula.), seedling germination and growth parameters (Plumule and Radicle length) were observed (Fig. 2.2 to Fig. 2.18).

(I) WHEAT PARAMETERS

(i) Wheat Germination percentage (%) & seedling growth parameters (Fig. 2.2 to 2.7)

Percentage Germination of Seeds

Fig. 2.2 shows that in dark, 25% sugar mill effluent concentration is promotry & promotes percentage germination by 50% & 100% in dark respectively over the control. The declines the percentage germination of seeds was in 50% & 100%.

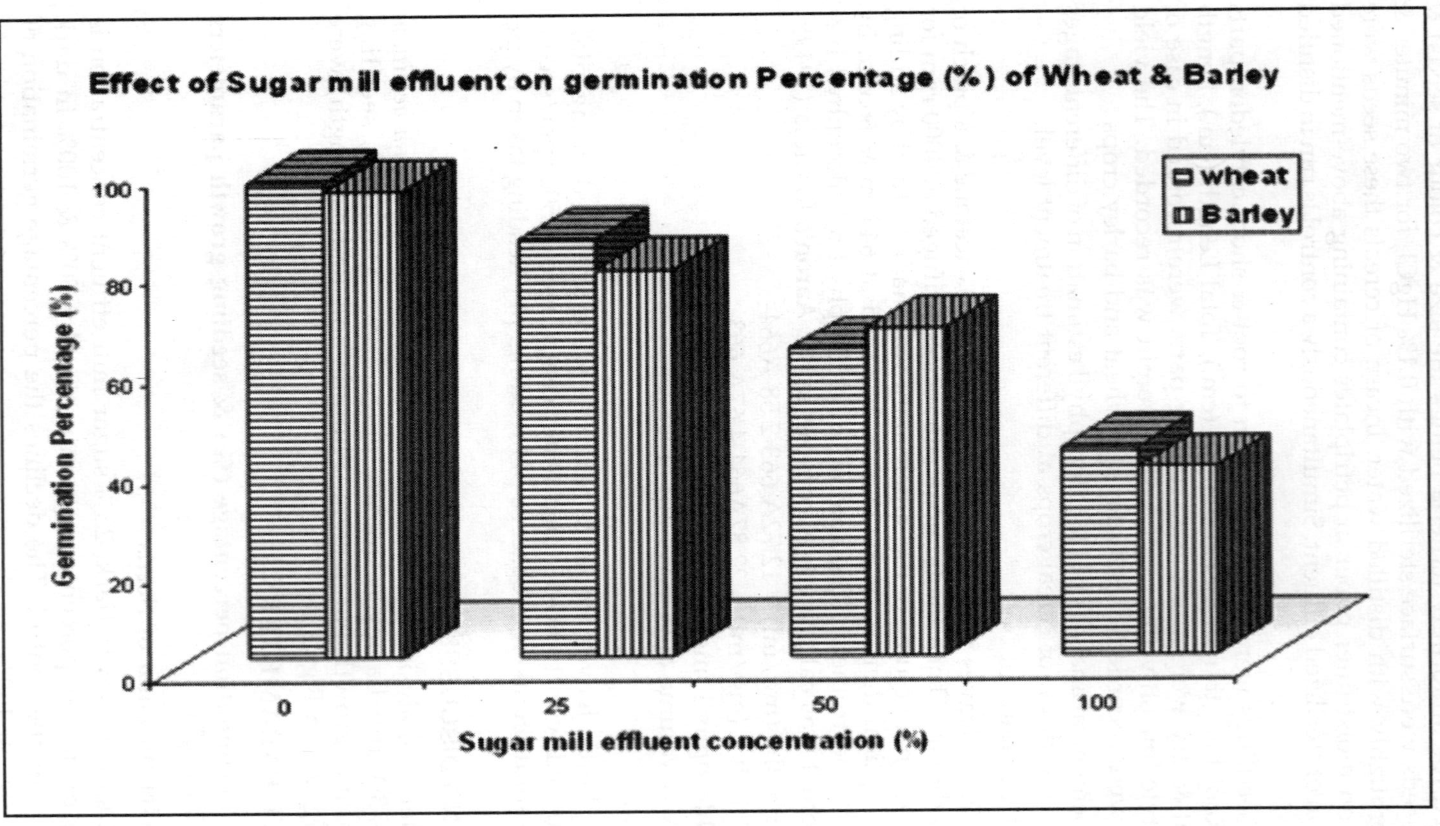
Effect of Sugar mill effluent on germination Percentage (%) of Wheat & Barley
wheat
Barley
Germination Percentage (%)
100
80
60
40
20
0
0
25
50
100
Sugar mill effluent concentration (%)

Fig. 2.2

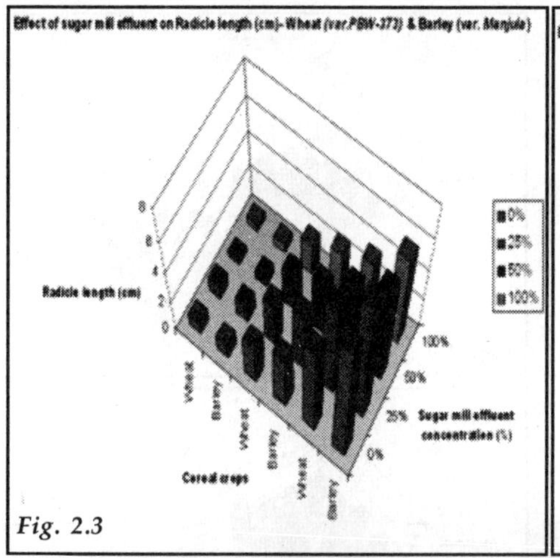

Fig. 2.3

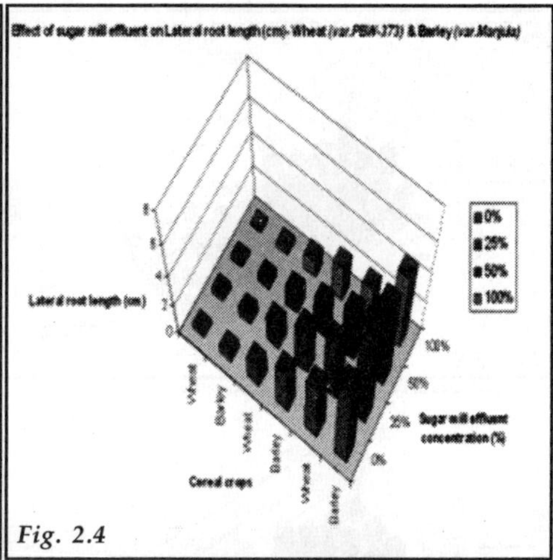

Fig. 2.4

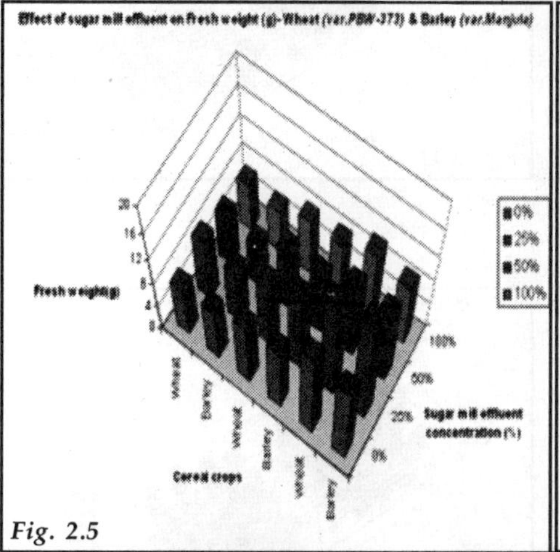

Fig. 2.5

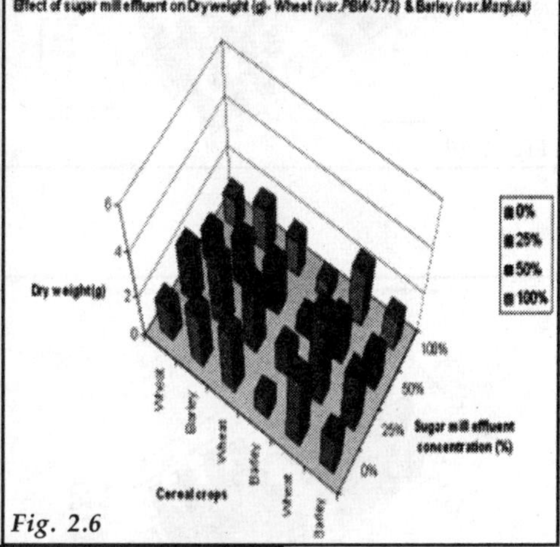

Fig. 2.6

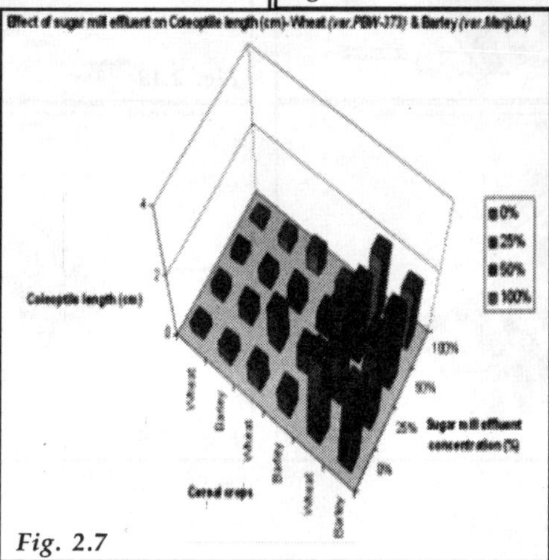

Fig. 2.7

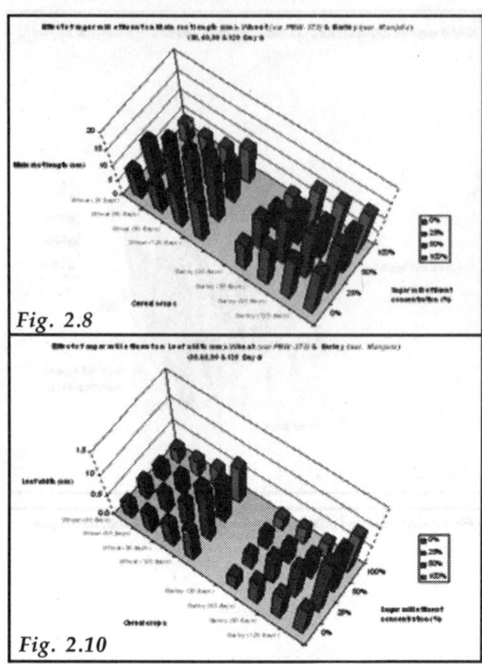

Fig. 2.8

Fig. 2.10

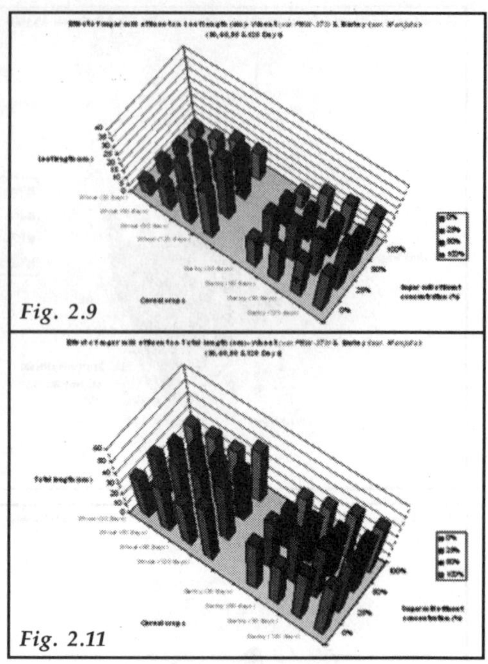

Fig. 2.9

Fig. 2.11

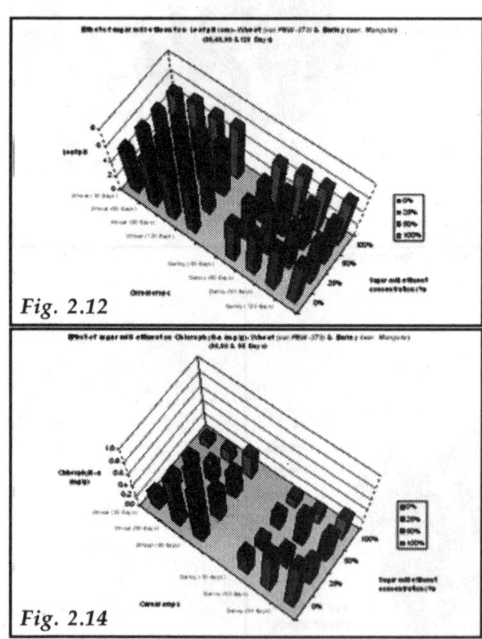

Fig. 2.12

Fig. 2.14

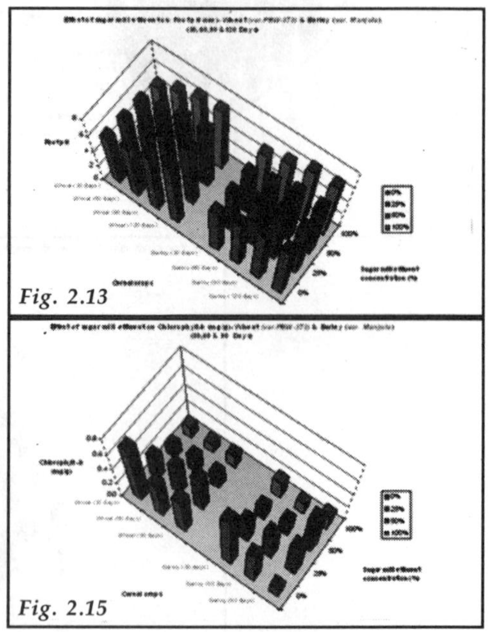

Fig. 2.13

Fig. 2.15

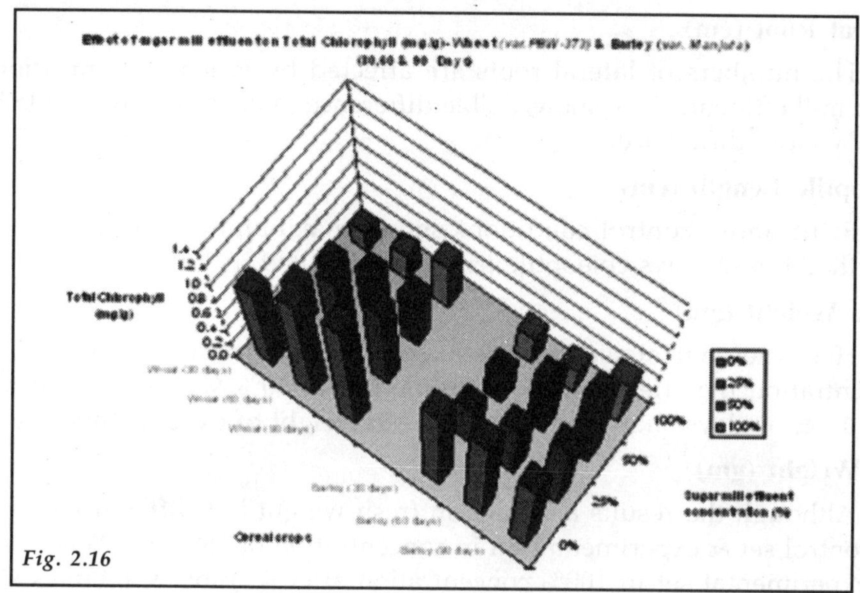

Fig. 2.16

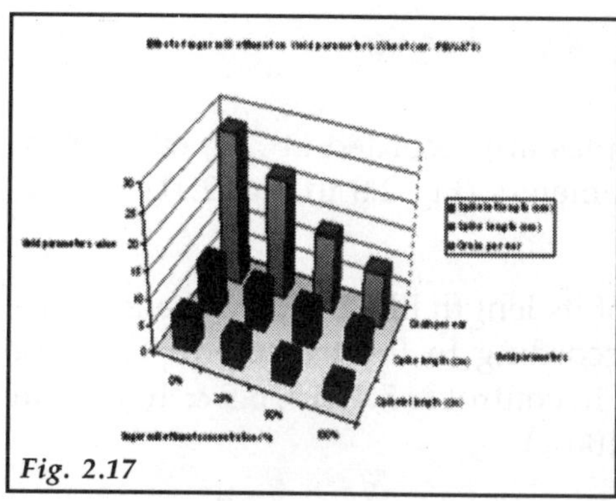

Fig. 2.17

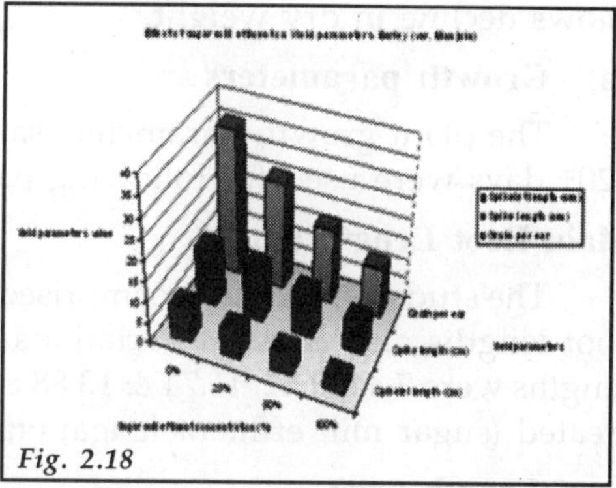

Fig. 2.18

Seedling Growth Parameters

The seedling growth parameters like main root lateral root, coleoptile, fresh weight & dry weight observed at 2nd, 4th & 6th days. The main root length, lateral root, coleoptile, fresh weight & dry weights are observed in different treatment of plants.

Radicle Length (cm)

An analysis of the data obtained on root length reveal that the length in maximum in control set & in 25% & 50% concentration shows a decrease in length & also in 100% concentration.

Lateral Root (cm)

The numbers of lateral roots are affected by much concentration of sugar mill effluent. They show visible difference in 2nd & 6th days while 50% &100% show difference.

Coleoptile Length (cm)

Plant under control conditions shows maximum length in coleoptile growth. After 6th days coleoptile length is inhibited in 100% concentration.

Fresh Weight (gm)

Here the control seed shows maximum weight but fewer than 25% concentration the effect not more visible but in 50% &100% concentration after 4th & 6th days shows decrease in fresh weight of experimental sets.

Dry Weight (gm)

Although the results are same in fresh weight but difference between the control set & experimental set in concentration of 25% & 50% is less but the experimental set in 100% concentration after 4th days & 6th days show clear difference in dry weight. The experimental sets of concentration 100% shows decline in dry weight.

(ii) Growth parameters

The plant growth parameters samples are recorded at 30th, 60th, 90th & 120th days were used for following parameters (Fig 2.8 to Fig. 2.11).

Main Root Length (cm)

The study on root was comprised of its length like the plant height. The root lengths also showed variations according to the treatment. The root lengths were 7.44, 9.22, 11.74 & 13.88 cm in control & 5.4, 5.5, 6.5 & 10.7 cm in treated (sugar mill effluent irrigation, 100%).

Leaf Length (cm)

It was observed that the values of leaf length were 9.6, 17.5, 23.8 & 38.5 cm in control, 8.8, 16.2, 22.8, & 32.3 cm in 25% & in 50% 7.1, 15.0, 16.8 & 30.6 cm where as in 100% effluent water these were 6.3, 8.4, 15.9 & 16.8 cm.

Leaf Width (cm)

Some what some result is obtained as in number of leaves i.e. 100% is more affect able to plants leaves.

Total Length (cm)

The total lengths of plants are affected by very much concentration of (100%) of sugar mill effluent. They show visible difference after 60th, 90th, & 120 days while 50% & 100% show much effect on the total length.

(iii) Bio-chemical parameters

To analysis of data obtained show-interesting results that are clearly showing difference between control sets & experimental set in chlorophyll a, chlorophyll b & pH (Fig. 2.12 to Fig. 2.16).

Chlorophyll a

The plants under experiment controlled conditions shows less maximum amount of chlorophyll a, then the controlled plants. The plants by 50% & 100% effluent concentrations show clear reduction in chlorophyll amount after 30 days. A further reduction is observed with high concentration of sugar mill effluent after 60th & 90th days respectively.

Chlorophyll b

Same results are obtained as in amount of chlorophyll a after analysis. The plants have been affected by low & high concentration of sugar mill effluent. The plants under experimental conditions i.e. even the plants under 50% & 100% effluent water shows clear reduction in chlorophyll b amount.

Total chlorophyll

Higher concentration of effluent water i.e. 50% & 100% shows inhibitory affect & decrease highly the amount of chlorophyll in their leaves after 60th & 90th days.

pH

Here also showed the results that is concentration of sugar mill effluent water acts as inhibitor & inhibit the pH value shows the leaves contained high amount pH after 90 days. Root pH higher than leaves, which inhibit the plant growth.

(iv) Yield parameters

Yield parameters were recorded on 120 days (Fig. 2.17 & Fig. 2.18).

Grains per ear

Grains counted per ear were 28 in control & reduced number 22, 14 &10 in 25%, 50% % 100% treated plant at 120 days respectively.

Spike Length (cm)

Spike length recorded after 120 days 9.80 cm in control & 5.85 cm in 100% higher concentration (%) decrease the spike length.

Spikelet Length (cm)

Spikelet length also decreases increase the concentration of sugar mill effluent treatment (%), after 120th days spikelet length. in control & reduced in 50% & 100% concentration.

(II) BARELY PARAMETERS

(i) Barley Germination percentage (%) & seedling growth parameters (Fig. 2.2 to 2.7)

Percentage Germination of Seeds

Fig. 2.2 shows that in dark, 25% sugar mill effluent concentration is promotry & promotes percentage germination by 50% & 100% in dark respectively over the control. The declines the percentage germination of seeds was in 50% & 100%.

Seedling Growth Parameters

The seedling growth parameters like main root lateral root, coleoptile, fresh weight & dry weight observed at 2nd, 4th & 6th days. Seedling growth parameters are observed in different percentage of treatment plants. The plant samples recorded at 2nd 4th &6th days were used for following parameters.

Radicle Length (cm)

An analysis of the data obtained on root length reveal that the length in maximum in control set & in 25% & 50% concentration shows a decrease in length & also in 1000% concentration.

Lateral Root (cm)

The numbers of lateral roots are affected by much concentration of sugar mill effluent. They show visible difference in 2nd & 6th days while 50% & 100% show difference.

Coleoptile Length (cm)

Plant under control conditions shows maximum length in coleoptile growth. After 6th days coleoptile length is inhibited in 100% concentration.

Fresh Weight (gm)

Here the control seed shows maximum weight but fewer than 25% concentration the effect not more visible but in 50% &100% concentration after 4th & 6th days shows decrease in fresh weight of experimental sets.

Dry Weight (gm)

Although the results are same in fresh weight but difference between the control set & experimental set in concentration of 25% & 50% is less but the experimental set in 100% concentration after 4th days & 6th days show clear difference in dry weight. The experimental sets of concentration 100% shows decline in dry weight.

(ii) Growth parameters

The plant growth parameters samples are recorded at 30th, 60th, 90th & 120th days were used for following parameters (Fig. 2.8 to Fig. 2.11).

Main Root Length (cm)

The study on root was comprised of its length like the plant height. The root lengths also showed variations according to the treatment. The root lengths were 11.5, 16.4, 17.4 & 19.4 cm in control & 4.7, 11.4, 12.6 & 13.9 cm in treated (sugar mill effluent irrigation,100%).

Leaf Length (cm)

It was observed that the values of leaf length were 23.8, 27.4, 29.4 & 35.7 cm in control 20.3, 24.7, 28.6 & 31.6 cm in 25% & in 50% 17.9, 21.4, 23.8 & 26.3 cm where as in 100% effluent water these were 8.6, 18.6, 22.1 & 25.3 cm.

Leaf Width (cm)

Some what some result is obtained as in number of leaves i.e. 100% is more affect able to plants leaves.

Total Length (cm)

The total length of plants are affected by very much concentration of (100%) of sugar mill effluent. They show visible difference after 60th, 90th & 120 days while 50% & 100% show much effect on the total length.

(iii) Bio-chemical parameters

To analysis of data obtained show-interesting results that are clearly showing difference between control sets & experimental set in chlorophyll a, chlorophyll b & pH (Fig. 2.12 to 2.16).

Chlorophyll a

The plants under experiment controlled conditions shows less maximum amount of chlorophyll a, then the controlled plants. The plant by 50% & 100% effluent concentrations shows clear reduction in chlorophyll amount after 30 days. A further reduction is observed with high concentration of sugar mill effluent after 60th & 90th days respectively.

Chlorophyll b

Same results are obtained as in amount of chlorophyll a after analysis. The plants have been affected by low & high concentration of sugar mill effluent. The plants under experimental conditions i.e. even the plants under 50% & 100% effluent water shows clear reduction in chlorophyll b amount.

Total chlorophyll

Higher concentration of effluent water i.e. 50% & 100% shows inhibitory affect & decrease highly the amount of chlorophyll in their leaves after 60th & 90th days.

pH

Here also showed the results that is concentration of sugar mill effluent water acts as inhibitor & inhibit the pH value shows the leaves contained high amount pH after 90 days. Root pH higher than leaves, which inhibit the plant growth.

(iv) Yield parameters

Yield parameters were recorded on 120 days (Fig. 2.17 & Fig. 2.18).

Grains per ear

Grains counted per ear were 36 in control & reduced number 26, 18 & 12 in 25%, 50% & 100% treated plant at 120 days respectively.

Spike Length (cm)

Spike length recorded after 120 days 14.25 cm in control & 7.72 cm in 100% higher concentration (100%) decrease the spike length.

Spikelet Length (cm)

Spikelet length also decreases, increase the concentration of sugar mill effluent treatment (%), after 120th days spikelet length 8.32cm in control & 5.45 & 3.37cm reduced in 50% & 100% concentration respectively.

CONCLUSIONS

Today we are success fully entered in to 21st century. We are facing lot of many environmental problem, basic problems are air, water and soil pollution it is critical problem The development of industry is like pesticides, urea, steel, sugar and distillery etc. in this industries water are used huge amount. In this water many toxic substances are mixed which are toxic for soil and plants. Many farmers used that effluent water for irrigation of crop that, that water reduced the yield of production and growth. This creates big problem for human beings and plants. Many of these by products waste materials and products of man's activities are extremely toxic and unless adequate precautions are taken they have disastrous effect on the plants and environment.

Water is essential for every living being. Every living organism directly linked with water. Water is essential requirements so water pollution is problems, which are directly, concern all of us. It is not only highly industrializes and advanced countries that are threatened with water pollution, the menace of growing in India too. Industrial effluent (sugar mill effluent) is one of the major wastes which posses great ecological crises. Its toxicity to plant growth is well known. Toxicity of effluent is considered due to its poisonous nature, high concentration of organic and inorganic pollutants. Its high BOD and COD make it deficient in dissolved oxygen pressure. This high concentration in the effluent causes a high osmotic pressure this high concentration in the effluent causes a high pressure. It is responsible for reduced in up take of water (Bhumla et al. 1968).

The present study reveals that in general sugar effluents depressed plant growth at the adult vegetative stage too and produced deleterious effects on plants and consequently reduces the field. The photosynthetic surface i.e. new leaf area is also reduced by sugar mill effluent (Overman,1975).

The growth and yield in term of fresh weight and biological yield per plant also reduced by irrigation of sugar mill effluents. The results given in the preceding selections and the available reports Overman, 1975, Rajanan & Oblisami (1979) etc. indicate that industrial effluents effect several vital processes. The plant growth stunted, leaves are yellow, and plant yield reduced germination percentage inhibits. Root length decreases node or inter node length reduces chlorophyll content less pH of root & leaf range between 5 to 8 so in to growth proper manner and yield percentage decrease. At the germination time fresh weight and dry weight lesser then normal plants.

Plants are not much healthy not resistant to better to environment, flowering later than normal plant. Seeds of the cereals are major source of food. The cereals & their products contribute substantially to the world's food supply & make an important source of carbohydrate in human diet. Wheat & barley, an important staple food crops is rich in carbohydrate & glutins. All seeds show biochemical & physiological activities after absorbing water but if some how toxic substances is absorbed by seeds than it will interfere in basic physiological activities of the germinating seeds. Generally all these activities are adversely affected by these toxic elements. It has been observed in our experiment that industrial effluents in general, inhibits the seed germination & seedling growth in Wheat var.PBW-373 & Barley var. Manjula which has been taken in this study. High osmotic pressure caused due to high salt concentration in the effluents might be major cause for a rapid decrease in percentage of germination.

The presented data clearly demonstrate that sugar mill effluent water cause considerable reduction in different growth parameters & at the end of the experiment of seedling growth analysis, all the dry weight fraction measured were found to be significantly decreased with regard to chlorophyll it was seen that the reduction in chlorophyll a was almost more as comparison to reduction in chlorophyll b. These data evidence that chlorophyll a is more sensitive that chlorophyll b. Thus according to observations, the higher concentration of sugar mill effluent water shows more adverse effective & destructive effect to plants. In Meerut City, main causes of water pollution, Modi rubber Ltd., Modipuram, Daurala sugar works, Daurala, Daurala Organic and Daurala Distillery. It produced large-scale water pollution. So that pollution keep under control, not only government organisation, every citizen awake up to pollution must be keep under control the pollution we area facing many health problem.

On the basis of the present study it could be suggested the out let conc. effluent is normally toxic to plant growth and his effluent cannot be used for irrigation. In spite of the rules and regulations the industrialists do not wish to spend a part of their profit to ensure that environment is not degraded. That pollution slowly-slowly affects on the soil and plants. When that is irrigated to polluted water we do not know how effects on the human beings when that plants are used by human populations. So we can not stop industrialization but we help the save of an environment we must be adopt Eco-friendly technology which produced low quantity air, water and soil pollutants.

We can help the save of the environment for future generation. We tried up to our generation for away this "devil problem" pollution is slow poison for environment, save the environment, stops the pollution. We can make better future life.

REFERENCES

Arnon, D.L. (1949). Copper Enzymes in Isolated Chloroplasts Poly Phenol Oxidase in *Beta vulgaris*. *Pl.* Physiol., 24: 1-15.

Bhumla, D.R., Singh, B. & Singh, T.N.(1968). Effects of Salt on Seed Germination. *Indian J. Agri.* 15:181-185.

Koshal, A.K. (2010): Effect of Sugar Mill Effluent on Cereal Crops. Zonal Seminar on Physiological and Molecular Interventions for Yield & Quality Improvement in Crop Plants. S.V.B.P.U.A. & T., Meerut, 17-18 September 2010, pp. 224-225.

Manivaskam, N. (1987): Industrial Effluents, Origin, Characteristics, Effects Analysis and Treatment, *Shakti publ.*, Coimbatore. 461-463.

Overman, A.R. (1975). Effluent Irrigation Pearl Millet. *J. Environ. Engg. Dev. Amer. Soc. Civ. Engg.*, 101: 193.

Rajannan, G. & Oblisami, G. (1979). Effect of Paper Factory Effluent on Soil and Crop Plants. Indian J. Environ. Health. 21: 120-130.

Sharma, P.D. (1995). Ecology & Environment. *Rastogi Publ.* Meerut. 1- 511.

Swaminathan, K. & Vaidheeswaran, P.(1991). Effect of Dye Factory Effluent on Seed Germination & Seedling Development of Groundnut (*Aarchis hypogea*). J. *Environ. Biol.* 12 (4): 353-358.

3

Tuber Yield and Storability of Processed Chips of Some Newly Developed Cassava (*Manihot esculenta* Crantz) Genotypes in Nigeria

B.C. Echezona*; G.O. Edebo; K.P. Baiyeri

ABSTRACT

One sure way of extending the shelf-life of any harvested cassava tuber is to process it into dry edible chips. Ten newly developed cassava genotypes emanating from the breeding programmes of two root crop research institutes in Nigeria (National Root Crops Research Institute, NRCRI, Umudike, Umuahia and International Institute of Tropical Agriculture, IITA, Ibadan) were therefore evaluated for their relative storability as dry chips. A local cultivar ("Otupam") and an improved variety (TMS 30572) were added as checks. In the first of our experiments, factorial combinations of 12 cassava accessions and three harvesting ages (6, 9 and 12 months after planting, MAP) were laid out in a randomized complete block design. A second experiment comprised factorial combinations of dry cassava chips processed from the 12 cassava accessions and three cassava harvesting ages laid out in a completely randomized design. There were three replications each.

The total biomass, tuber weight and yield of a newly developed genotype, TMS 96/1432, increased by 39%, 41%, 41% respectively, over the local cultivar. The tuber weight and yield was each increased by 21% over the improved check. Conversely, weight loss of dry chips and damage by

Department of Crop Science, University of Nigeria, Nsukka, Nigeria.

store pests (assessed as weight of powdery wastes produced, number of exit holes, and weevil count) were each reduced by about 97 % in TMS 96/1672 and TMS 96/1432 compared to the local and the improved varieties. Harvesting at 12 MAP ensured better storability of cassava chips and therefore should be adopted by farmers using TMS 96/1432 or TMS 96/1672 to extend the shelf-life of cassava in form of dry chips.

Key words: Genotype; Harvest index; Local best; Shelf-life; Store pest; Tuber yield.

INTRODUCTION

Cassava, *Manihot esculenta* Crantz., belongs to dicotyledonous family Euphorbiaceae, a family that also include the rubber plant, *Harvae braziliensis* and castor plant, *Ricinus communis.* It is a major staple food in south-eastern Nigeria (Olojede *et al., 2002*). Cassava constitutes about 90% of starchy staples widely accepted by the local farmers, which is attributed to it's width of ecological amplitude, such as it's adaptability to a wide variety of ecological and agronomic conditions (Carter *et al.,* 1992 and Nweke, 1996).

Nigeria through her new agricultural programme plans to boost cassava production up to 33 million metric tons yearly. The country is rated the world largest producer and consumer of cassava (IITA, 1998; Guardian Newspaper, July 22, 2005). Because of the importance of cassava in the agricultural sub-sector, the federal Government has funded a research exercise which produced five high yielding cassava varieties that can adapt to all ecological zones of the country. Adetunji (2005) reported that federal government was set to end farmers experience in the area of glut, low price regimes and post-harvest related problems.

With these emphasis and support in the production of cassava, there is every indication that its production will appreciably increase, but the seemingly major problem would be in the area of storage of surplus tubers to be produced. Cassava does not store well especially in fresh form. Fresh cassava tubers can not store for long because they rot within 3-4 days after harvest (Nweke, 1996). They are bulky with about 70% moisture content, thus transportation of fresh roots from rural centres to urban areas is usually very difficult and expensive. Consequently, there is need for tubers to be processed into storage products like garri, "akpu", chips and flour. This will also reduce the pressure on land especially where tenure system is in vogue through the reduction of on-farm-in-ground storage practices. Processed cassava products have longer shelf, easier to transport and market, contains low cyanide and are more palatable (Nweke, 1996). According to Asiedu (1989), processing is undertaken to detoxify cassava product, improve its palatability, and convert it to a storage form. Most processing methods (soaking/fermentation, heating, drying, boiling etc), however, eliminate the toxic components (Osiru, *et al.*, 1995). However, much labour is required in processing cassava roots into garri unlike into other forms like chips (IITA, 1998).

Fermentation is a key process in cyanide elimination and they have been supported by the ability of micro-organisms to hydrate linamarin (Okafor and Ejiofor, 1986). The flavour, aroma and texture of the fermented cassava products vary with season, location and the producer. Three types of fermentation are generally distinguished. They are a submerged fermentation. Here, cassava roots after manual peeling whole or in large pieces are deepen in water for 3-5 days. The second type is mash fermentation, in which a mash is obtained by grating or rasping fresh cassava root, and leaving it to ferment in a container for several days. The third type is a low moisture fermentation, whereby peeled cassava roots are heaped together and fungal growth allowed to develop at the surface of the roots. Submerged fermentation is 'most efficient' process of reducing the level of cyanogenis in cassava and the reduction rate of 95-100% was reported by Ayernor (1985); Ezeala and Okoro (1986) and Bakanga *et al.*, (1990).

Cassava chips are important intermediate product, making up a major proportion of marketed cassava in Africa (Berry, 1993). IITA (2005) reported that cassava chips are an alternative source of raw materials for producing alcoholic drinks as well as medicinal and industrial alcohol. To produce chips, the fresh tubers are peeled, washed and cut into slices between 3 and 6 cm long. The slices are sun dried or oven dried and bagged for storage. When dried, chips are produced and about 98% of the linamarin is destroyed during the process (IITA, 1990; Rehm and Espig, 1991). Most recently produced chips are mechanized and export oriented. One of the major constraints in cassava chips production is that very few of the producing factories and outfits have efficient means for artificial drying and preservation. Chips when not properly dried and preserved are still prone to attack by storage pests. The vulnerability of chips to storage pests and diseases are related to the internal composition of the chips, the age of the cassava tuber before being used, method of preparation and storage facilities as well as the prevailing environmental factors at its storage (Nweke, 1996).

The present study therefore evaluates some of the newly developed cassava genotypes in the country for possible production into chips. The specific objective was to evaluate the yield and post-harvest qualities of some newly developed cassava genotypes at different harvesting ages.

MATERIALS AND METHODS

Experimental Site

Both field and laboratory studies were carried out. The studies were conducted at the teaching and research farm and the physiology laboratory of Department of Crop Science, University of Nigeria, Nsukka. Nsukka is in the derived savannah of agro-ecology. The vegetation is predominantly grass with interspersed trees. It is located on latitude 06°52'N, longitude 07°24'E and altitude 447.2 m. a. s. l. Rainfall is bimodal with annual total of about 1500 mm. Rain stabilizes in May and often stops completely in late November. Relative humidity ranges from 70%-80%, while the ambient temperature ranges from 20°C-30°C, during the rainy months of the year.

Field Experimental Design

Treatments of the field experiment comprised factorial combinations of 12 cassava genotypes and three harvesting ages. Each treatment was replicated three times and laid out in a randomized complete block design (RCBD). The cassava genotypes used were ten new genotypes comprising five NR-series from National Root Crops Research Institute (NUCRI), Umudike, Umuahia (NR 93/0061, NR 93.0199, NR 93/0162, NR 93/0127 and NR 93/0225) and five TMS-series from International Institutes of Tropical Agriculture (IITA) Ibadan (TMS 96/0160 TMS 96/1672, TMS 96/1432, TMS 96/1087 and TMS 96/0304). They were evaluated along side the local best "Otupam" (as a local check) and TMS 30572, a widely cultivated genotype (as an improved check). The three harvesting ages were 6, 9 and 12 months after planting (MAP).

Field Layout

A total land area of 0.2 ha was ploughed, harrowed and ridged using tractor. The plot size of 5 ridges by 6 crop stand (5 × 6) m^2, that is 30 m^2, was made. The plots were 1 m apart while the blocks were 2 m apart. Soil samples of the research area were colleted at random from twelve (12) points on the field using auger sampler at a depth of 0-20 cm. The samples were bulked together to form a composite sample, which was sent to the laboratory for physico-chemical analysis. A detailed physico-chemical property of the site is shown in Table 3.1. A planting distance of 1 m between-row and 1 m within-rows was adopted. Thirty (30) cuttings per genotype per replication were planted. The plots were weeded manually throughout the experimental period when necessary. Compound fertilizer (NPK 15:15:15) was applied at the rate of 400 $kgha^{-1}$.

Data Collection from the Field Experiment

Tubers were harvested at different harvesting ages of 6, 9 and 12 months after planting and assessed for fresh and dry tuber yield (t ha^{-1}), fresh and dry weight and harvested indices. Pest/disease responses of the plant in the field were also assessed.

Laboratory Study

Preparations of Dry Cassava Chips

Cassava tubers were harvested at different harvesting ages of 6, 9 and 12 MAP. A known sample weight of freshly harvested cassava tubers per genotype per replication were washed with clean water, peeled, cut into thin slices, and later oven dried to a constant weight. The dried cassava chips so produced were enclosed in cellophane bags, sealed, labeled and stored in a refrigerator (-5 ± 2°C) until all the samples were ready for the study. Chips were stored in cellophane bags of equal sizes for six months. Initial weight of the chips before bagging was recorded.

Laboratory Experimental Design

Treatment comprised factorial combinations of the 12 cassava genotypes and the 3 harvesting ages replicated three times. The treatments were laid out in a completely randomized design (CRD) on a laboratory bench.

Data Collection from the Laboratory Experiment

Incidence of mould was assessed visually using a 5 point scale rating of 0-5 where 0 = no mould or 0% incidence and 5 = 100% incidence or most severe. Incidence of insects was by visual counting of adult insects and entry/exit holes. The incidence of powdery wastes and final weight of chips were taken six (6) months after storage.

Data Analysis

Insect counts and disease incidence were normalized using appropriate transformation procedures prior to analysis of variance with GENSTAT (2007). Detection of differences among treatment means for significant effect was done using Fisher's least significant difference (F-LSD = LSD) procedure as outlined by Obi (2002).

RESULTS

The various genotypes assessed significantly ($p<0.05$) affected total cassava biomass (dry weight) (Table 3.2). The total biomass ranged from 438 g in NR 93 0127 to 893 g in TMS 96/1087. Also, plants harvested 9 MAP produced significantly ($p<0.05$) lower biomass compared to either those harvested 6 MAP or 12 MAP with 12 MAP producing the highest biomass. There was no significant genotype (G) × Age of harvest (A) interaction. Similarly, there was a significant ($p<0.05$) genotype effect on fresh weight harvest index (Table 3.3). This is such that TMS 96/1432 produced significantly ($p<0.05$) higher harvest index (fresh weight) compared with other genotypes. TMS 96/1087 produced the least harvest index. Also, the harvest index obtained at 9 MAP was significantly ($p < 0.05$) lower than those of 12 MAP, but not with those of 6 MAP. On dry weight basis, the trend was similar as in fresh weight of the harvest index (Table 3.4).

Table 3.1: Chemical and Physical Properties of Soil of the Experimental Site

Properties	Values
Total Sand (%)	71.2
Total Silt (%)	14.0
Total Clay (%)	14.8
Available Water Content (%)	15.0
Field Bulk Density (gcm^{-3}) 0-10 cm 10-20 cm	1.5 1.65
pH in water	5.02
pH in KCl	4.14
Total nitrogen (%)	0.30
Organic matter content (%)	1.41
Available phosphorus (ppm)	6.50
CEC (meq/100g Soil)	4.40

Table 3.2: The Effect of Genotypes (G), Ages of Harvest (A) and G × A Interaction on Total Plant Biomass (Dry Weight) (g)

	Months After Planting			
Genotypes	6	9	12	Mean
NR 930061	381.62	369.60	670.97	474.60
NR 930199	468.98	594.92	1383.12	815.55
Local Best	418.89	365.79	755.35	513.34
NR 930163	790.60	592.63	1179.95	854.39
TMS 96/0160	795.09	643.55	998.32	812.32
NR 930127	372.50	240.67	703.44	438.87
TMS 96/1672	635.40	457.17	895.71	692.76
TMS 96/1432	727.54	546.83	1229.80	834.72
NR 930255	765.61	627.84	1138.78	844.08
TMS 96/1087	687.10	665.34	1326.58	893.00
TMS 30572	768.85	486.68	987.58	747.70
TMS 96/0304	748.57	634.07	1145.70	842.78
Mean	630.03	518.76	1042.11	730.34

F-LSD $_{0.05}$ for comparing any 2 Genotype means	278.70
F-LSD $_{0.05}$ for comparing any 2 Age of growth means	139.35
F-LSD $_{0.05}$ for comparing any G × A interaction means	Ns

Table 3.3: The Effect of Genotypes (G), Age at Harvest (A) and G x A Interaction on Fresh Weight Harvest Index (%)

	Months After Planting			
Genotypes	6	9	12	Mean
NR 930061	76.44	73.20	79.56	76.40
NR 930199	61.54	69.69	85.56	72.25
Local Best	69.41	63.22	82.35	71.66
NR 930163	72.25	67.87	82.59	74.24
TMS 96/0160	71.97	66.71	75.49	71.39
NR930127	78.06	68.38	83.87	76.77
TMS 96/1672	78.30	71.44	83.60	77.78
TMS 96/1432	75.56	71.57	85.14	77.42

	Months After Planting			
Genotypes	6	9	12	Mean
NR 930061	74.71	75.14	79.67	76.51
NR 930199	56.63	69.61	84.55	70.26
Local Best	70.24	67.93	82.74	73.64
NR 930163	72.34	69.69	82.69	74.90
TMS 96/0160	67.41	67.72	78.60	71.24
NR930127	76.54	71.73	84.44	77.57
TMS 96/1672	72.72	70.30	82.47	75.16
TMS 96/1432	74.22	74.76	86.04	78.34
NR 930255	63.83	59.75	72.92	65.50
TMS 96/1087	55.09	61.31	74.25	63.55
TMS 30572	64.64	60.00	77.85	67.50
TMS 96/0304	73.59	72.96	81.78	76.11
Mean	68.50	68.41	80.67	72.52
F-LSD $_{0.05}$ for comparing any 2 Genotype means			5.621	
F-LSD $_{0.05}$ for comparing any 2 Age of growth means			2.810	
F-LSD $_{0.05}$ for comparing any G x A interaction means			NS	

Genotypes	6	9	12	Mean
NR 930255	62.27	58.02	72.69	64.32
TMS 96/1087	57.76	61.77	74.03	64.52
TMS 30572	69.56	57.27	75.69	67.51
TMS 96/0304	77.29	75.30	84.41	79.00
Mean	70.87	67.04	80.41	72.77

(Contd...)

	Months After Planting			
Genotypes	6	9	12	Mean
NR 930061	855.7	1013.7	1733.3	1200.9
NR 930199	631.7	1138.0	3200.0	1656.6
Local Best	766.7	794.6	2000.0	1187.1
NR 930163	1409.1	1052.2	2433.3	1631.5
TMS 96/0160	1350.3	1302.3	2766.7	1806.4
NR930127	711.5	543.9	1783.3	1012.9
TMS 96/1672	1205.5	983.1	2400.0	1529.5
TMS 96/1432	1429.1	1297.6	2300.0	2008.9
NR 930255	1313.8	975.5	2200.0	1496.4
TMS/96/1087	1017.0	1142.6	2966.0	1708.7
TMS/30572	1260.5	880.9	2600.0	1580.5

Table 3.4: The Effect of Genotypes (G), Age at Harvest (A) and G × A Interaction on Harvest Index (%) on Dry Weight Basis

F-LSD $_{0.05}$ for comparing any 2 Genotype means	6.142
F-LSD $_{0.05}$ for comparing any 2 Age of growth means	3.071
F-LSD $_{0.05}$ for comparing any G x A interaction means	NS

However, TMS 96/0304 had significantly ($p<0.05$) higher harvest index (dry wt.) compared with other genotypes, while NR 930258 produced the least dry weight harvest index. The harvest index (dry wt.) also dropped significantly ($p<0.05$) at 9 MAP compared with 12 MAP, but did not differ significantly with that at 6 MAP. Combinations of genotype and age of harvest did not attain any level of statistical significance with respect to harvest index (fresh wt. or dry wt.). Neither the genotype nor their interaction with harvesting age significantly affected tuber fresh weight of cassava significantly (Table 3.5). Nevertheless, fresh tuber yield harvested at 9 MAP were significantly ($p<0.05$) lower than those harvested at 12 MAP, but not statistically lower than those at 6 MAP. Similarly, the fresh tuber yield (tons per ha) was not significantly influenced by either the genotypes or their interaction with harvesting age (Table 3.6). Nonetheless, the tuber yields at 9 MAP were significantly ($p<0.05$) lower compared with those harvested at 12 MAP, but did not differ with those harvested at 6 MAP.

Both the genotypes of cassava and ages at harvest significantly ($p<0.05$) affected pulp-to-peel ratio on fresh and dry weight bases (Table 3.7).

Table 3.5: The Effect of Genotypes (G), Age at Harvest (A) and G × A Interaction on Fresh Weight (g) of Tubers

TMS 96/1087	1017.0	1142.6	2966.0	1708.7
TMS 30572	1260.5	880.9	2600.0	1580.5
TMS 96/0304	1527.3	1224.6	3415.7	1722.9
Mean	1123.2	1029.1	2483.3	1545.2

F-LSD $_{0.05}$ for comparing any 2 genotype means	NS
F-LSD $_{0.05}$ for comparing any 2 Age of growth means	312.25
F-LSD $_{0.05}$ for comparing any G x A interaction means	NS

Table 3.6: The Effect of Genotype (G), Age at Harvest (A) and G × A Interaction on Fresh Tuber Yield (Tons per Hectare)

	Months After Planting			
Genotypes	6	9	12	Mean
NR 930061	8.6	10.1	17.3	12.0
NR 930199	6.3	11.4	32.0	16.6
Local Best	7.7	8.0	20.0	11.9
NR 930163	14.1	10.5	24.3	16.3
TMS 96/0160	13.5	13.0	27.7	18.1
NR930127	7.1	5.4	17.8	10.1
TMS 96/1672	12.0	9.8	24.0	15.3
TMS 96/1432	14.3	13.0	33.0	20.1
NR 930255	13.2	9.8	22.0	15.0
TMS 96/1087	10.2	11.4	29.7	17.1
TMS 30572	12.6	8.8	26.0	15.8
TMS 96/0304	15.3	12.2	24.2	17.2
Mean	11.2	10.2	24.8	15.5

F-LSD $_{0.05}$ for comparing any 2 Genotype means	NS
F-LSD $_{0.05}$ for comparing any 2 Age of growth means	3.12
F-LSD $_{0.05}$ for comparing any G x A interaction means	NS

Table 3.7: The Effect of Genotype (G), Age at Harvest (A) and G x A Interaction on Fresh and Dry Weight Pulp-to-peel Ratio

*Fresh and Dry weight pulp-to-peel ratio				
	Months After Planting			
Genotypes	6	9	12	Mean
NR 930061	3.5(5.1)	2.8(5.0)	2.6(3.5)	3.0(4.5)
NR 930199	3.0(4.4)	3.4(4.9)	2.9(4.4)	3.1(4.6)
Local Best	3.6(5.7)	4.4(6.1)	3.3(4.8)	3.7(5.6)
NR 930163	3.9(5.0)	5.2(7.2)	3.8(4.6)	4.3(5.6)
TMS 96/0160	4.2(6.6)	4.3(7.9)	3.3(4.9)	4.0(6.5)
NR930127	3.9(5.6)	3.8(6.7)	3.4(4.8)	3.7(5.7)
TMS 96/1672	3.8(6.5)	3.8(6.9)	3.1(4.5)	3.5(6.0)
TMS 96/1432	3.6(5.5)	3.7(5.3)	2.9(4.5)	3.4(5.1)
NR 930255	3.4(5.0)	4.2(7.2)	3.4(5.2)	3.7(5.8)
TMS 96/1087	3.6(5.5)	4.4(7.3)	3.7(6.1)	3.9(6.3)
TMS 30572	3.6(5.0)	4.6(5.3)	4.2(5.5)	4.1(5.2)
TMS 96/0304	4.4(6.1)	5.2(7.4)	4.3(6.5)	4.6(6.7)
Mean	3.7(5.5)	4.1(6.4)	3.4(4.9)	3.8(5.6)

	Fresh Weight	Dry Weight
F-LSD $_{0.05}$ for comparing any 2 Genotype means	0.47	0.88
F-LSD $_{0.05}$ for comparing any 2 Age of growth means	0.24	0.44
F-LSD $_{0.05}$ for comparing any G x A interaction means	NS	NS

* Dry weight pulp-to-peel ratio in parentheses.

The TMS 96/0304 produced significantly ($p<0.05$) higher fresh and dry pulp-to-peel weights ratio compared with other genotypes. There was an increase in fresh and dry pulp-to-peel ratio as harvest age increased but later decreased at 12 MAP. Consequently, 6 MAP had higher fresh and dry pulp-to-peel ratio, while the lowest was obtained at 12 MAP. Generally, the interaction of genotypes and age of harvest did not attain any level of statistical significance with respect to pulp-to-peel ratio on fresh and dry weight bases.

There was no significant difference also on the severity ratings of anthracnose and mosaic disease symptoms obtained on the cassava leaves amongst the sampling period (6, 9 and 12 MAP) (Table 3.8). However, cassava blight symptoms were significantly ($p<0.05$) more severe at 12 MAP (3.5) than at the other sampling periods. The green spider mites and mealy bug populations were not statistically affected by the genotypes in the field

(Table 3.9). On the other hand, the severities of cassava anthracnose disease (CAD), cassava bacteria blight (CBB) and cassava mosaic disease (CMD) were significantly ($p<0.05$) affected by the various genotypes screened. This is such that genotype NR 930255 recorded significantly ($p<0.05$) higher mosaic disease rating (2.4) than other genotypes, while NR 930127, TMS 96/1087 and TMS 30572 were less severely infected (1.0). The result also showed that the local best cultivar had significantly ($p<0.05$) higher CBB severity rating (3.4) than the other genotypes with NR 930127 harboring the least CBB infection rating (2.2). Mosaic disease severity rating from the same result was significantly ($p<0.05$) higher also on NR 930127 compared with other genotypes, while TMS 96/1432 had the least severity rating of 1.2.

Table 3.8: Periodic Disease Severity of CAD, CBB and CMD on Plant Age

Months After Planting	CAD	CBB	CMD
6	1.6	2.2	2.0
9	1.6	2.4	2.4
12	1.8	3.5	2.2
F-LSD$_{(0.05)}$	NS	0.24	NS

CAD Cassava Anthracnose Disease
CBB Cassava Bacterial Blight
CMB Cassava Mosaic Disease

Table 3.9: Disease and Pest Responses of 12 Cassava Genotypes Evaluated in the Field

Genotypes	CAD	CBB	CMD	CGSM	CM
NR 930061	1.4	2.3	2.8	3.0	1.7
NR 930199	1.8	2.7	1.3	3.0	1.3
Local Best	1.8	3.4	2.9	3.7	1.0
NR 930163	1.8	2.6	2.7	3.3	1.7
TMS 96/0160	1.7	2.4	1.8	3.0	1.0
NR930127	1.0	2.2	3.0	3.0	1.7
TMS 96/1672	1.9	2.8	1.9	3.7	1.7
TMS 96/1432	1.4	2.7	1.2	4.0	1.3
NR 930255	2.4	3.0	2.7	3.3	1.0
TMS 96/1087	1.0	2.9	2.0	3.7	1.7
TMS 30572	1.0	2.7	2.1	3.3	1.0
TMS 96/0304	2.8	2.7	2.1	2.3	1.7
F-LSD$_{(0.05)}$	0.42	0.39	0.62	NS	NS

CAD Cassava Anthracnose Disease
CBB Cassava Bacterial Blight
CMD Cassava Mosaic Disease
CGSM Cassava Green Spider Mite
CM Cassava Mealy bug

Although the weight loss of cassava chips, quantity of powdery substances produced over time, the number of exit holes produced and number of weevils sampled during post-harvest storage were significantly ($p<0.05$) affected by the genotypes, the mould incidence on the various genotypes were statistically similar (Table 3.10). The local best ("Otupam") experienced significantly ($p<0.05$) higher weight loss (4.31 g) compared to the other genotypes. This was followed by TMS 96/0304 with (3.16 g), while the lowest (0.14g) was obtained from the TMS 96/1672, followed by TMS 96/1432 with 0.17g. The percentage weight loss was higher in the TMS 96/0304 which ranked second in the weight loss followed by TMS 30572, the positive check. The negative check local best ("Otupam') which ranked first in weight loss was third in per cent weight loss. The least per cent weight loss was obtained from TMS 96/1672 followed by the TMS 96/1432, resulting in the genotypes with less percentage weight loss performing better under storage with minimal loss in weight. On the basis of powdery substances production during storage, the local best ("Otupam") which was among the genotypes that recorded the highest weight loss and percentage weight loss, produced the highest quantity of powdery substances followed by the NR 93/30162.

Table 3.10: The Main Effects of Genotypes of Storage Qualities of Cassava Chips

Genotypes	Weight Loss (g)	Weight Loss (%)	PW Weight (g)	NEH	NW	MI
NR 930061	0.30	2.29	0.15	0.41	0.24	0.30
NR 930199	1.74	1.69	1.25	23.52	4.97	0.30
Local Best	4.37	4.58	4.37	36.48	15.21	0.30
NR 930163	3.53	2.76	3.35	118.75	7.56	0.40
TMS 96/0160	2.66	2.66	2.50	24.40	8.82	0.38
NR930127	1.21	1.08	1.02	11.16	4.04	0.42
TMS 96/1672	0.14	0.12	0.04	0.04	0.10	0.30
TMS 96/1432	0.17	0.16	0.06	0.04	0.04	0.42
NR 930255	0.98	0.88	0.42	4.67	1.99	0.42
TMS 96/1087	2.59	2.43	2.40	54.02	14.59	0.42
TMS 30572	2.50	9.30	2.16	28.41	10.83	0.42
TMS 96/0304	3.61	17.22	2.96	58.52	12.07	0.42
Mean	1.98	3.60	1.72	21.70	6.71	0.38
$F\text{-}LSD_{(0.05)}$	0.45	2.20	0.09	13.26	0.45	NS

PW Weight (g) Powdery waste weight (g)
NEH Number of exit holes
NW Number of weevils
MI Mould incidence

The TMS 96/1672 and the TMS 96/1432 that had a significantly ($p<0.05$) lower weight loss and percentage weight loss recorded the least quantity of powdery substances. TMS 96/0304 had the highest number of exit holes followed by the TMS 96/1087. The least number of exit holes came from both the TMS 96/1672 and the TMS 96/1432.The highest number of weevils was sampled from the local best cultivar, followed by the TMS 96/1087, while the least was sampled from the TMS 96/1432 followed by the TMS 96/1672, which sustained lowest number of weevils.

Harvesting cassava tubers at 9 MAP significantly ($p<0.05$) increased the weight loss of dry chips, production of powdery dust, number of exit holes and number of weevils compared with when harvested at either 6 MAP or 12 MAP (Table 3.11). The mould incidence found on the dry chips was however not significantly affected by harvesting time of cassava tubers.

Table 3.11: The Main Effect of Age on Storage Qualities of Cassava Chips

Plant Age at Harvest (Months)	Weight Loss (g)	Weight Loss (%)	PW Weight (g)	NEH	NW	MI
6	0.30	3.35	0.62	3.84	0.76	0.66
9	5.34	15.52	4.75	59.14	4.48	0.52
12	0.83	1.10	0.26	4.45	0.41	0.10
Mean	2.16	6.66	1.88	22.48	2.00	0.43
$F\text{-}LSD_{0.05}$	0.01	0.24	0.16	2.47	0.01	NS

PW Weight (g) Powdery waste weight in grams
NEH Number of exit holes
NW Number of weevils
MI Mould incidence

DISCUSSION

In agriculture, the ultimate yield of the production is very important as this determines if one is operating at a loss or not. Yield per hectare (fresh tuber) was not significant among the genotypes; however, TMS 96/1432 gave the highest fresh tuber yield. In plantain and banana, many environmental factors interact to determine the final fruit size. These include adequate moisture, light and mineral utilization (Dennis, 1982). The performance of any crop is usually affected by the properties of the soil in which the crop is grown (Morton, 1987; Nweke *et al.,* 1998). Age at harvest was statistically significant. Instead of a continuous upward trend in fresh tuber yield as harvest age increases, there was a decline at 9 MAP, with 12 MAP having the highest fresh tuber yield. The decline at 9 MAP may be attributed to the dry spell caused by harmattan around that period. Under such stress conditions, there will be higher accumulations of dry matter in the tubers. Onwueme

(1978) noted that in regions that have distinct wet and dry seasons, cassava planting should be done as early as possible in the wet season. In this way, the plants will be able to make appreciable growth before the onset of the adverse dry season. The report further stated that it is however possible to get reasonable yields from plantings made at any time during the rainy season.

The actual yield and the consistency of yield of adapted cultivars in a particular environment is its ultimate index of adaptation, but yield is an outcome of several processes at all stages in the growth and development of a crop including response to pests and diseases. The newly developed genotypes compared favourably with the local cultivar in terms of total biomass, harvest index, pulp-to-peel ratio and tolerance to CBB and CMD. Similarly, they compared favourably with the improved in terms of total biomass, tuber yield, and tolerance to CBB and CMD. On the other hand, they performed better than either the local or the improved varieties in terms of fresh tuber yield, weight loss of tuber, resistance to damage by stored pests (assessed by weight of powdery wastes produced, number of exit holes, and weevil count). This suggests that the new genotypes are well adapted to the new environment (by comparing favourably with the local in terms of yield), but better than either the local or the improved variety in terms of storability as chips. This could be attributed to the genetic compositions of these newly developed genotypes. The periodic disease severity was not significant for both CAD and CMD, but CBB was statistically significant with 9 MAP being seriously affected. There were significant genetic responses to the diseases but severity indices for the pests were similar. TMS 96/0304 had the highest severity rating for CAD. Local best ("Otupam") sustained the most severe attack of CBB, while NR 930127 was most susceptible to CMD. Asiegbu (2000) estimated crop losses to pest and disease in developing countries to about 30%, with losses of up to 50-70% in tubers, and 40-60% in cereals due to uncontrolled weed growth in maize. Tuber harvest age effect on storage quality attributes of cassava chips was statistically significant among the various cassava genotypes. Nine (9) months old plants in storage performed worse than to those of 6 months and 12 months old plant. However, storage was best among 12 MAP, probably because the tubers were older and more lignified at 12 MAP than other preceding dates. Meanwhile, TMS 96/1672, TMS 96/1432 and NR 930061 had the best storage attributes of cassava chips because they recorded the least weight loss, powdery waste, exit holes, number of weevils and mould incidence. This could probably be attributed to some inherent genetic make-up of the genotypes.

CONCLUSION

The fresh tuber yield, although did not significantly differ among the genotypes, TMS 96/1432, a newly developed genotype, gave the highest yield. This genotype with TMS 96/1672 and NR 930061 also had the best storage attributes as cassava chips. While TMS 96/0304 had the highest severity rating for CAD, the local best "Otupam" sustained the most severe CBB attack and NR 930127 was most susceptible to CMD. Newly developed genotypes compared favourably with the local in terms of total biomass, harvest index, pulp-to-peel ratio and tolerance to CBB and CMD damage. It compared also favourably with improved genotypes in terms of total biomass, tuber yield and tolerance to CBB and CMD damage. The new genotypes were superior to either the local or the improved genotypes in terms of fresh tuber yield, weight loss of tuber, and storability as chips.

REFERENCES

Adejunji CM (2005). Nigerian Cassava Chips in China Market. Agric Business Today. May, 2005. pp. 2.

Asiedu, JJ (1989). Processing Tropical Crops: A Technological Approach. Macmillian Publishers. Hong Kong.

Asiegbu JE (2000). The Challenges of Crop Production in Nigeria for the 21st Century. Agro-Science J. Trop. Agric. Fd. Environt and Ext. 1 (1) 47.

Ayernor GS (1985). Fffect of the Gratting of Cassava on Product Yield and Cyanide Detoxification. J. Fd Techn. 20: 89-96.

Berry SS (1993). Socio-economic Aspects of Cassava Cultivation and Use in Africa: Implication for the Development of Appropriate Technology: COSCA Working Paper No. 8. Collaborative Study of Cassava in Africa, International Institute of Tropical Agriculture, Ibadan, Nigeria.

Bokanga MO, Hair SK, Naraganan KR, Steinkraus KH (1990). Cyanide Detoxification and Nutritional Changes during Cassava (*Manihot esculenta* Crantz) Fermentation pp. 385-392. In: Proceedings of the 8th Symposium of International Society for Tropical Root Crops, Bangkok, Thailand, 30 October to 5 November 1988, Edited by Howeler, RH. Centro International de Agricultura Tropical, Cali, Columbia.

Carter SE, Jones PG, Fairbarin JN (1989). An Atlas of Cassava in Africa. Historical Agro-ecological and Demographic Aspects of Crop Distribution. Cal. Colombia: International de Agricultura Tropical, (CIAT) Cali, Columbia.

Dennis FG (1982). Fruit Development. In: Physiological Basis of Crop Growth and Development. Am. Soc. Agron. USA. pp. 265-289.

Ezeala DO, Okoro, N (1986). Processing Techniques and Hydrocyanic Acid Content of Cassava Based Human Food Stuffs in Nigeria J. Fd Bioch. 10: 125-132.

GENSTAT (2007). GENSTAT Release 7.2 DE, Discovery Edition 3, Lawes Agricultural Trust. Rothamsted Experimental Station. U.K.

Guardian Newspaper (Nigerian Newspaper) (2005).Vol. 22. No. 9739 of Friday July 22, 2005. p. 63.

IITA (International Institute of Tropical Agriculture, Ibadan Nigeria) (1990). Annual Report. 1990.

IITA (International Institute of Tropical Agriculture, Ibadan Nigeria) (1998). Annual Report. 1998.

IITA (International Institute of Tropical Agriculture, Ibadan Nigeria) (2005). Annual Report. 2005.

Morton J (1987). Banana. In: Fruits of Warm Climate. Edited by Julia F. Morton, Miami. pp. 29-46.

Nweke FI (1996). Cassava Processing in Sub-Saharan Africa: Implications for Expanding Cassava Production. IITA Research Number 12, March 1996 pp. 7-13.

Nweke FI, Kapinga RE, Dxon AGP, Ajobo O, Asadu CLA (1998). COSCA No. 16 Production Process Cassava Prospects for Cassava in Tanzania. pp. 9-18.

Obi IU (2002) Statistical Method of Detecting Differences Between Treatment Means and Research Methodology Issues in Laboratory and Field Experiment. AP Express Publishers, Nsukka 28 pp. 39-44.

Okafor N, Ejiofor MAN (1986). The Microbial Breakdown of Linamarin in Fermenting Cassava Pulp (*Manihot esculenta* Crantz) MIRCEN J 2: 327-338.

Olojede AO, Okereke OU, Ikeorgu JEG (2002). Evaluation of New Cassava Genotypes for Intercropping in a Cassava Based System of South Eastern Nigeria. Nigeria Agric. J. 33: 50-70.

Onwueme IC (1972). The Influence of the Weight of the Planted Tuber on the Vegetative Performance of White Yam (*Dioscora rotundata* Poir) Plants. Nigeria Agric. J. pp. 170-173.

Osiru DSO, Porto, MCM, Ekenayake, IJ (1995). IITA Research Guide 55. Physiology of Cassava.

Rehm, S. and Espig, G (1991). The Cultivated Plants of the Tropics and Subtropic. Cultivation, Economic Value Utilization IAT (Institute of Agronomy in the Tropics) University of Gottingen. pp. 37-44.

4

Use of Ash to Improve the Nutrient Content of an Ultisol and its Effect on Maize (Zea mays L.) Growth and Dry Matter Yield

C.N. Mbah[1*]; Njoku C.[1]; Ngene P.[1]; Oludare C.G.[2]

ABSTRACT

This study evaluated the effect of ash from different sources on soil properties, growth and dry matter yield of maize (Zea mays L) in 2010 and 2011 cropping seasons. The experiment was laid out as a randomized complete block design with four treatments [wood ash (WA), coconut shell ash (CA) and mixture of WA+CA (WCA)] and five replications and a control. Ash application significantly (p=0.05) increased soil pH, % OM, available P,and Total N in both seasons. Results also show increased Ca, K, Na, Mg and ECEC in ash amended plots relative to the control in both seasons. Similarly significantly higher plant height and dry matter yield were observed in ash amended plot compared to the control in both seasons. Observed results show highest improvement in dry matter yield, plant height and soil properties in plots amended with mixed ash (WCA) in both seasons.

Keywords: Ash, dry matter yield, plant height, maize, soil properties.

---

1. Department of Soil Science and Environmental Management, Ebonyi State University, P.M.B. 053, Abakaliki – Nigeria.
2. Department of Soil Science and Technology, Federal University of Technology, Owerri – Nigeria.

INTRODUCTION

Changes in mineral composition of soils and plants usually result in serious alterations in the plant metabolism. Ash is as valuable as fertilizers and herbicides. It is used as liming materials to reduce the effect of acidity which hinders proper agricultural production in the tropics. According to Jayalakshmi *et al.*, (2007) ash improves soil texture, bulk density, permeability, water holding capacity/aeration, fertility status, resistance to pest attack and reduce crust formation. Research results (Jacobson, 2001; Vuorinen and Kurkela, 2000; Demeyer *et al.*, 2001) revealed positive effects of woodash on Ca and K contents of the soil as well as increase of K, Mg, S, Bo, Fe, and Zinc in tissues of the Scott pine. Adekayode and Olujugba (2010) reported significantly higher maize grain yield in a plot with a mixture of ash and 200 $kgha^{-1}$ NPK 15 – 15 – 15 fertilizer. Mbah *et al.*, (2010) reported reduction in soil acidity to levels required for maize production in ash amended plots relative to the control. Similarly, Odedina *et al.*, (2003) observed reduced acidity and increased cation availability in soils amended with wood ash. Saarsalm *et al.*, (2001) reported increase in the concentration of soil nutrients except N in soil amended with woodash. Bramyrd and Fransman (1995) and Arvidson and Lunkvrst (2003) noted that the enrichment of soil due to ash would cause changes in the metabolism and physiological activity of plants which may manifest in crop yield. However, research efforts on ash have concentrated on wood with little or no research on other types of ash and their effect on soil properties and crop yield. The aim of this study was to find out the effect of ash from different sources and their combination on soil properties and maize dry matter yield.

MATERIALS AND METHODS

Study Area

The experiment was conducted during the growing seasons of 2010 and 2011 at the Teaching and Research Farm of the department of Soil Science and Technology, School of Agriculture and Agricultural Technology, Federal University of Technology, Owerri-Southeast Nigeria. The area lies between latitude 04°40'N and 08°15'N and longitude 06°40'E and 08°15'E. The area is characterized by high rainfall and high temperature with ranges of 2000-2500 mm and 26°C – 29°C, respectively. The predominant parent material underlying Imo State from which most of the soils are formed are the coastal plain sands popularly known as acid soil (Orajaka, 1975). The soil is classified as plinthic Tropudult/plinthic acrisol (FDALR, 1985). The main vegetation of the study area is rainforest with poor soil nutrient content as a result of high rainfall enhancing leaching. Farming constitutes a major socio-economic activity in the study area.

Field Methods

The site was slashed and cleared of grasses. A total land area of 15.0 m × 13.5 m (202.5 m^2) was mapped out on the same plots in the 2010 and 2011 planting seasons. The field was divided into four blocks with each block having five experimental units giving a total of 20 plots. The experimental units were demarcated by 1 m alleys and each plot measures 3 × 3 m (9 m^2). The experimental design was randomized complete block design (RCBD). The treatments were: 4 t ha^{-1} wood ash (WA), 4 t ha^{-1} coconut shell ash (CSA), 2 t ha^{-1} WA + 2 t ha^{-1} CSA (WCA) and 0 t ha^{-1} (C). The choice of 4 t ha^{-1} as the rate of the treatments was based on the recommendation of Mbah *et al.*, (2010). The experimental plots (raised beds 30 cm high) were prepared manually with traditional hoes and the treatments incorporated into the beds during tillage. The maize variety used was Oba Super 11. Two grains of maize were planted per hole at a depth of 5 cm using 50 cm apart intra and inter – row spacing. The maize plants were thinned to one stand/plot at two weeks after germination.

Observation and Data Collection

Composite soil samples were collected from ten points at a depth of 0-20 cm for pre-planting laboratory analysis. Similarly, auger samples were collected from each plot at 90 days after planting (DAP) for post harvest analysis. Maize dry matter yield was measured at harvest 90 DAP. For plant height and maize dry matter yield measurements, 10 plants were randomly selected, tagged and sampled. The ten plants were uprooted, air-dried and their root cut off. The dried plants were weighed for dried matter yield.

Laboratory Methods

The pre and post-harvest soil samples were analyzed in laboratory for N, P, K, Ca, Mg, Na, pH, organic carbon, and effective cation capacity(ECEC). Total N was determined by the macro-kjeldahl method (Bremner and Mulvaney, 1982). Available P was determined using Bray 11 method as outlined in Olsen (1982). Organic carbon was analyzed by Walkley/Black procedure (Nelson and Sommers, 1982). Soil pH in KCl was determined by the glass electrode pH meter (Mclean, 1982). The exchangeable cations were determined by the method described by Thomas (1982) while the ECEC was determined by summation. Particle size distribution was determined by hydrometer method (Gee and Bauder, 1986).

Data Analysis

The data collected from the study was analyzed using analysis of variance test based on RCBD (using F-LSD at $P < 0.05$ according to the procedure outlined by Steel and Torrie (1980).

RESULTS

Table 4.1 shows that the soil of the study area has low OM % content and medium total N and available P contents according to the ratings of Landon, (1991). Application of WA, CA, and WCA significantly ($p < 0.05$) increased the soil organic matter (OM%), total nitrogen (TN%), and available P relative to control in both planting seasons (Table 4.2). In the first planting season highest available P (73.27 $Mgkg^{-1}$) and OM% (2.33%) contents of the soil was observed in WCA amended plots. The observed OM% of 2.33% in WCA amended plot in 2010 planting season was 29%, 18% and 16 % higher than OM% values in C, CA and WA, respectively. The order of increase in TN% and available P values in 2011 planting season was WA>CA=WCA>C and WCA>WA>CA>C, respectively. Similarly, application of ash increased soil pH in amended plots relative to the control in both seasons. In 2010 planting season observed ash value in C plot was 9%, 6% and 10% lower than observed ash values in WA, CA and WCA amended plot, respectively. The order of decrease in soil pH in the 2011 planting season was C<CA<WA<WSA. Results of the study (Table 4.3) show significant ($P < 0.05$) higher exchangeable cations and ECEC values in ash amended plots relative to the control in both seasons. In 2010 planting season Mg and Ca content ranged between 1.83 – 2.98 $Cmolkg^{-1}$ and 4.56 – 6.01 $Cmolkg^{-1}$in ash amended plots, respectively. Similarly, Na, K, and ECEC values were observed to be within the range of 0.10 – 0.19 $Cmolkg^{-1}$, 0.12 – 0.17 $Cmolkg^{-1}$ and 6.06 – 13.19 $Cmolkg^{-1}$, respectively, in 2011 planting season. In both seasons lowest values of Na, K, Ca, Mg and ECEC were observed in the C plots. Table 4.4 shows that ash application as soil amendment significantly ($P < 0.05$) increased plant height and dry matter yield relative to the control in both seasons. In 2010 and 2011planting seasons observed plant height in ash amended plots ranged between 98.57 – 110.73 cm and 104.50 – 120.20 cm, respectively. Table 4 also show significantly higher dry matter yield in amended plots relative to the control. In both seasons WCA amendment gave highest plant height (110 cm and 120.2 cm) and highest dry matter yield (19.34g and 21.92g). The dry matter yield value of 21.92g observed in WCA amended plot in 2011 planting season was 640%, 21% and 7% higher than values in C, CA and WA amended plots, respectively. Higher values of the measured soil and plant parameters were observed in 2011 compared to 2010 planting season. For instance observed Ca, OM%, plant height and dry matter yield values in WCA amended plot in 2011 planting season were 2%, 17%, 9% and 13%, respectively higher than values obtained in 2010 cropping season.

DISCUSSIONS

The observed increase in soil pH in ash amended plots relative to the control could be attributed to the effect of ash (which contains Ca) on soil acidity.

Table 4.1: Initial Soil Properties of the Study Site

Parameter	Value
pH	5.30
Organic Matter (%)	1.99
Total N (%)	0.17
Available P ($Mgkg^{-1}$)	25.80
Exchangeable cations ($Cmolkg^{-1}$)	
Ca	4.80
Mg	1.93
Na	0.16
K	0.17
ECEC	8.91
Particle size (%)	
Sand	87.50
Silt	5.88
Clay	6.62

In a study on the response of maize (zea mays L.) to different rates of wood ash application in an acid ultisol in south east Nigeria, Mbah *et al.,* (2010) reported increase soil pH in ash amended plot. Similarly, Adetunji (1997) observed that ash application in soil reduces soil acidity and increases availability of K, Ca and Mg in soil. Furthermore, the increase in plant height and dry matter yield observed in ash amended plots could be due to improved soil condition as a result of increased levels of exchangeable bases (Ca, Na, K and Mg), OM%, and available P content of the soil. Using ash as amendments Jacobson (2001) and Demeyer *et al.,* (2001) revealed that application of ash has positive effect on the Ca and K content of the soil. Similarly, Saarsalmi (2001) reported increased concentration of soil nutrients in soil amended with ash while Arvidson and Lunkvist (2003) observed increased crop yield resulting from enrichment of soil due to ash application. Ojeniyi *et al.,*(2001) reported improved yield of vegetable crops and nutrient level of soil due to wood ash application. In a study on the effect of different crop residue management techniques on selected properties and grain production of maize, Mbah and Nneji (2011) reported improved pH and increased maize yield in plots incorporated with ash. The observed increase in ECEC in ash amended plots could be as a result of increase in soil exchangeable bases (Mg, Ca, K and Na) in line with the observations of Kayode and Agboola (1993).

Table 4.2: Effect of the Amendments on Soil pH, avail.P, Total N and Organic Matter

	2010 Planting Season				2011 Planting Season			
Treatment	pH	avail.P (Mgkg^{-1})	OM (%)	TN (%)	pH	avail.P (Mgkg^{-1})	OM (%)	TN (%)
WA	5.64	50.21	1.97	0.17	5.68	53.44	2.01	0.17
CA	5.32	37.02	1.93	0.16	5.29	38.26	1.97	0.16
WCA	5.63	68.71	1.99	0.14	5.74	73.27	2.33	0.16
Control (C)	5.18	25.46	1.86	0.12	5.20	25.03	1.80	0.15
LSD $_{0.05}$	0.11	1.20	0.06	0.03	0.12	0.53	0.15	0.02

WA = wood ash, CA = coconut palm ash, WCA = wood ash + coconut palm ash, C = control

Table 4.3: Effect of the Amendments on Soil Exchangeable Bases and ECEC (Cmolkg^{-1})

	2010 Planting Season					2011 Planting Season				
Treatment	Na	K	Mg	Ca	ECEC	Na	K	Mg	Ca	ECEC
WA	0.15	0.16	3.98	4.56	8.63	0.17	0.16	3.44	4.75	9.47
CA	0.17	0.17	1.83	6.06	10.00	0.19	0.16	1.92	8.32	11.01
WCA	0.18	0.17	2.00	6.00	12.03	0.20	0.17	2.16	6.12	13.19
Control (C)	0.11	0.13	1.70	4.50	6.32	0.10	0.12	1.66	4.06	6.06
LSD $_{0.05}$	0.02	0.01	0.38	0.61	1.20	0.03	0.02	0.09	0.19	0.05

WA = wood ash, CA = coconut palm ash, WCA = wood ash + coconut palm ash, C = control

Table 4.4: Effect of the Amendments on Maize Plant Height and Dry Matter Yield

	2010 Planting Season		2011 Planting Season	
Treatment	Height (cm)	Dry Matter Yield (g)	Height (cm)	Dry Matter Yield (g)
WA	105.60	18.33	110.50	20.37
CA	98.51	15.06	104.50	18.10
WCA	110.13	19.34	120.20	21.92
Control (C)	90.02	3.04	87.65	2.96
$LSD_{0.05}$	2.18	0.18	3.27	0.65

WA = wood ash, CA = coconut palm ash, WCA = wood ash + coconut palm ash, C = control

CONCLUSION

Result of this study shows that ash application improves soil chemical properties leading to increase in maize growth and dry matter yield. Results also show that highest improvement in soil properties, maize growth and dry matter yield were observed in WCA amended plots in both seasons, thus indicating that mixture of ash (from different sources) are better source of soil amendment compared to ash from single source.

REFERENCES

Adekayode F.O. and Olujugba. A.2010. The Utilization of Wood Ash Manure to Reduce the Use of Mineral Fertilizer for Improves Performance of Maize (Zea Mays L.) as Measured in the Chlorophyll Content and Grain Yield. *Journ. Soil Sci. and Environmental Management 1(3): 40-45.*

Adetunji M.T. 1997. Organic Residue Management and Nutrient Cycling. Agro – Ecosystems. 47: 189-195.

Arvidson H. and Lunkvist H. 2003. Using of Pulverized Fuel Ash from Victorian Brown Coal as a Source of Nutrients for Pasture Species. Australian Journ. of Experimental Agriculture, Animal Hushandary 20: 377-384.

Bramyrd T. and Fransman B. 1995. Silvicultural Use of Wood Ash. Effect of Nutrients and Heavy Metal Balance in a Pine (Pinus sylvestris L.). Forest, Soil and Air; Soil Pollution 85: 1039-1044.

Bremner J.M. and Mulvaney C.S. 1982. Total Nitrogen. In: Page A.L., Miller R.H. and Keeny D.R. eds. Methods of Soil Analysis. Part 1. ASA, No. 9 Madison.

Demeyer A., Voundikanas J.C. and Verloo M.C. 2001. Characteristics of Wood Ash and Influence on Soil Properties and Nutrient Uptake. Journ. of Soil Sc. 1(12) 112-116.

Federal Department of Agriculture and Land Resources 1985. Reconnaissance Soil Survey of Anambra State Nigeria; Soil Report. Federal Department of Agriculture and Land Resources, Lagos Nigeria.

Gee G.W. and Bauder J.W. (1986). Particle Size: In Klute A. (ed). Methods of Soil Analysis. Part 1: 2nd Edition. Agronomy Monograph No. 9 ASA and SSA, Madison WI pp. 383-411.

Jacobson K.S. 2001. The Effect of Fly Ash/Sewage Sludge Mixtures and Application Rates on Biomass Production. Journ. of Environmental Science and Health 30: 1327-1337.

Jayalakshmi M.J., Puspha K. and Murphy R.K. 2007. Flyash Improves Soil Fertility. The Hindu Online Edition of Indian's National Newspaper. www.hindu.com/thehindu/mp/index.htm.

Kayode G.S. and Agboola A.A. 1993. Investigation on the Use of Macro and Micro Nutrients to Improve Maize Yield in Southeastern Nigeria. Liming Research 4: 211-221.

Landon J.R. 1991. Booker Tropical Soil Manual. A Handbook for Soil Survey and Agricultural Land Evaluation in the Tropics and Sub-tropics. John Wiley and Sons Inc., 605 Third Avenue, New York 454-474.

Mbah C.N. and Nneji R.K. 2011. Effect of Different Crop Residue Management Techniques on Selected Soil Properties and Grain Production of Maize. African Journal of Agric Research 6 (17) 4149-4152.

Mbah C.N., Nwite J.N., Njoku C., and Nweke A.I. 2010. Response of Maize (Zea mays L.) to Different Rates of Wood-ash Application in Acid Ultisol in Southeast Nigeria; African Journal of Agricultural Research 5 (7) 580-583.

Mclean E.O. (1982). Soil pH and Lime Requirements: In Page A.L. (eds) Methods of Soil Analysis Part 2. Chemical and Microbial Properties Agronomy Series No. 9 ASA, SSSA Madison,W.I. USA.

Nelson D.W. and Sommers L.E. 1 982. Total Carbon and Organic Matter: In Page A.L., Miller R.H. and Keeny D.R. eds. Methods of Soil Analysis. Part 2: 2nd Edition. Agronomy Monograph No. 9 ASA and SSA, Madison 1: 539-579.

Odedina S.A., Odedina J.N., Ayeni S.O., Arowofolu S.A., Adeyeye S.D. and Ojeniyi S.O. 2003. Effect of Types of Ash on Soil Fertility, Nutrient Availability and Yield of Tomato and Pepper. Nigeria Journal of Soil Science 13, 61-67.

Ojeniyi S.O., Oso O.P. and Arotolu A.R. 2001. Response of Vegetables to Wood Ash Fertilizer. Proceedings of 35th Annual Conference of Agric. Society of Nigeria, pp 39-43.

Olsen S.R. 1982. Phosphorus. In Page A.L., Miller R.H. and Keeny D.R. eds. Methods of Soil Analysis. Part 2: 2nd edition. Agronomy Monograph No. 9 ASA and SSA, Madison WI, pp. 403-430.

Orajaka S.O. 1975. Geology: In Nigeria in Maps. Eastern States (GEK Ofomata ed.) Ethiope Publishers. Benin city – Nigeria; 1975: 5-7.

Saarsalmi S., Hedley M.J. and White K.O. 2001. A Simplified Resin Membrane Technique for Extracting Phosphorus from Soil. Fertilizer Research 24: 173-180.

Steel G.O. and Torrie J.N. 1980. Process and Procedures of Statistics. A Biometric Approach. 2nd Edition. New York; Mcgraw Hill Book p. 63.

Thomas G.W. 1982. Exchangeable Cations: In Page A.L., Miller R.H. and Keeny D.R. eds. Methods of Soil Analysis. Part 2: 2nd Edition. Agronomy Monograph No. 9 ASA and SSA, Madison WI pp. 159-165.

Vuorien M. and Kurkela J.C. 2000. Granulated Wood Ash and a N – Free Fertilizer to a Forest Soil. Effects on Phosphorus Availability. Forest Ecology and Management 66: 127-136.

5

Haematological and Serum Enzymes Biomarkers of Heavy Metals in *Chrysichthys nigrodigitatus* and *Cynoglossus senegalensis*

Ayoola, S.O*; Adekunbi, F.O

ABSTRACT

Haematological, serum enzymes activity and heavy metal concentrations in feral populations of *Chrysichthys nigrodigitatus* (Lacepede:1803) and *Cynoglossus senegalensis* (Kaup: 1858) from Ebute-Oba section of the Lagos Lagoon, Lagos, Nigeria were evaluated from July-September, 2012 in order to determine and establish the relationship between heavy metal levels, serum enzymes activity and haematological parameters in *Chrysichthys nigrodigitatus* and *Cynoglossus senegalensis*. Levels of metals in *Chrysichthys nigrodigitatus* and *Cynoglossus senegalensis* in mg/l were as follows: (Cr: 0.07 ± 0.001, Cu: 0.027 ± 0.01, Fe: 0.481 ± 0.214, Pb: 0.001 ± 0.001, Zn: 0.316 ± 0.575) and (Cr: 0.010 ± 0.07, Cu: 0.029 ± 0.01, Fe: 0.467 ± 0.217, Pb: 0.021 ± 0.044, Zn: 0.433 ± 0.499) respectively.

Cadmium was not detected in any of the fish and all results were below the limits for fish consumption proposed by WHO/FAO/FEPA. Serum alanineaminotransferase (ALT), Aspartate aminotransferase (AST) and Alkalinephosphase (ALP) activities in *Chrysichthys nigrodigitatus* and *Cynoglossus senegalensis* measured in IU/l were as follows: (AST: 64.995±44.123, ALT: 16.345 ±166, ALP: 157.787±34.88) and (AST: 73.758±48.768, ALT: 29.532±20.100, ALP: 45.707±285) respectively. ALP

Department of Marine Sciences, University of Lagos, Lagos State, Nigeria.

activity between the two species showed a statistical significance at ($P<0.05$). Haematological parameters recorded for *C. nigrodigitatus* were Haemoglobin (Hb) 13.325±8.293g/dl, Packed Cell Volume (PCV) 25.53±11.79%, Red Blood Cell (RBC) 2.95±0.73 10^6mm^3, White Blood Cells (WBC) 124.19±56.41x10^4mm^3, Mean Corpuscular Heamoglobin Concentration (MCHC) 32.46±2.18g/l, Neutrophils 41.00±27.91% and Lymphocyte 64.33±31.94%. While values for *C. senegalensis* were: Hb 11.33±8.04 g/dl, PCV 34.00±22.83%, RBC 2.70±1.98x10^6mm^3, WBC 275.20±167.27 10^4mm^{-3}, MCV 178.94±126fl, MCH 59.63±44.50 Pg, MCHC 33.33±33.28g/l, Neutrophils 39.00±30.33% and Lymphocytes 80.00±71.77%.

Negligible number of Monocytes, Eosinophils and Basophils were recorded and is characteristic of fish blood. No statistical significant difference ($P>0.05$) for all haematological parameters recorded for both fish species. There was a strong inverse correlation ($r = -0.88$) between mean haemoglobin and iron only in *C. nigrodigitatus* and a strong direct correlation between mean MCV and copper in *C. senegalensis*. Accumulation of heavy metals in both fish species leads to an increased ALT, AST and decreased ALP activities. Conversely, accumulation resulted to reduced Haemoglobin and an increased Red Blood Cell and Lymphocyte counts Haematological and serum enzymes activities are predilective biomarkers for the detection and monitoring of aquatic ecosystems pollution.

Keywords: Biomarkers, Haematological, Serum Enzymes, Heavy Metals, Fish.

INTRODUCTION

Aquatic systems are exposed to a number of pollutants that are mainly released from effluents discharged from industries, sewage treatment plants, and drainage from urban and agricultural areas. These pollutants cause serious damage to aquatic life (Karbassi *et al.*, 2006). The tremendous increase in the use of heavy metals over the past few decades has inevitably resulted in an increased flux of metallic substances in the aquatic environment (Yang and Rose, 2003).

A large part of these elements exert their toxic effects by generating reactive oxygen species (ROS), causing oxidative stress. Most of the heavy metal ions are toxic or carcinogenic in nature and pose a threat to human health and the environment.

According to Olatunji and Abimbola (2010), the city of Lagos is the most populous in Nigeria and is projected to be the fifth most populous in the world by 2015. The city harbours over 75% of the industrial outfits within the country which include textile industries, chemical and paint industries, breweries and bottling companies, metal industries, ship yards, plastic and petro-chemical factories, paper mill and sawmills.

These industries discharge untreated wastes into the several drainages and canals that find their way into the Lagos lagoon (Okoye, 1989).

The Lagos Lagoon which lies within longitudes 6°25′ and 6°43′E and latitudes 3°22′ and 3°40′N is the largest of the three lagoon systems occurring in the Lagos area receiving over 80% of the land-derived run-offs laden with various types of wastes.

An estimated 10,000m^3 of industrial effluents are discharged into the Lagos Lagoon per day (Singh *et al.*, 1995; Don-pedro *et al*; 2004).

According to Oyewo (1998), an estimated level of heavy metals discharged into drains/canals/streams and subsequently into the Lagos Lagoon is as follow: Fe – 161, 718 kg, Mn-205, 989 kg, Co-15,683 kg, Zn-7026 kg, Cr-5286 kg, Pb-2251 kg, Ni-6124 kg, Cd-538 kg and Hg-278 kg per annum.

Consequent to the aforementioned level of heavy metals, the resources of the Lagos Lagoon are being exposed to high degree of heavy metal contaminants and toxicants which when consumed leads' to conditions such as anaemia, renal toxicity, hearing loss, low intelligent Quotient (IQ), hypertension and behavioural disorders (Bellinger, 2004; Ajagbe *et al.*, 2012). The consumption of fisheries species with high concentrations of heavy metals has been reported to have caused serious cases of human tragedies such as the Minamata disease and Itai-Itai disease tragedies (Kurdland, 1960; Ajagbe *et al.*, 2012).

However, there has been growing interests in the determination of the levels of heavy metals in fish (Kalay *et al.*, 1999). Fishes are good bioindicators of the degree of pollution in the aquatic environment due to their propensity to bio-accumulate toxic metals and other contaminants in their internal organs, most especially their edible muscle tissues which could reach toxic concentrations leading to serious health hazards.

Fish has attracted much attention in biomonitoring water pollution due to its special biological characters such as relatively big body size, long life cycle, easy to raise etc. More importantly fish species are at the top position in the aquatic food chain and may directly affect the health of humans, which make it much significant for biomonitoring.

According to Qunfang *et al.*, (2008), a comprehensive review article described fish bioaccumulation and biomarkers in environmental risk assessment and a suite of fish biomarkers such as metallothioneins (MTs), haematological parameters, immunological parameters, reproductive and endocrine parameters, histological parameters and morphological parameters were involved to assess exposure to or effects of environmental pollution on aquatic ecosystems.

In natural aquatic ecosystems metals occur in low concentrations. As they cannot be degraded, they are deposited, assimilated or transported in water, sediment and aquatic animals and thus causing heavy metal pollution in water bodies.

Metals entering aquatic ecosystem can be deposited in aquatic organisms through the effects of bio-concentration, bio-accumulation via the food-chain process and become toxic when accumulation reach a substantially high level.

Fish which is at high trophic level of the aquatic food chain accumulate substantial amount of metals in their soft and hard tissues (Mansour and Sidky, 2002), Pollutants enter fish through a number of routes: via skin, gills, oral consumption of water, food and non-food particles. Once absorbed, pollutants are transported in blood stream to either a storage point i.e. (bone) or to the liver for transformations and/or storage (Obasohan, 2008).

Oxidative stress is an imbalance between the pro-oxidant/antioxidant steady state in the cell, with the excess of pro-oxidants being available to cause damage to the cell often resulting in cell death (Hodgson, 2004). It is an unavoidable aspect of aerobic life which results due to an imbalance between the production of reactive oxygen species (ROS) and antioxidant defences in living organisms (Nishida, 2011). Reactive oxygen species are induced by substances such as transitional metal ions, pesticides and petroleum pollutants (Slaninova *et al.*, 2009; Lushchak, 2011). Free radicals are also produced by endogenous cellular sources during normal cell metabolism. Mitochondrial respiration is the main endogenous source of ROS. Elevated production of ROS can cause oxidation of protein and lipids, alteration in gene expression and changes in cell redox status (Livingstone 2003).

Mechanisms of anti-oxidant defences in fish include the enzyme system and low molecular weight anti-oxidants. Superoxide dismutase (SOD), Catalase (CAT) and glutathione – s- transferase (GST) are the main anti – oxidant enzymes, while metal-binding proteins such as ferritin, ceruloplasmin and metallothioneins (MTs) are low molecular weight non-enzyme anti-oxidants which have special functions in the detoxification of toxic metals, and also play a role in the metabolism and homeostasis of essential metals (Kelly *et al.*, 1998).

Heavy metals are high priority pollutants because of their relative high toxicity and persistent nature in the environment. A sound understanding of dynamics of the concentration and distribution of heavy metals and their compounds in various compartments of the environment is a priority for good environmental management programmes all over the world (Don-pedro *et al.*, 2004). Hence it is important to regularly monitor the levels of metals and other contaminants that are being discharged into the aquatic ecosystems which can in turn be accumulated by fisheries resources.

Field and laboratory toxicological studies investigating heavy metal toxicities combining liver enzymes activity and haematological parameters as biomarkers of effect in fish are scanty. To this end however, the present study was undertaken to examine the relationship between heavy metal levels with alanineanino transferase (ALT), Aspartateamino tansferase (AST), Alkalinephosphatase (ALP) activities and haematological parameters in *Chrysicthys nigrodigiatus* and *Cynoglosnus senegalensis*.

The focus of this research is to investigate the levels of heavy metals (Cd, Cr, Cu, Fe, Pb and Zn) in the flesh of fish of commercially importance and to determine the liver enzymes activity and haematological parameters in C *nigrodigitatus* and C *senegalensis*.

MATERIALS AND METHODS

Description of Study Area

Ebute-Oba is a fish landing site located along the shores of the Lagos Lagoon, situated between latitudes 6°27^{1}58.3^{11} N and 6°27^{1}55.9^{11}N and longitudes 3°29^{1}32.2^{11} E and 3°23^{1}49.0^{11} E in the vicinity of the Third Mainland Bridge in Isale-Eko Lagos Island (Fig. 5.1). The landing site experience similar environmental conditions characteristic of the Lagos Lagoon notably semi-diurnal tidal regime and seasonal salinity variations due to rainfall. Both finfish and shell fish commonly found in the market around Lagos Island come from landings from this site. Fisher- folk which comprise of Eguns make their catch from a wide expanse of the Lagos Lagoon making use of cast and seine nets with motorized canoes. Amongst the notable species caught and landed are; *Chrysichthys nigrodigitatus, Ilisha africana, Cynoglossus senegalensis, Penaeus notialis, Machrobrachium machrobrachium* and *M. vollenhovenii*.

A common scene around this landing site is a constant vehicular movement which is predominant throughout the day.

FIELD SAMPLING AND MEASUREMENT OF MOPHOMETRIC FEATURES

Samples of *Chrysichthys nigrodigitatus* and *Cynoglossus senegalensis* were collected twice a month between July and September, 2012 between 09.00-12.00 hours on each sampling day.

Total length (cm) and body weight (g) was measured using a measuring board and an electric weighing balance respectively. A total of 30 samples of *C.nigrodigitatus* and 30 samples of *C.senegalensis* were collected.

After blood collection, fish samples were transported to the ecotoxicology laboratory of the Marine Sciences Department, University of Lagos in ice-chest for heavy metal analysis of the tissues.

Surface water samples were collected using I litre water sampling bottles. The bottles were preserved in a cool dry place and transported to the laboratory for further analysis of water quality parameters not measured in-situ.

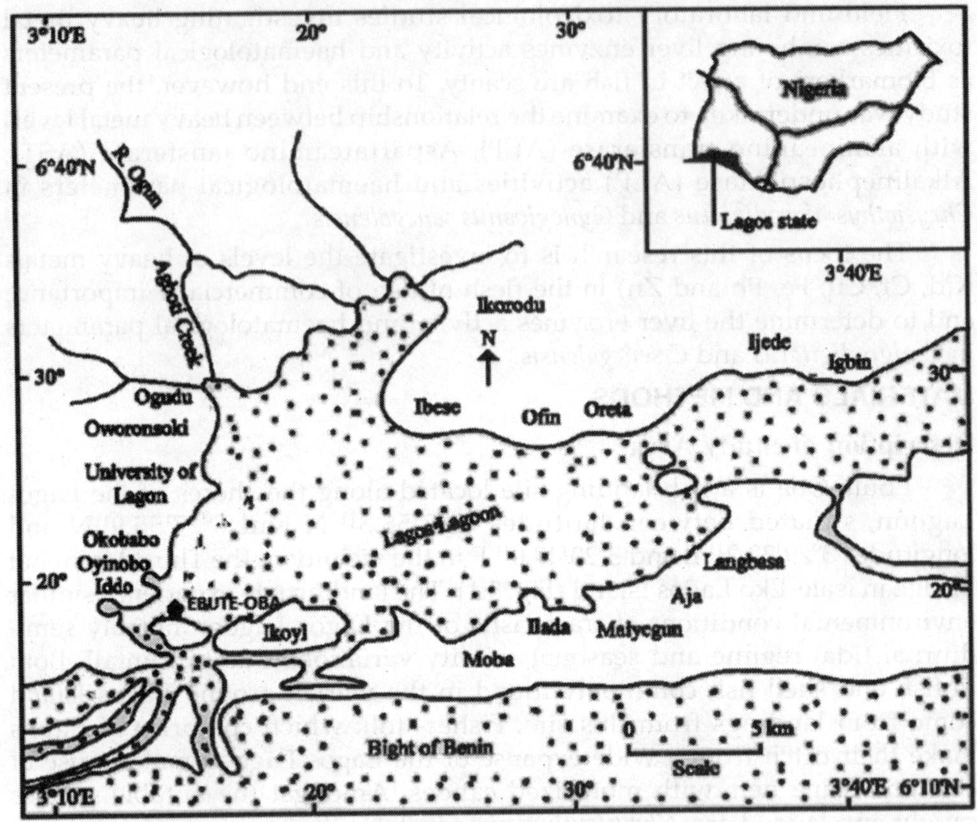

Fig 5.1: **Map of Lagos Lagoon Showing Study Location**

Parameters measured in-situ include surface water temperature, hydrogen ion concentration, electrical conductivity, salinity, turbidity and dissolved oxygen. Chemical oxygen demand was measured ex-situ in the laboratory.

The surface water temperature of the water sample was determinate in-situ by using mercury-in-glass thermometer calibrated in degree centigrade (°C).

The thermometer was immersed in the water for about five (5) minutes and the height of the mercury was read on the graduated glass tube.

pH measures hydrogen ion activity in water. The pH of the water was determined with the aid of a pH meter. This was done by dipping the probe in the water and reading off the values from the meter.

The conductivity of the water samples was measured using the Horiba U-10 water quality checker and values were read off from the meter. This was done in-situ with the use of a hand held refractometer. A drop of the water sample was placed on the prime of the meter of the refractometer and the meter was adjusted to $‰_0$ mark and viewed through the eye piece. The daylight plate was closed and the salinity of the water sample read on the scale.

Turbidity is a measure of the amount of light. This was measured at the study site using the Horiba water checker, model U-10 probe.

The dissolved oxygen level was measures in-situ using a DO meter. The probe was placed in the water and the reading was recorded from the meter.

The measurement of COD is based on the principle that almost all organic compounds in water can be oxidized to CO_2 and water by the action of strong oxidizing agents under acid condition. This was done in the laboratory.

HAEMATOLOGICAL PARAMETERS

Blood Collection

Blood was collected from the caudal blood vessels on the field to avoid stress and this lasted for about 5minute following the procedure of Kori-Siakpere and Egor, 1997.

Approximately 3ml of blood was collected using 5ml sterile plastic disposable syringe fitted with 0.8 × 40mm hypodermic needle. 1.5ml of the recovered blood was expressed into a vial containing potassium salt of ethelenediaminetetra-acetic acid (EDTA) for haematology and another 1.5m into a vial containing lithium heparin anticoagulant for enzymatic assay. The blood sample was gently rocked in the vial to allow thorough mixing of its contents.

Blood sample was taken in the morning (between 09.00 and 11.00 hours) and held on ice chest to help avoid possibility of coagulation due to increased temperature. The blood was then takes to laboratory for analysis.

LABORATORY ANALYSES OF HEAVY METALS

Determination of Heavy Metals in Fish Samples

Five grammes (g) each of *C. nigrodigitatus* and *C. senegalensis* fish flesh tissue were placed in a beaker and 15ml of freshly prepared mixture of HNO_3/H_2O_2 (I: I, v/v) were added to each one. The beakers were covered with a wash glass and set aside for about 1hr. The beakers and contents were placed on a hot plate whose temperature was allowed to rise gradually until it attained a maximum of 160°C in a fume cupboard. Heating continued for about 2 hrs., reducing the volume of the beaker contents to about 2-5ml. The contents in the beakers were allowed to cool and transferred with Whatman filtration into a 25ml volumetric flask. Reagent blanks were prepared accordingly to test the purity of the reagents. Metal concentrations for all extracts were determined using Perkin Elmer Model 200 Atomic Absorption Spectrophotometer (air-acetylene flame). Accuracy was assessed by analyzing three replicates of selected samples yielding standard deviations lower than 10% for all the metals (Cd, Cr, Cu, Fe, Pb and Zn). To validate the analytical methods employed in sample preparation and analyses for this study, percentage recovery was calculated for each of the metals in a series of three (3) repeat analysis of fish sample. This was made by spiking the samples with a known concentration of a mixed standard of the metals.

DETERMINATION OF HEAVY METALS IN WATER SAMPLES

Water sample is first aspirated into the flame or electrothermal device where it is vaporized and atomized. Ration of the proper wavelength is then passed through the vapour containing the ground state atoms of the metal where absorption occurs. The magnitude of the AAS absorption signal is directly proportional to the concentration of the analyze metal in the sample solution.

STATISTICAL ANALYSIS

Variations in heavy metal levels in C. *nigrodigitatus*, C. senegalensis and water were tested by one-way Analysis of Variance (ANOVA) at 5% level of significance. Post-hoc comparison of means between fish species were carried out using Least Square Difference (LSD) test to determine which values differed significantly. Comparison of mean heavy metal levels between C. *nigrodigitatus* and C. *senegalensis* was carried out by independent T-test. Pearson correlation analysis was carried out to determine the relationship between heavy metals in fish, serum enzymes activity and haematological parameters. The analysis and graphical representations was performed using the SPSS 17.0 package.

RESULTS

Heavy Metals in Fish Species and Water

Heavy metals contents in the flesh of *Chrysichthys nigrodigitatus*, *Cynoglossus senegalensis* and water during the sampling periods is presented in table 5.1.

Table 5.1: Heavy Metals Concentration in Flesh of *C. nigrodigitatus*. *C.senegalensis* and Water

Species	Mean ± SD (mg/l)					
	Cd	Cr	Cu	Fe	Pb	Zn
C.nigrodigitatus	–	0.007±0.003	0.027±0.011	0.481±0.214	0.001±0.001	0.316±0.575
C.senegalensis	–	0.010±0.007	0.029±0.011	0.467±0.217	0.021±0.044	0.433±0.499
Water	–	0.014±0.003	0.020±0.044	1.098±0.448	0.001±0.001	0.458±0.683
WHO Guidelines for fish	2.0	0.15	0.15-1.0	–	2.0	1.5
WHO Guidelines for Water	0.005	0.05	–	–	0.01	3.0

The results on the table reveals that heavy metals concentration in the flesh of both fish species and water is generally low and are below WHO/FAO/FEPA allowable limits. No Cadmium was detected in all matrices measured.

Analysis of Variance (ANOVA) of the mean values of the heavy metals concentration of *C.nigrodigitatus*, *C. senegalensis* and water showed a significant difference. There was a significant difference (P<0.05) in Cr and Fe between *C. nigrodigitatus* and water for the sampling periods. There was a significant difference (P<0.05) between Fe concentration in *C. senegalensis* and water all through the sampling period.

Table 5.2: Accumulation Factor from Water for the Two Fish Species

Species	Metals (mg/l)					
	Cd	Cr	Cu	Fe	Pb	Zn
C.nigrodigitatus	–	0.5	1.35*	0.43	1.00*	0.70
C.senegalensis	–	0.7	1.45*	0.43	21.0*	1.00*

* Bioaccumulation of Heavy metals.

SERUM ENZYMES ACTIVITY IN FISH SPECIES

Table 5.3: Summary of Serum Enzymes Activity in *C. nigrodigitatus* and *C. Senegalensis*

Species	Mean IU/L ± SD		
	AST	ALT	ALP
C.nigrodigitatus	64.995±44.123	16.345±12.166	157.787±34.88
C.nigrodigitatus	73..758±48.768	29.532±20.100	45.707±35.285

T-test analysis showed no statistical significant difference (P>0.05) between mean serum AST activity value in *C.nigrodigitatus* (65.00U/l±44.12) and *C.senegalensis* (73.76U/L±48.77). No statistical difference (P>0.05) was recorded between mean serum ALT activity value in *C. nigrodigitatus* (16.35 IU/l±12.16) and *C. senegalensis* (29.53U/l±20.10). A statistical significant difference was recorded (P< 0.05) between mean serum ALP activity value in *C.nigrodigitatus* (157.79 IU/l±34.89) and *C.senegalensis* (45.71U/l±35.29) for the sampling periods.

Table 5.4: Reference Plasma Enzymes Activity Level in some Osteichthys

Species	AST	ALT	ALP	Source
-	IU/L			
Oreochromis niloticus	18.62	14.30	–	Younis *et al* 2012
Acanthopagrus latus	135.00	6.91	–	Aliakbar *et al* 2010
Synodontis membranacea	16.80	11.79	63.01	Owolabi *et al* 2011
Labeo rohita	24.5	26.00	99.00	Kumari *et al* 2011

HAEMATOLOGICAL PARAMETERS IN FISH SPECIES

Table 5.5: Summary of Haematological Parameters in *C. nigrodigitatus* and *C.senegalensis*

Species	Mean±SD											
	Hb g/dl	PCV %	RBC 10^6 mm^{-3}	WBC 10^4 mm^{-3}	MCV Fl	MCH Pg	MCHC g/l	Neutrophil %	Lymphocytes %	Monocytes %	Eosinophils %	Basophils %
C.nirodigitatus	13.325±8.293	25.53±11.79	2.95±0.73	124.19±56.41	97.89±50.56	36.46±12.55	32.46±2.18	41.00±27.91	64.33±31.94	–	–	–
C.senegalensis	11.33±8.04	34.00±22.83	2.70±1.98	275.20±167.27	178.94±126	59.63±44.50	33.33±33.28	39.00±30.33	80.00±71.17	–	–	–

T-test showed no statistically significant difference (P>0.05) for all haematological parameters recorded between *C. nigrodigitatus* and *C. senegalensis*.

CORRELATION

The relationship between the concentrations of the heavy metals in flesh of *C. nigrodigitatus* and *C. senegalensis* was plotted against the respective serum enzymes activity and haematological parameters. The coefficient of correlation (r=-0.88) showed a strong inverse relationship between mean haemoglobin and iron in *C.nigrodigitatus*. A strong and positive coefficient of correlation (r=0.90) was recorded between mean MCV and Cu in *C.senegalensis*.

Correlation between Heavy Metals Concentration, Serum Enzymes Activity and Haematological Parameters in C. nigrodigitatus

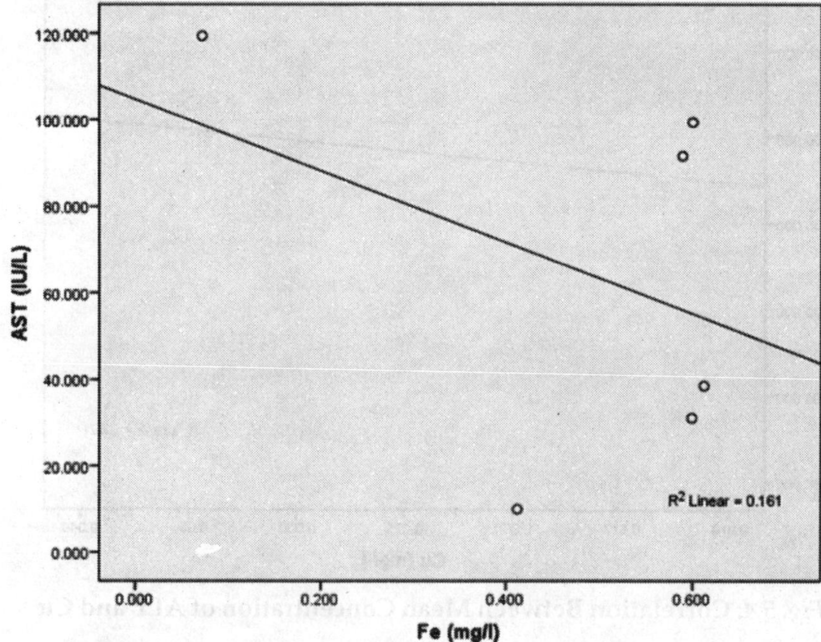

Fig. 5.2: Correlation Between Mean Concentration of AST and Fe

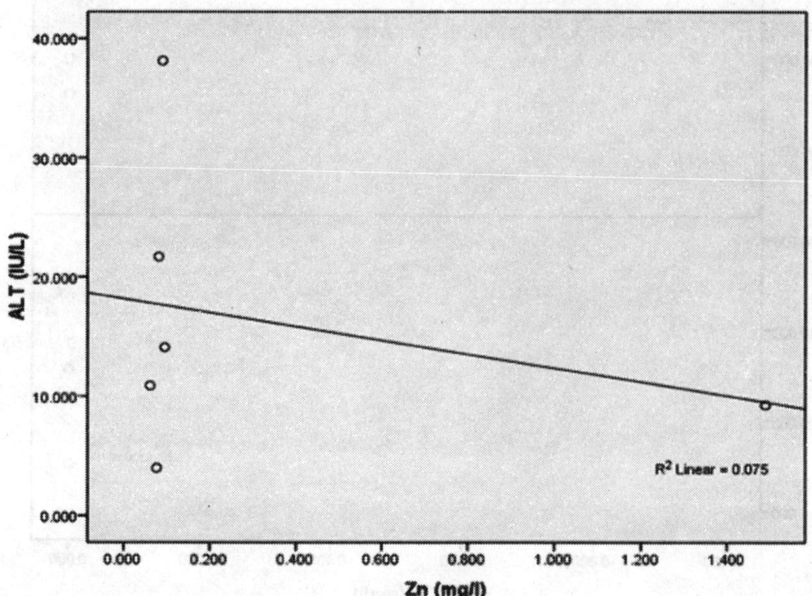

Fig. 5.3: Correlation Between Mean Concentration of ALT and Zn

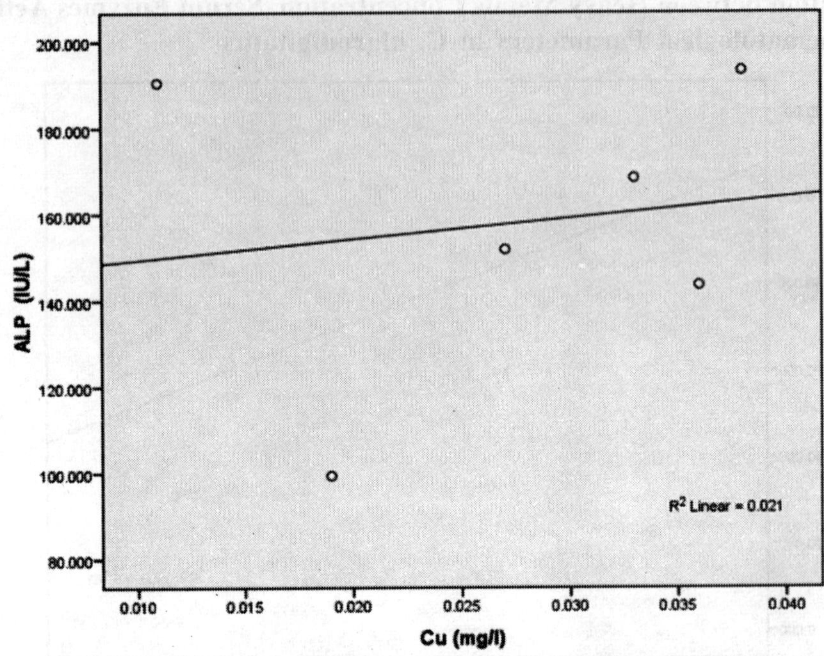

Fig. 5.4: Correlation Between Mean Concentration of ALP and Cu

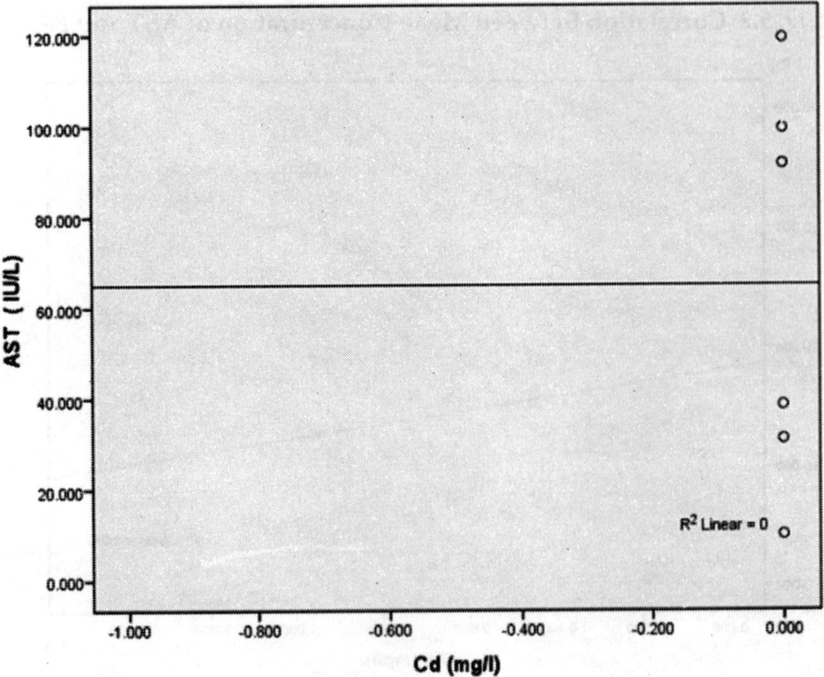

Fig. 5.5: Correlation Between Mean Concentration of AST and Cd

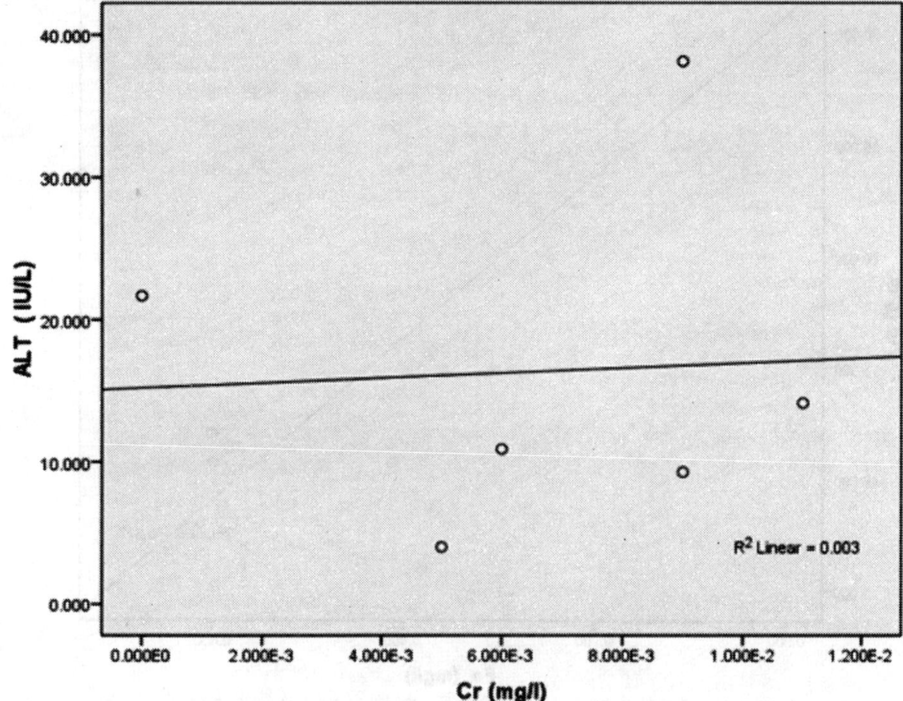

Fig. 5.6: **Correlation Between Mean Concentration of ALT and Cr**

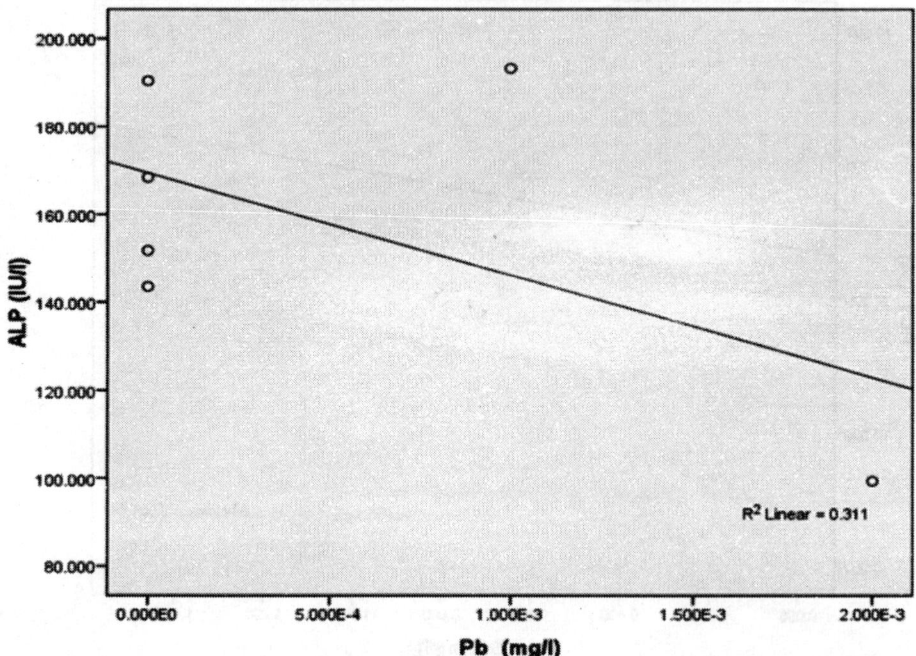

Fig. 5.7: **Correlation Between Mean Concentration of ALP and Pb**

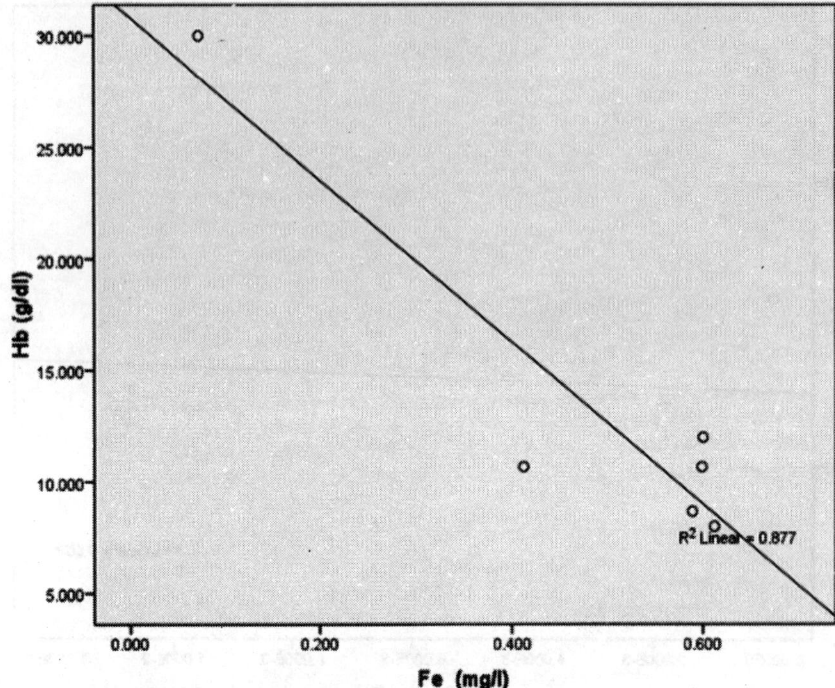

Fig. 5.8: **Correlation Between Mean Concentration of Hb and Fe**

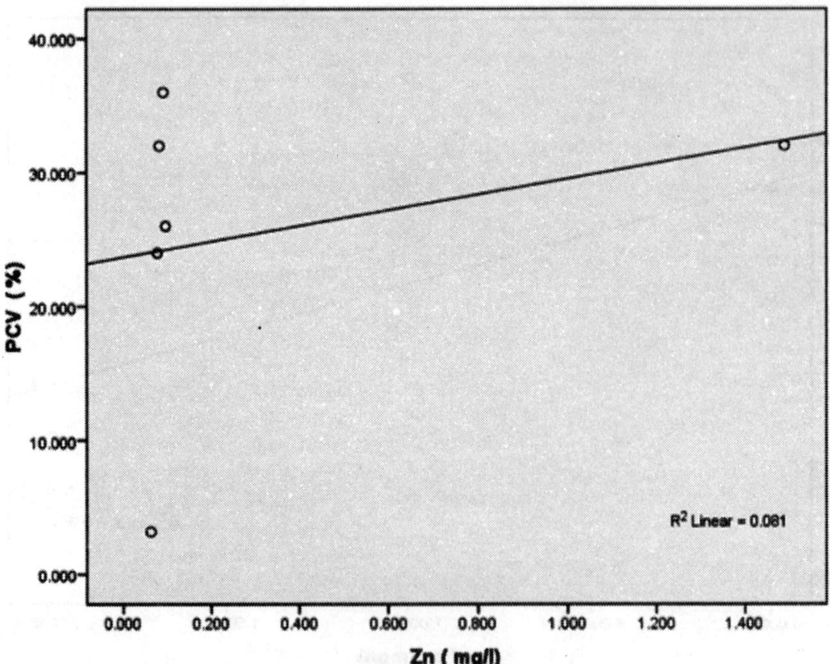

Fig. 5.9: **Correlation Between Mean Concentration PCV and Zn**

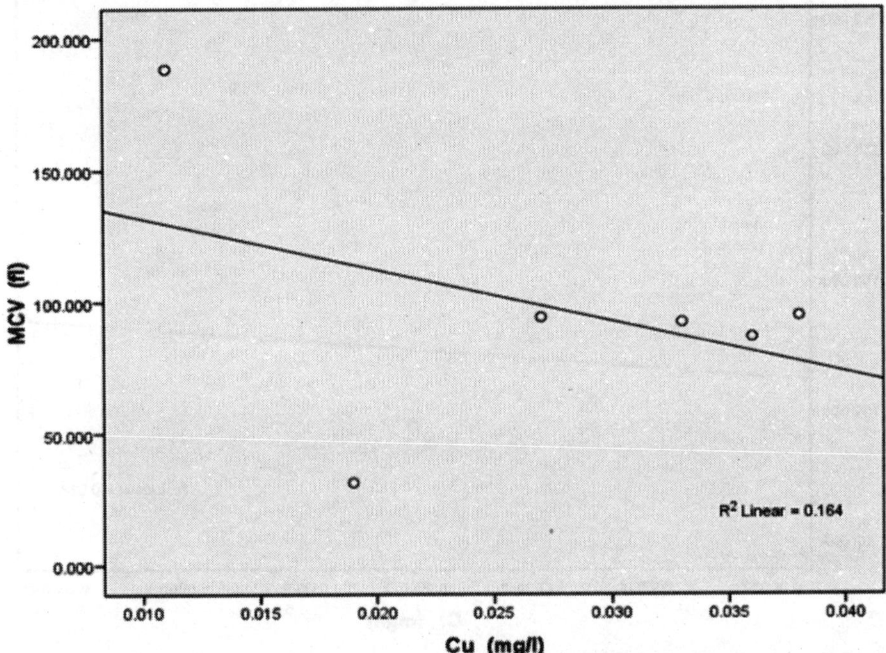

Fig. 5.10: **Correlation Between Mean Concentration of MCV and Cu**

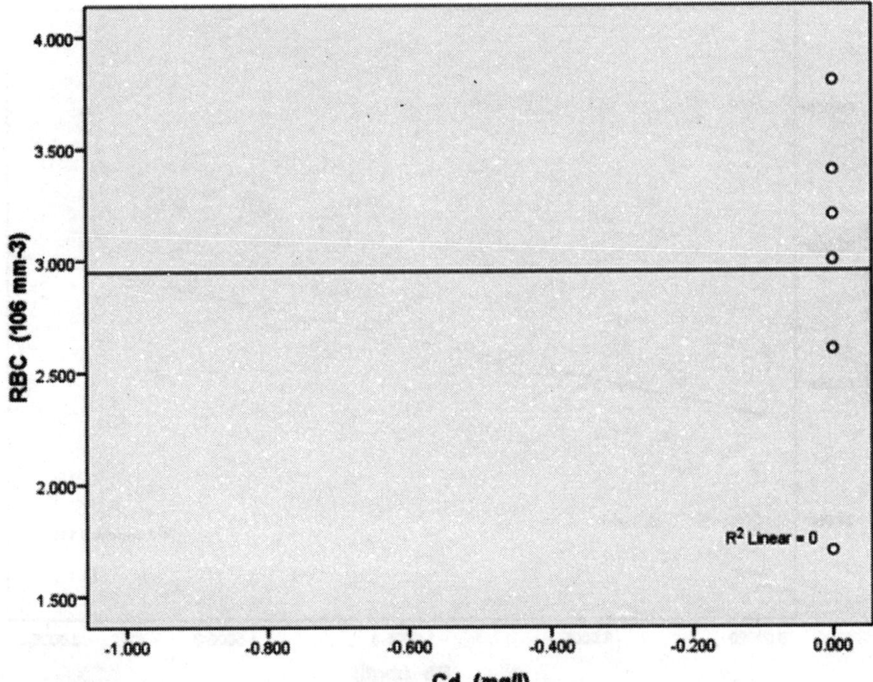

Fig. 5.11: **Correlation Between Mean Concentration of RBC and Cd**

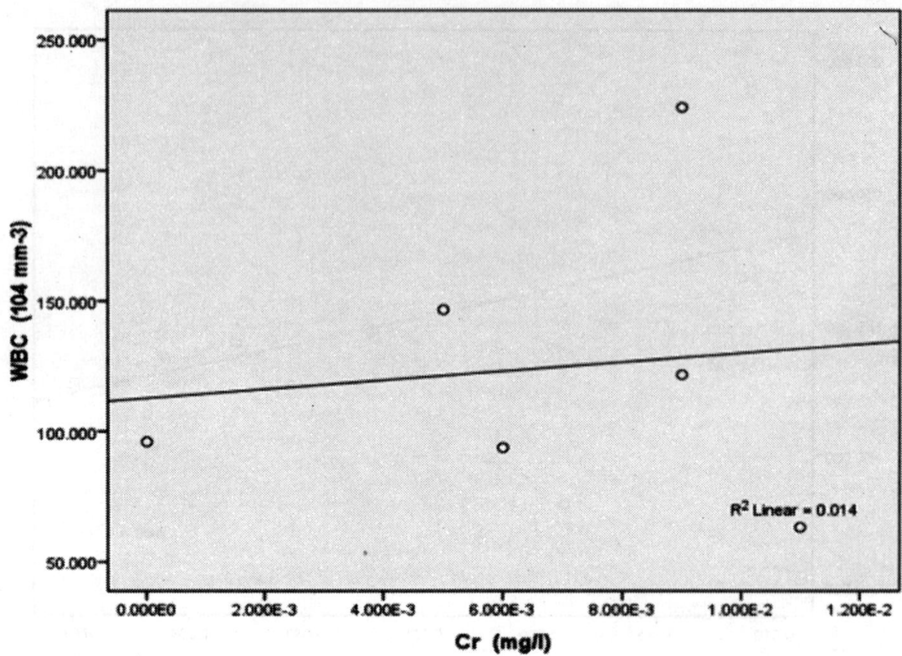

Fig. 5.12: Correlation Between Mean Concentration of WBC and Cr

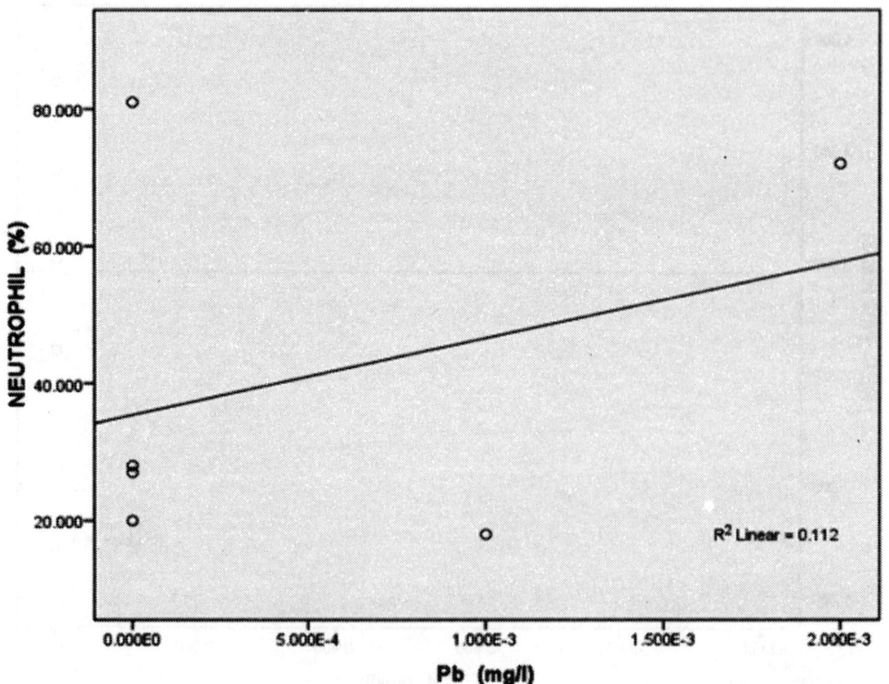

Fig. 5.13: Correlation Between Mean Concentration of neutrophil and Pb

Correlation between Heavy Metals Concentration, Serum Enzymes Activity and Haematological Parameters in C. senegalensis

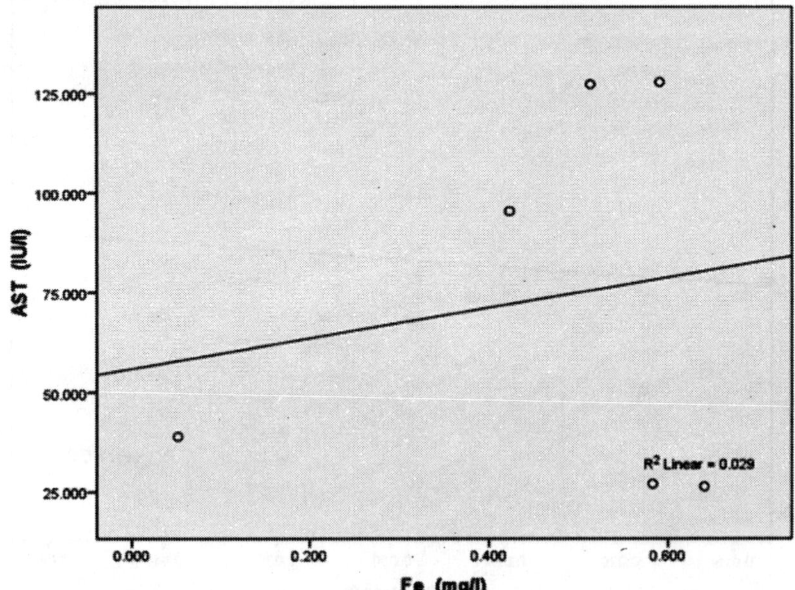

Fig. 5.14: Correlation Between Mean Concentration of AST and Fe

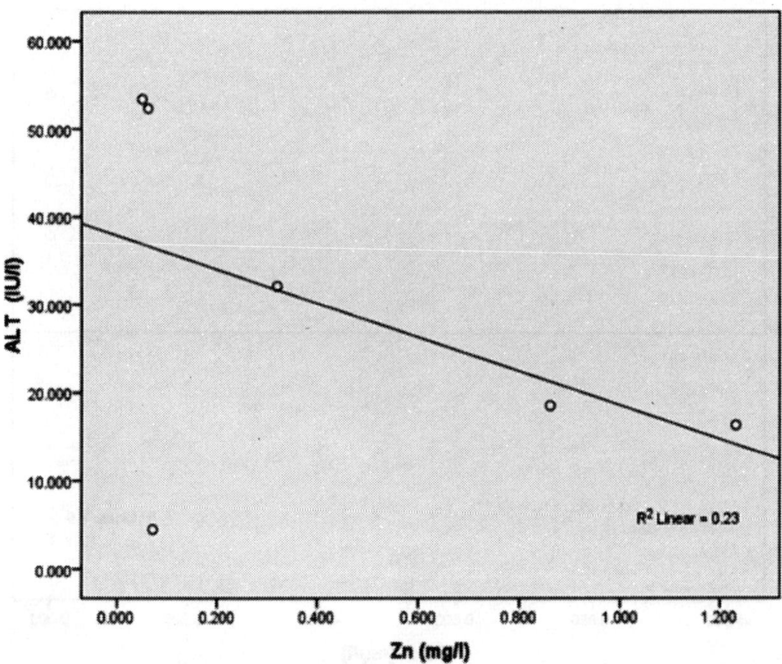

Fig. 5.15: Correlation Between Mean Concentration of ALT and Zn

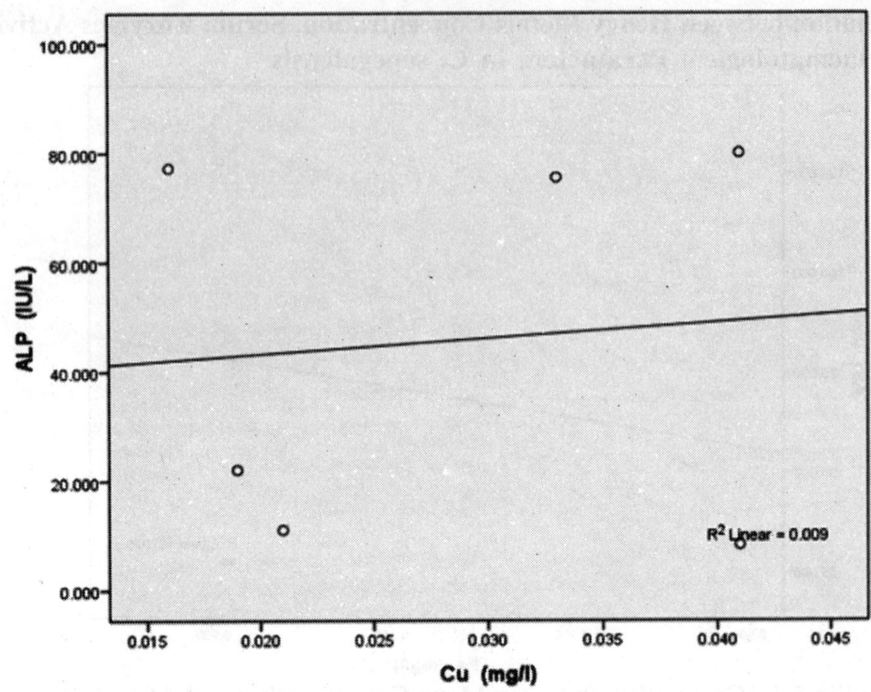

Fig. 5.16: **Correlation Between Mean Concentration of ALP and Cu**

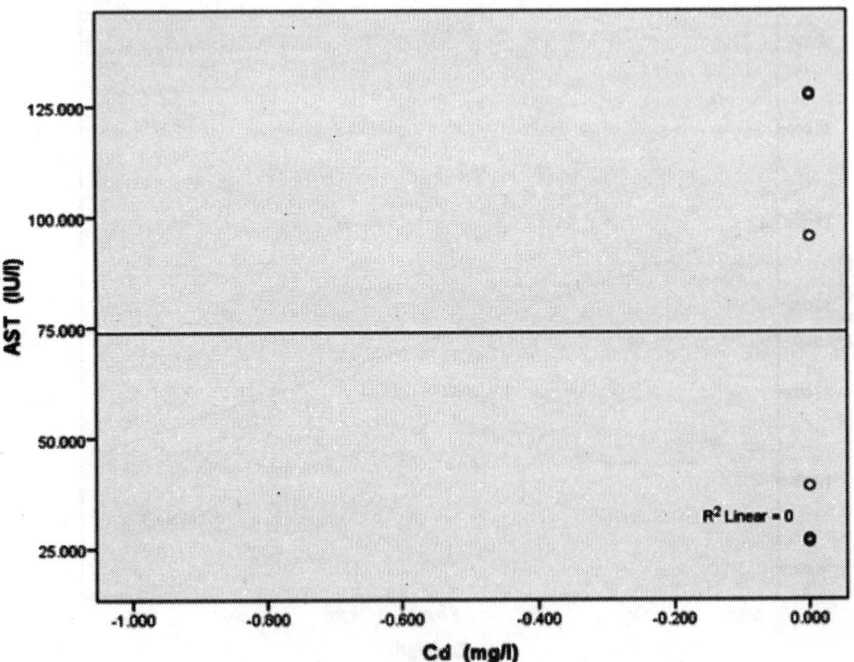

Fig. 5.17: **Correlation Between Mean Concentration of AST and Cd**

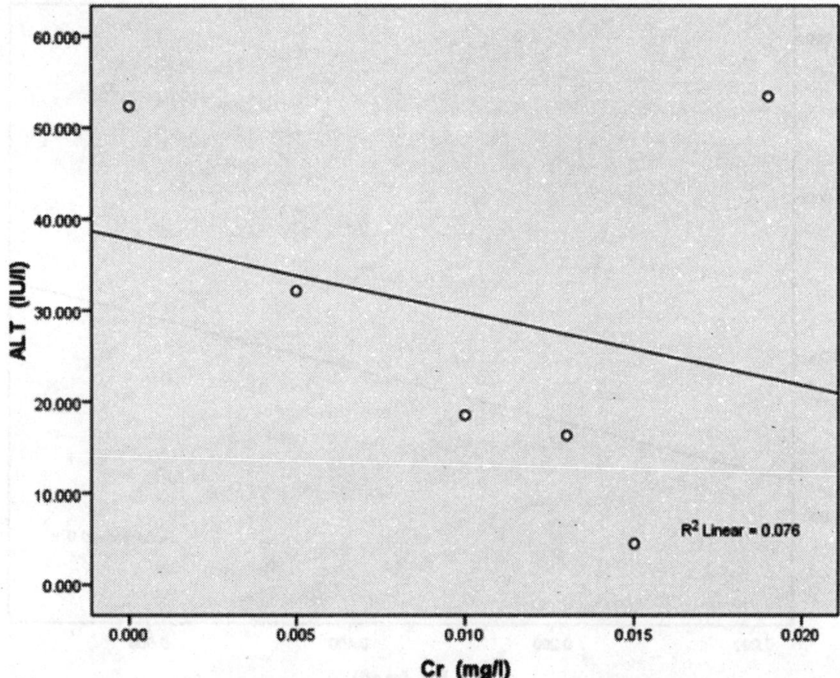

Fig. 5.18: Correlation Between Mean Concentration of ALT and Cr

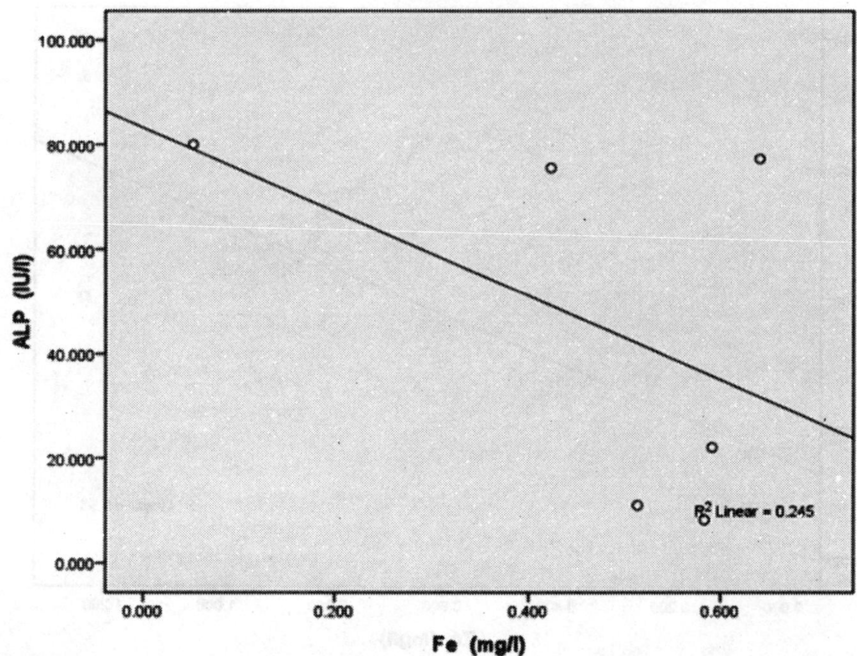

Fig. 5.19: Correlation Between Mean Concentration of ALP and Fe

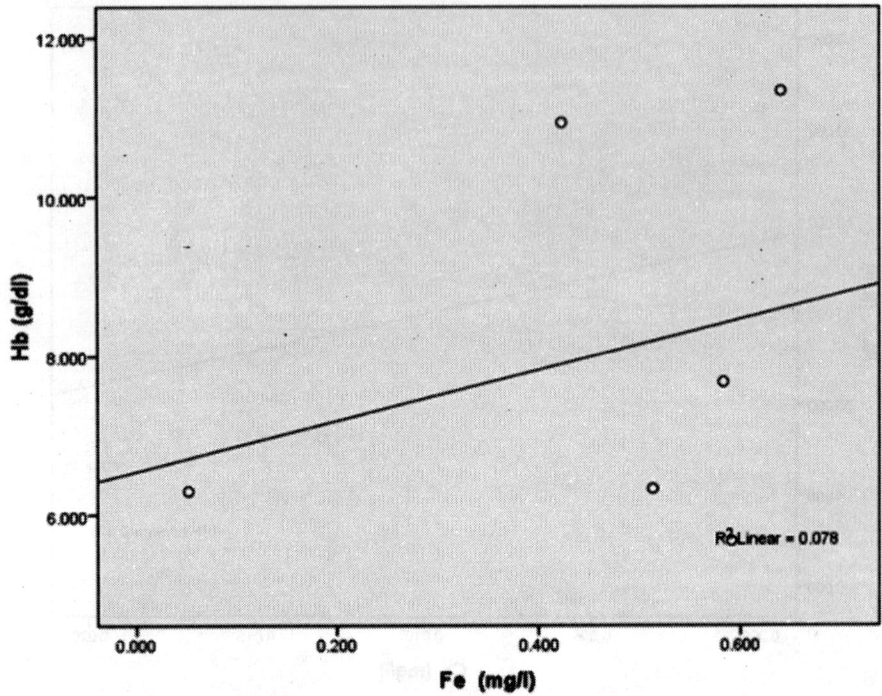

Fig. 5.20: **Correlation Between Mean Concentration of Hb and Fe**

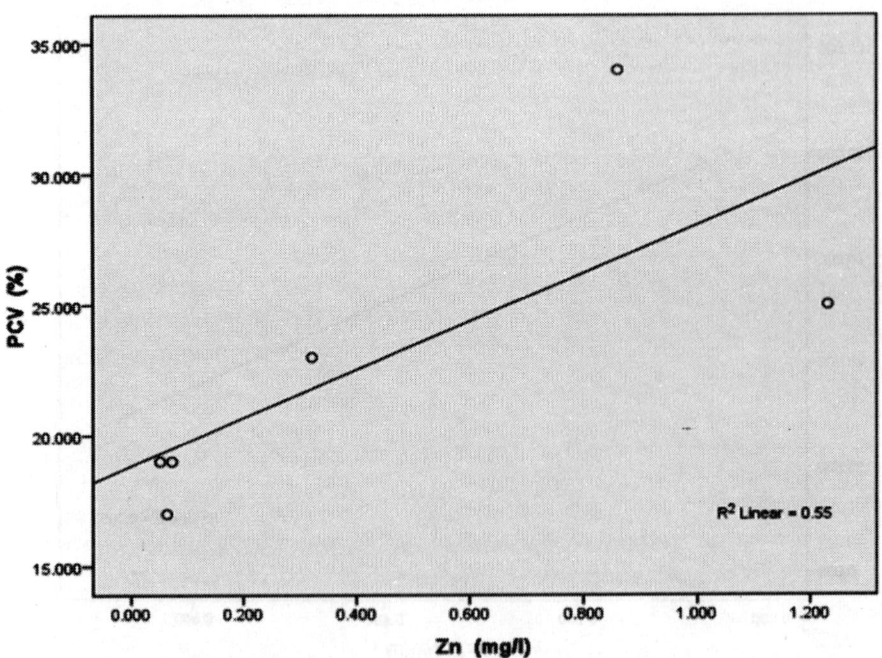

Fig. 5.21: **Correlation Between Mean Concentration of PCV and Zn**

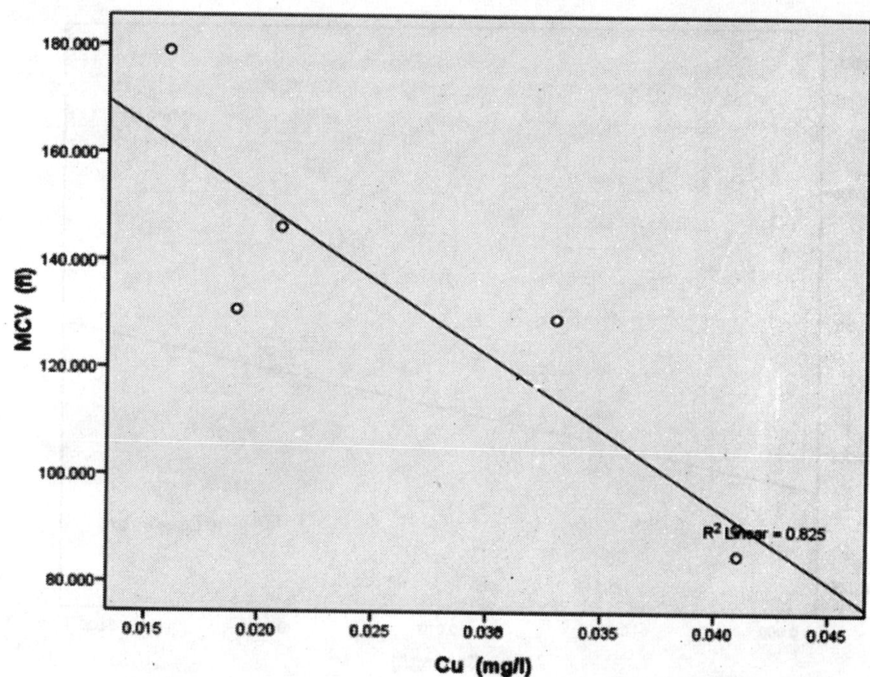

Fig. 5.22: **Correlation Between Mean Concentration of MCV and Cu**

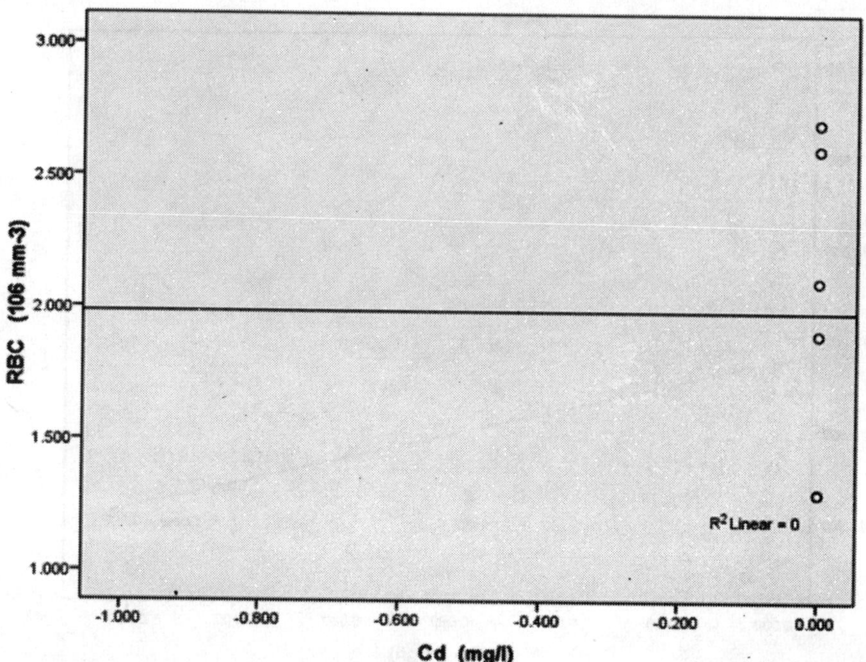

Fig. 5.23: **Correlation Between Mean Concentration of RBC and Cd**

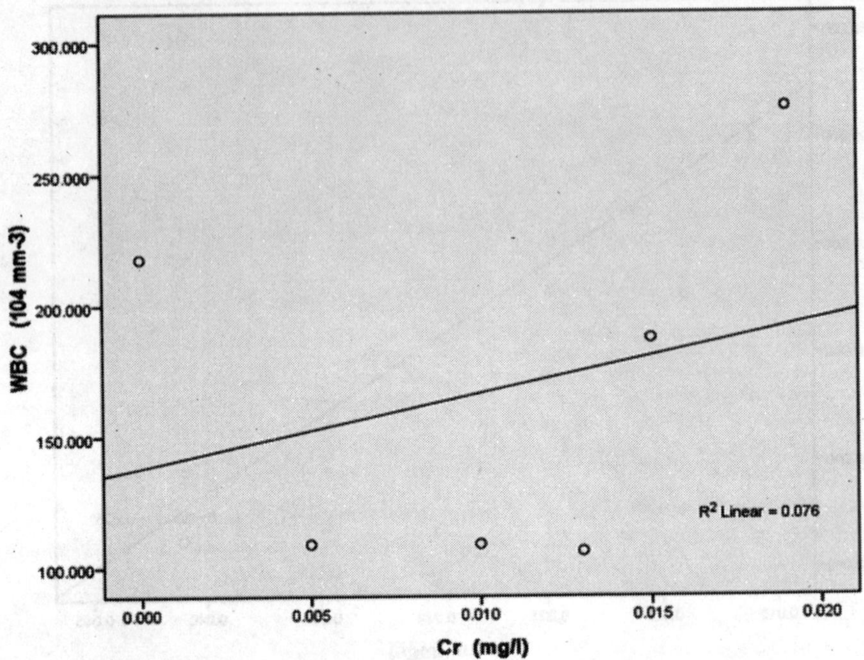

Fig. 5.24: **Correlation Between Mean Concentration of WBC and Cr**

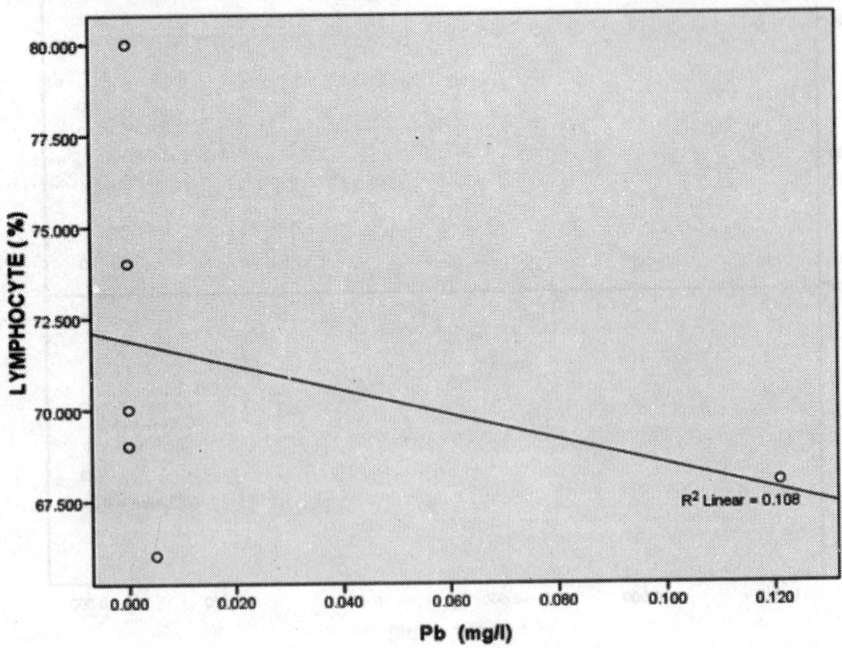

Fig. 5.25: **Correlation Between Mean Concentration of Lymphocyte and Pb**

MORPHOMETRIC PARAMETERS

Table 5.6: Summary of Length and Weight of *C. nigrodigitatus* and *C. senegalensis*

Species	Morphometric Parameters	Range	Minimum	Maximum	Mean	Standard Deviation
C.nigrodigitatus	Length (cm)	27.000	26.000	53.000	37.41667	9.520592
	Weight (g)	1133.000	522.000	1655.000	859.50000	409.992073
C.senegalensis	Length (cm)	14.000	29.000	43.000	36.93333	5.485131
	Weight (g)	942.000	473.000	1415.000	748.71667	385.156749

WATER QUALITY PARAMETERS

Table 5.7: Summary of Water Quality Parameters

Parameters	Range	Minimum	Maximum	Mean	Standard Deviation
Water Temperature (°C)	1.00	24.00	25.00	24.17	0.41
Dissolved Oxygen (mg/l)	0.57	1.40	1.97	1.71	0.22
PH	1.50	6.30	7.80	7.08	0.59
Conductivity (µScm)	1100.00	6900.00	8000.00	7650.00	393.70
Turbidity (FTU)	2.00	1.00	3.00	2.00	0.89
Salinity (‰)	2.00	3.00	5.00	4.17	0.98
COD (mg/l)	16.00	24.00	24.00	32.33	5.43

Pearson Rank Correlation (P=0.05) showed no statistical significance (P>0.05) for all water quality parameters recorded for the sampling periods.

DISCUSSION

Heavy metals are constituents of marine environment that occur as a result of pollution principally due to the discharge of untreated wastes into water bodies by many industries. Bioaccumulation of heavy metals in tissues of marine organisms has been identified as an indirect measure of the abundance and availability of metals in the marine environments (Kucuksegin *et al.*, 2006).For this reason, monitoring fish tissue contamination serves an important function as an early warning indicator of sediments contamination or related water quality problems (Mansour and Sidky 2002; Babatunde 2012) and enables appropriate action to protect public health and the environment. Several studies (Ademoroti 1996; Allen 1995; Karthikayan *et al.*, 2007) have indicated that fish are able to accumulate and retain heavy metals from their environment. Adeyeye *et al.*, (1996) also showed that the concentration of metals was a function of fish species as it accumulates more in some fish species than others.

Apparently, *C.nigrodigitatus* and *C,senegalensis* accumulated heavy metals in the flesh with essential metals in higher levels than non-essential metals. The average concentrations of Cd, Cr, Cu, Fe, Pb and Zn in flesh of the two species showed the following trend (*C.nigrodigitatus*); Fe>Zn>Cu>Cr>Pb>Cd and (*C.senegalensis*); Fe>ZN>Cu>Pb>Cr>Cd. Except for Fe, mean concentration of heavy metals were higher in *C. senegalensis* compared to *C. nigrodigitatus*. From the study, the concentration of Cr, Pb, and Zn in *C, nigrodigitatus* and *C. senegalensis* showed lower levels compared to WHO maximum permissible limits. An important observation was the elevated levels of metals especially Cr, Fe and Zn in both species which could be directly attributable to bioaccumulation as evidently depicted by the accumulation factors. Metals (Copper and Zinc) play an important role in cellular metabolism acting as co-factor in a number of important enzymes. However, they can become toxic when elevated concentrations are introduced into the environment (Younis *et al.*, 2012). The concentrations of the metals (Cd, Cr, Cu, Fe, Pb, and Zn) in flesh of the two fishes were lower than WHO limit and pose no potential threats to public health.

Pollution monitoring using enzyme inducement or enzyme dispersion in fish or other aquatic organisms have been proposed for studying polluted environments.. Various organic and inorganic wastes in industrial and domestic effluents are responsible for water pollution. Conventional laboratory toxicity studies cannot be extrapolated to the natural environment because they lack natural ecological realism (Abdelmeguid *et al.*, 2002) Since fish often respond to toxicants in a similar way to higher vertebrates they can be used to screen for chemicals that are potentially teratogenic and carcinogenic in humans. Plasma enzymes depends on the rate of release of enzymes from damaged cells, which in turn depend on the rate at which damage is occurring and at the extent of cell damage. The varied levels of aminotransferase observed in the two species investigated in the present study when compared to the mean levels recorded in other species (Younis *et al.*, 2012; Aliakbar *et al., 2010)* suggest high activity levels in these species. It has been reported that the variation in enzyme activities in heavy metals exposed fish is due to increased permeability of the cells as well as the direct effect of heavy metal on the tissues (Roy 2002).

The pattern of AST and ALT activities recorded in this study showed that cellular damage could arise due to chronic exposure to heavy metals in the environment of the test species. Albeit, no significant difference between plasma enzymes activity between the fish species occurred in the study, the results of this investigation showed a relatively high levels of AST and ALT activities which is a consequent of tissue impairment due to heavy metal exposures.

Alkalinephosphatase (ALP) activity varied significantly between the two species with the activity higher in *C. nigrodigitatus* and lower in

C. senegalensis. This may imply that *C. senegalensis* is less sensitive to heavy metals exposure compared to *C. nigrodigitatus*, since reduction in ALP activity may be taken as an index of hepatic parenchymal damage and hepatocytic necrosis (Onikienko, 1963; Kori-Siiakpere *et al.*, 2010). Reduced ALP activity by stressors probably indicates an altered transport of phosphate and an inhibitory effect on the cell growth and proliferation. Conversely, elevated plasma ALP activity as observed in *C. nigrodigitatus* may be as a consequence of osteoblastic activity increase or due to intra and extra hepatic obstruction of bilary passage (Jyotti and Narayanan 1999).

Blood parameters in fish have been studied to elucidate physiological adaptation and to assess the health of fishes (Vazquez and Guerrero 2007; Yildz 2009) Blaxhall and Diasley (1973) reported the use of haematocrit (PCV) and haemoglobin in checking anaemic conditions and reported values for fish usually vary from 20% to 35% (Pietse *et al.*, 1981) and do not exceed 50% (Clarke *et al.*,1979).

The mean PCV value of 34.00% for *C. senegalensis* and 25.52% for *C,nigrodigitatus* recorded in the present study is within this range but this value for *C.nigrodigitatus* is lower than *C. nigrodigitatus* (35.52%) and *C.furcatus* (35.5%) from kwa River (Etim *et al.*, 1999) The difference in mean haemoglobin, PCV and RBC values between *C.senegalensis* and *C. nigrodigitatus* could be attributed to differential responses caused by heavy metal exposures as it is well known that some metals cause early mortality of mature red blood cells and inhibition of haemoglobin formation through inhibition of erythrocyte alpha-amino levulinic acid dehydrogenase (ALA-D).

RBC counts of 2.71×10^6 mm^3 for *C. senegalensis* and 2.95×10^6 mm^3 for *C. nigrodigitatus* was significantly high, according to Lenfant and Johnson (1972) erythrocyte counts greater than 1×10^6 mm^3 is considered high and indicative of high oxygen carrying capacity of the blood which is characteristic of fishes capable of aerial respiration and high metabolic rate. A strong inverse correlation (r=-0.94) which occurred between haemoglobin and Iron in *C. nigrodigitaus* compared to a weak positive correlation (r=0.28) recorded between haemoglobin and Iron in *C. senegalensis* could indicate that haemoglobin increased with a fall in Iron and vice- versa in *C. nigrodigitatus* while there was a very slight increase in Iron with a corresponding slight increase in haemoglobin concentration, this observed relationship could imply that *C. nigrodigitatus* is more sensitive to Iron contamination compared to *C.senegalensis*.

This is reflected in the slight difference between mean RBC count of *C. nigrodigitatus* (2.95×10^6 mm^3) and *C. senegalensis* (2.7×10^6 mm^3). The mean haemoglobin value of *C. senegalensis* (11.33±8.04g/dl) and *C. nigrodigitatus* (13.32±8.29g/dl) was high and fell within the range (5.6-15.8g/dl) reported for *C. gariepinus* (8.70g/dl) (Sowunmi 2003). This values are also higher than

4g/dl recorded for *Heterotis niloticus* (Fagbenro *et al.*, 2000). This observed haemoglobin level may be connected to an adaptive response to heavy metal contamination or low dissolved oxygen recorded.

The observed lymphocytes that were numerous than any other differential cells for C. nigrodigitatus (64.33±31.94%) and *C. senegalensis* (80.00±71.17%) and basophils that were seldomly seen are typical of most fishes (Ezzat *et al.*, 1974; Kori-Siakpere and Ake 2005). Abundance of neutrophils in both species is similar to the observations of Breazile *et al* (1982) and Kori-Siakpere and Ake (2005) and thought to be normal picture for fish blood.

The major findings of this study are that heavy metals were accumulated by both species at concentration below WHO/FAO/FEPA permissible limits for human consumption. Heavy metals are toxic substances, with changes in enzymes activities in serum of fish exposed to various concentrations. Results of the study indicated that sub-lethal and chronic concentrations observed may cause changes in the haematological parameters and enzymztic activities of the studied fishes, hence could be used as biomarkers of metal contamination and detection in aquatic systems such as the Lagos Lagoon.

CONCLUSION AND RECOMMENDATION

Although results of heavy metal concentrations studied showed that consumption of the two species would not have any potential health implications, recommendations should be taken (Shareef 2011). Similar studies may be performed to check contamination with other toxic metals such as mercury, cobalt, nickel and arsenic in commercial fish.

Periodical monitoring of contaminants levels in fish by using enzymatic activities and haematological parameters in both commercial and feral fish is needful to checkmate any possible future accumulation and/or increase as a result of waste and effluents discharge into the Lagoon. The use of feral fish species in local water bodies should be utilized as sentinel organisms for monitoring and management of the contamination status of these aquatic systems and should be complementary with conventional physico-chemical water monitoring regimes.

REFERENCES

Abdelmeguid, N. Kheirallah, A.M. Abou-Shabana, K. and Abdel-Moneim, A. (2002). Histochemical and Biochemical Changes in Liver of *Tilapia zill.G* as a Consequence of Water Pollution. *J. Biol. Sci.* 2 (4): 224-229.

Abowei, J.F.N. (2009). The Abundance, Condition Factor and Length – Weight Relationship of *Cynoglossus senegalensis* from Nkoro River Delta, Nigeria. *Adv. J. Food. Sci..Tech.* 1 (1): 57-62.

Adakole, J.A. (2012). Changes in Some Haematological Parameters of the African Catfish (*Clarias gariepinus*) Exposed to Metal Finishing Company Effluents. *Indian. J. Sci. Tech.* 2510-1514.

Ademoroti, C.M.A. (1996). *Environmental Chemistry and Toxicology*, Foludex Press Ltd., Ibadan. 171-204.

Adeyeye, E.I. Akinyugha, R.J. Febosi, M.E. and Tenabe, V.O. (1996). Determination of Some Metals in *Clarias gariepinus* (Cuvier and Valenciemes), *Cyprinus carpio* (L) and *Oreochromis niloticus* (L) Fishes in a Polyculture Fresh Water Pond and Their Environment. *Aquacut*. 47. 205-214.

Ajagbe, F.E. Osibona, A.O and Otitoloju, A.A. (2012). Discovery of the Edible Fishes of the Lagos Lagoon, Nigeria and the Public Health Concerns Based on Their Lead (Pb) Content. *Int. J. Fish. Aquacut*. 2 (3): 55-62.

Ali, M.H. Sayed and Golian, M.E. (2006). Studies of Water Quality and Some Heavy Metals in Hyper Saline Mediterranean Lagoon (Badawil Lagoon, Egypt). *Egypt. J. Aquatic Biol. Fish*. 10: 45-64.

Aliakbar, H. Alireza, S. Ahmad, S and Jasem, G.M. (2010). Assessment of Amino Transferase Enzymes in Yellow Sea Bream (*Acanthopagrus latus*) Under Experimental Condition as Biomarkers of Mercury Pollution. *World. J.Fish. Mar.Sci*. 2(3): 196-192.

Allen, P. (1995). Chronic Accumulation of Cadmium in the Edible Tissues of *Oreochromis aureus* (Steindachner): Modification by Mercury and Lead. *Arch. Environ. Contam. Toxicol*. 29. 8-14.

American Public Health Association APHA (1998). Standard Methods for the Examination of Water and Waste Water. 20th ed. Clesceri LS, Greenberg AE. And Eaton A.D (Eds). American Public Health Association. Washington D.C.

ATSDR, (2005). Draft Toxicological Profile for Lead, US Department of Health and Human Services. Atlanta, Georgia, USA. 102-225.

Babatunde, A.M. Waidi, O.A. and Adeolu, A.A. (2012). Bioaccumulation of Heavy Metals in Fish : *Hydrocynus forskalii, Hyparoisus bebe occidentalis* and *Clarias gariepinus* Organs in Down Stream Ogun Coastal Water, Nigeria. *Transintl. J. Sci. Tech*. 2 (6): 119-133.

Bayne, B.L., Brown, D.A., Burns, K., Dixon, D.R., Ivanovici, A., Livingstone, D.A., Lowe, D.M., Moore, M.N., Stebbing, A.R.D. and Widdings, J., (1985). The Effects of Stress and Pollution on Marine Animals. *Praeger*, New York, USA.

Bellinger, D.C. (2004). Lead Pediatrics, 113: 1016-1022.

Blaxhall, P.C. and Daisley, K.W. (1973). Routine Haemotological Methods for Use with Fish Blood. *J. fish Biol*, 5: 771-781.

Boge, G. Leydet, M. and Houvet, V. (1992) The Effects of Hexavalent Chromium on the Activity of Alkaline Phosphatase in the Intestine of Rainbow Trout (*Oncorhynchus mykiss*), *Aquatic. Toxicol*, 23:247.

Breazile, J.E. Zinn, L.L.Yauk, J.C, Mass, H.J. Wollscheid, J. (1982). A Study of Haematological Profiles of Channel Catfish, *Ictalurus punctatus* (Rafinesque). *J. Fish. Biol*. 21: 305-309.

Campbell, T.W. (2004). Hematology of Lower Vertebrates. In: Proceedings of the 55th Annual Meeting of the American College of Veterinary Pathologists (ACVPC) and 39th Annual Meeting of the American Society of Clinical Pathology (ASVCP). ACVP and ASVCP, USA.

Clark S, Whitmore, D.H. McMahon, R.F. (1979). Considerations of Blood Parameters of Largemouth Bass, *Micropterus salmoides*. *J. Fish. Biol*. 14: 147-158.

Don-Pedro KN, Oyewo OE, Otitoloju AA (2004). Trend Measurement of Heavy Metals in Lagos Lagoon Ecosystems, Nigeria. *W. Afr. J. Appl. Ecol*., 5: 103-114.

Duruibe, J. O., Ogwuegbu, M.C. and Egwurugwu, J. N (2007). Heavy Metal Pollution and Human Biotoxic Effects. *Int. J. Physical. Sci*. 2: 112-118.

Dyhrman, S.T. and Palanik, B.(1999). Phosphate Stress in Cultures and Field Populations of the Dinoflagellate *Propocentrum minimum* Detected by Single Cell Alkaline Phosphatase Assay. *App.environ. Microbiol*, 65: 3205.

ECETOC, (1993). Environmental Hazard Assessment of Substances. European Centre for Ecotoxicology and Toxicology of Chemicals: *Technical Report* No. 51. Brussels, Belgium.

Emerit, J. Beaumont, C, Trivin, F. (2001). Iron Metabolism, Free Radicals, and Oxidative Injury. Biomedicine and Pharmacotherapy 55: 333-339.

Etim, L. Lebo, P.E. and King, R.P (1999). The Dynamics of an Exploited Population of a Siluroid Catfish (*Schilbe intermedius* Ruppell, 1832) in the Cross River, Nigeria. *Fisheries Res*., 40: 295-307.

Eze, L.C (1983). Isoniazid Inhibition of Liver Glutamic Oxaloacetic Transaminase from Goat (*Carpa hercus*). *Int. J. Biochem*. 15: 13-16.

Ezenwa, B.I.O. (1978). Studies on the Distribution, Age and Growth of the Catfish, *Chrysichthys nigrodigitatus* (Lacepede). M.Sc. Thesis. University of Lagos, Nigeria.

Ezenwa, B. (1981). A Study of the Reproductive Biology of the Catfish *Chrysichthys nigrodigitatus* (Lacepede) in Nigeria. University of Lagos, Lagos, Nigeria.

Ezenwa, B.I.O, Alegbeleye, W.O, Anyanwu, P.E. Uzukwu, E.O. (1990). Culturable Fish Seeds in Nigerian Coastal Waters. A research Survey (Second Phase: 1986-1989). Nigerian Institute for Oceanography and Marine Research. (N.I.O.M.R.) *Tech. p*. 66, 37.

Ezzat, A.A, Shabana, M.B. Farghaly, A.M. (1974) Studies on the Blood Characteristics of *Tilapia zillii* (Gervias) I. Blood cells. *J. Fish. Biol*. 6: 1-12.

Falaye, A. (1981). Brackish Water Culture of Catfish. Chrysichihys nigrodigUamus (Lacepede) Nigeria. University of Ibadon, Nigeria. *MSc. Thesis*.

F.A.O. (1990). Field Guide to the Commercial Marine Resources of the Gulf of Guinea. FAO Species Identification Sheets of Fisheries Resources. *FAO Regional Office for Africa*. 229 pp.

Fagbenro, O, Adedire, C.O. Ayotunde, E.O. Faminu, E.O. (2000). Haematological Profile, Food Composition and Enzyme Assay in the Gut of the African Bony-tongue Fish, *Heterotis* (Clupisudis) *niloticus* (Cuvier 1829) (Osteoglossidae). *Trop. Zool*. 13: 1-9.

FAO, (1983). Compilation of Legal Limits for Hazardous Substances in Fish and Fishery Products. FAO Fishery Circular, 464: 5-100.

FEPA, (2003) Guideline and Standards for Environmental Pollution and Control in Nigeria. Federal Environmental Agency, Nigeria.

Gül, S. Belge-Kurutas, E. Yildiz, E. Sahan, A. Doran, F. (2004). Pollution Correlated Modifications of Liver Antioxidant Systems and Histopathology of Fish (Cyprinidae) Living in Seyhan Dam Lake, *Turkey. Environ. Int*. 30: 605-609.

Herreros, M. Inigo-Nunez, S. Sanchez-Perez, E. Encinas, T. and Gonzalez Bulnes.A. (2008) Contribution of Fish Consumption to Heavy Metals Exposure in Women of Childbearing Age from a Mediterranean Country (Spain). *Food*.

Hill, M.B. and Webb. J.E. (1958). The Ecology of Lagos Lagoon ll. The Topography and Phyical Features of Lagos Harbour and Lagos Lagoon. *Phil. Trans. R. Soc. B*. 241, 319-333.

Hodgson, E.(2004). *A Text Book of Modern Toxicology*.3rd Edition. John Wiley and Son Inc, New Jersey. 557 pp.

Holden M, Reed W (1991). *West African Freshwater Fish*. Longman Publishers Ltd., Singapore. 68 p.

Holdway, D.A (1988). *The Toxicity of Chromium to Fish*,.In: Nriagu, J.O, Nieboer, E. (Eds). Chromium in the Natural and Human Environments. John Wiley and Sons Inc, New York.

Jyothi, B. and Narayan, G. (1999). Certain Pesticide-induced Carbohydrate Metabolic Disorders in the Serum of Freshwater Fish *Clarias batrachus* (Linn.). *Food Chem. Toxicol.* 37: 417-421.

Kalay, M. Aly. O. and Canil, M.(1999) Heavy Metal Concentrations in Fish Tissues from the Northeast Mediterranean Sea. *Bull. Environ. Contam. Toxicol.* 63: 673-681.

Karbassi, R. Bayati, I. Moattar, F. (2006). Origin and Chemical Partioning of Heavy Metals in Riverbed Sediments. *Int. J. Environ. Sci. Tech*, 3(1): 35-42.

Karthikeyan, S. Palaniappan, P.L.R.M. and Sabhanayakan, S. (2007) Influence of pH and Water Hardness Upon Nickel Accumulation in Edible Fish *Cirrhinus mrigala. J. Environ. Biol.*, 28, 484-492.

Kelly, S.A. Havrilla, C.H.M. Brady, T.C, Abramo, K.H, Levin, E.D (1998). Oxidative Stress in Toxicology: Established Mammalian and Emerging Piscine Model Systems. Environmental Health Perspectives 106: 375-384.

Kim, S.G. and Kang, J. C (2004). Effect of Dietary Copper Exposure on Accumulation, Growth and Hematological Parameters of the Juvenile Rockfish, *Sebastes schlegeli. Mar. Environ. Res.* 58: 65-82.

Kori-Siakpere, O. Adamu, K.M. Okobi, I.J (2012). Sublethal Effects of Chromium on Enzymatic Activities of the African Catfish: Clarias gariepinus. *Nor. Sci. Biol* 4(1): 24-30.

Kori-Siakpere, O. and Ake, J.E.G. (2005) Blood Cell Types, Morphology and Dimensions of the African Snakehead; *Parachanna obscura* (Osteichthyes: Channidae). *The Zoologist.* 3: 89-98.

Kori-Siakpere, O. and Egor, V.E. (1997). Haematological Characteristics of the African Mudfish, *Clarias buthupugon* (Pisces : Clariidae). *Bull. Sci. Assoc. Nig.* 21: 177-185.

Kori-Siakpere, O. Ikom, R.B. and Ogbe, M. G. (2010). Variation in Alanine Aminotransferase Activities in African Catfish : *Clarias gariepinus* at Different Sublethal Concentrations of Potassium Permangate. *Sci. Res. Essay.* 5(12). 1501-1505.

Kucuksezgin, F.A., Kontas, O., Altay, E. and Uluturhan, D. E. (2006). Assessment of Marine Pollution in Izmir Bay; Nutrient Heavy Metal and Total Hydrocarbon Concentrations. *Environ. Int.*, 32: 41-51.

Kumari, K. and Sinha, R.C. (2011). LDH and SDH Activity as Potential Biomarkers in the Fish *Labeo rohita*. Proc. International Conference on Biodiversity and Aquatic Toxicology, A.N. University, Andhra Pradesh.

Kurldand, L.T. Faro, S.W. and Siedler, H. (1960). Minamata Disease: The Outbreak of a Neurological Disorder in Minamata, Japan and its Relation to Ingestion of Sea Food Containing Mercury Compounds: *World Neurol.* 1: 370-395.

Kusemiju, K. and Olaniyan, C.I.O. (1977). The Food and Feeding Habits of the Catfishes, *Chrysichthys walkeri* (Gunther), *Chrysichthys nigrodigitatus* (Lacepede), *Chrysichthys filamentosus* (Buolenger) in the Lekki lagoon, Nigeria. *J. Fish. Biol.* 8: 453-458.

Kusemiju, K. and Olaniyan, C.I.O. (1989). The Length-weight Relationship, Condition Factor and Feeding Habits of the Catfish, Chrysichthys Nigrodigitatus (L) in Lagos lagoon, Nigeria. *Nig. J. Nat. Sci.* 4(1-2): 144-149.

Kusemiju, K. (1991). *Fishes, Man and the Aquatic Environment*. Inaugural Lecture Series. University of Lagos Press. 36 pp.

Lawal, M.O. Sangolesye, O.J and Seriki, B.M.(2010). Morphometry and Diet of Chrysichthys Nigrodigitatus in Epe Lagoon, Nigeria. Afr. J. Biotechnol. 9 (46): 7955-7960.

Lenfant, C. Johansen, K. (1972). Gas Exchange in Gill, Skin and Lung Breathing. *Respi.r Physiol.* 14: 211-218.

Levesque, H.M. Moon, T.W. Campbell, P. G. C. Hontela, A. (2002). Seasonal Variation in Carbohydrate and Lipid Metabolism of Yellow Perch (*Perca flavescens*) Chronically Exposed to Metals in the Field. *Aquat. Toxicol*, 60: 257-267.

Livingstone, D.R. (2003). Oxidative Stress in Aquatic Organism in Relation to Pollution and Agriculture. *Revue de Medecine Veterinaire* 154: 427-430.

Lushchak, V.I. (2011). Environmentally Induced Oxidative Stress in Aquatic Animals. *Aquat.Toxicol* 1, 13-30.

Mansour, S.A. and Sidky, M.M. (2002) Heavy Metals Contaminating Water and Fish from Fayoum Governorate, Egypt. *Food Chememistry*, 78: 15-22.

McCarthy, J.F.(1990). Implementation of a Biomarker-based Environmental Monitoring Programme. In: McCarthy, J.F., Shugart, L.R. (Eds.), *Biomarkers of Environmental Contamination*. Lewis Publishers, Boca Raton, FL, USA, 429-440.

McCarthy, J.F., Shugart, L.R.(1990). Biological Markers of Environmental Contamination. In: McCarthy, J.F., Shugart, L.R. (Eds.), *Biomarkers of Environmental Contamination*. Lewis Publishers, Boca Raton, FL, USA, 3-16.

Nishida, Y. (2011) The Chemical Process of Oxidative Stress by Copper (II) and Iron (III) Ions in Several Neu-rodegenerative Disorders. *Monatshefte. Fur. Chemie* 142: 375-384.

Obasohan, E.E. (2008). Bioaccumulation of Chromium, Copper, Manganese, Nickel and Lead in a Freshwater Cichlid, *hemichromis fasciatus* from Ogba River in Benin City, Nigeria. *Afr.J. General Agriculture*. 4(3): 141-152.

Okoye, B.C.O. (1989). A Study of Some Heavy Metals in Lagos Lagoon. *Ph.D., Thesis*. Obafemi Awolowo University, Ile-Ife. 142 pp.

Olatunji, A.S. and Abimbola, A.F. (2010). Geochemical Evaluatin of the Lagos Lagoon Sediments and Water. *World. Appl. Sci. J*. 9 (2): 118-198.

Onikienko, F.A., (1963). Enzymatic Changes from Early Stages of Intoxication with Small Doses of Chloroorganic Insecticides. *Giginea. I. Fiziol. Ruda. Pro. Toksilol. Klinika* (Kietcv: Gos IZ. *Med. Lit*. 77 p.

Oribhabor, B. and Ezenwa, B. (2005). Inventory of Fisheries and Fishes of the Lagos Lagoon, Lagos Nigeria. *Trop. Freshwater. Biol*. 14: 19-36.

Oyewo, E.O. (1998). Industrial Sources and Distribution of Heavy Metals in Lagos Lagoon and Their Biological Effects on Estuarine Animals. *Ph.D. Thesis*, University of Lagos, Nigeria.278 pp.

Paris-Palacios, S. Biagianti-Risbourg, S. Vernet, G. (2000). Biochemical and (ultra) Structural Hepatic Perturbation of *Brachydanio rerio* (Teleostei, Cyprinidae) Exposed to Two Sublethal Concentrations of Copper Sulphate. *Aquat Toxicol* 50: 109-124.

Pietse, J.J. Smit, G.L. van Viiet, K.J, Schoobee, H.J, Hattingh, J. (1981). Some Blood Parameters of the Chinese Grass Carp, *Ctenopharygodon idella* (Valenciennes). *S. Afr. J. Zool*. 16(2):124-126.

Quanfang, Z. Jianbin, Z. Jianjie, F. Jianbo shi. Guibin, J. (2008). Biomonitoring: An Appealing Tool for Assessment of Metal Pollution in the Aquatic Systems. *Analytica. Chimica. Acta*. 606: 135-150.

Reitman, S. and Frankel S. (1957). A Colorimetric Method for the Determination of Serum Glutamic-oxaloacetic and Glutamic-pyruvic Transaminases. *Am. J. Clinical.Pathol*. 28: 56-63.

Roy, S.S (2002). Some Toxicological Aspects of Chloropyrifos to the Intertidal Fish *Boleopthalmus dussumieri*. *Ph.D. Thesis*, University of Mumbai, India. 52-71.

Shareef, K.M. (2011). Heavy Metal Concentration in Commercially Available Fishes in Gaza Strip Markets.M.Sc Thesis. The Islamic University of Gaza, Palestine.

Shukor, M.Y. Masdor, N. Baharom, N.A. Jamal, J.A. Abdullah, M.P. (2008) An Inhibitive Determination Method for Heavy Metals Using Bromelain, a Cysteine Protease. *Appl Biochem Biotechnol* 144: 283-291.

Shukor, M.Y.B, Rahman, N.A, Abdullah, F.A, Shamaan, M.P. Syed, M.A (2006) Development of Heavy Metals Enzymatic Based Assay Using Papain. *Anal. Chem. Acta* 566: 283-289.

Sikoki, F.D. and Otobotekere, A.J.T. (1999). Fisheries. In: *The Land People of Bayelsa State Central Niger Delta*. Alagoa, E.C. (Ed.). Port Harcourt. 301-319.

Singh, A. Sharma, R. Agrawal, M. and Marshall, F.(2012) Risk Assessment of Heavy Metal Toxicity Through Contaminated Vegetables from Waste Water Irrigated Area of Varanasi, India. *Trop. Ecol.* 51(2S): 375-387.

Singh, J, Hewawassam, H. Moffat, D. (1995). Nigeria: Strategic Options for Redressing Industrial Pollution. Industry and Energy Division, *West Central Africa Department,* 1: 45 pp.

Slaninova, A. Smutna, M. Modra, H. Svobodova, Z. (2009) A Review: Oxidative Stress in Fish Induced by Pesticides. Neuroendocrinol. 30: 2-12.

Sowunmi, A.A. (2003). Haematology of the African Catfish, *Clarias gariepinus* (Burchell, 1822) from Eleiyele Reservoir, Ibadan, Southwest Nigeria. *The Zoologist* 2(1): 40-44.

Stickel, F. Patsenker, E. and Schuppan D.(2005) Herbal Hepatotoxicity. *J. Hepatol.* 43: 901-910.

Tasaduq, S.A. Sing, K. Sethi, S. Sharma, S.C. Berdi K. L. (2003). Hepatocurative and Antioxidant Profile of HP-1, a Polyherbal Phytomedicine. *Human Experimental Toxicol.* 22 (12): 639-645.

Torre, F.R. Salibián, A. Ferrari, L. (2000). Biomarkers Assessment in Juvenile *Cyprinus carpio* Exposed to Waterborne Cadmium. *Environ. Pollut.* 109: 277-282.

Valko M, Morris H, Cronin, M.T.D (2005). Metals, Toxicity and Oxidative Stress. Current Medicinal Chemistry 12: 1161-1208.

Van der Oost, R., J. Beyer, and N.P.E. Vermeulen (2003). Fish Bioaccumulation and Biomarkers in Environmental Risk Assessment: A Review. *Environ. Toxicol. and Pharmacol.* 13: 57-149.

Vazquez, G.R. Guerrero, G.A. (2007). Characterization of Blood Cells and Haematological Parameters in *Cichlasoma dimerus* (Teleostei, Perciformes). *Tissue and Cell* 39:151-160.

Vinodhini R and Narayanan M (2009) The Impact of Toxic Heavy Metals on the Hematological Parameters in Common Carp (*Cyprinus carpio* L.). *Iran. J. Environ. Health. Sci. Eng.* 6(1), 23-28.

W.H.O. (World Health Organisation) (1985). Guidelines for Drinking Water Quality (ii): Health Criteria and Supporting Information. Vol. 1, Recommendations. WHO, Geneva. 130 pp.

WHO International Programme on Chemical Safety (IPCS), (1993). Biomarkers and Risk Assessment: Concepts and Principles. Environmental Health Criteria 155, World Health Organisation, Geneva.

Witeska, M., and Kosciuk, B. (2003). Changes in Common Carp Blood After Short-term Zinc Exposure. *Environ. Sci. Pollut. Res,* 3: 15-24.

Yang, H. and Rose, N.L. (2003). Distribution of Hg in the Lake Sediments Across the UK. *Sci. Total Environ,* 304: 391-404.

Yildiz, H.Y. (2009). Reference Biochemical Values for Three Cultured Sparid Fish: Striped Sea Bream, *Lithognathus mormyrus*; Common Dentex, *Dentex dentex*; and Gilthead Sea Bream, *Sparus aurata*. *Comp Clin Pathol* 18: 23-27.

Younis, E.M. Abdel-Warith, A.A and Al-Asgah, N.A. (2012). Hematological and Enzymatic Response of Nile Tilapia : *Oreochromis niloticus* during Short and Long Term Sublethal Exposure to Zinc. *Afr. J.Biotechnol.* 11 (19). 4442-4446.

6

Eco-friendly Management of Shoot and Fruit Borer, *Leucinodes orbonalis* (Guenee) Infesting Eggplant (*Solanum melongena* L.)

Sunil Kumar Ghosh

ABSTRACT

Eggplant (also known as brinjal), *Solanum melongena* L. is one of the most common vegetable crops grown in India and other parts of the world. The crop is said to have originated in India and is known to have been cultivated for over 4000 years. The brinjal belongs to the family Solanaceous and to the genus Solanum, species melongena. The egg plant, Guinea squash are some synonyms to brinjal. *Leucinodes orbonalis* (brinjal shoot and fruit borer) is the key pest infesting eggplant, with international importance as it causes heavy damage in all eggplant growing areas. It is very difficult to control this pest since it feeds inside the shoot and fruit, and there is every possibility of toxic residues remaining in the fruits as they are harvested at frequent intervals and are consumed after little cooking.

In the sub-himalayan region of West Bengal, India the pest was found to be most active during summer and the rainy season, particularly during May-August, and caused 49.5-81.0% damage to fruits. Peak infestation (81.0% fruit damage) was noticed in the first week of June (22nd standard week), when the mean temperature, mean relative humidity and weekly

Department of Agricultural Entomology, Uttar Banga Krishi Viswavidyalaya, Po: Pundibari, Dist: Cooch Behar, West Bengal - 736 165, (India).

rainfall were 27.8°C, 79.2% and 81.2 mm respectively. The pest became less active during winter months particularly in December-January. Borer infestation showed a significant positive correlation (p = 0.05) with maximum and mean temperature, minimum and mean relative humidity and rainfall, whereas with maximum relative humidity the correlation was negative but non-significant.

The yield loss varies from season to season and from location to location. Damage to the fruits in India, particularly in autumn, is very severe and the whole crop can be destroyed. Study of seasonal incidence and biology is very important to formulate suitable and eco-friendly control measures. The control of this pest through the use of synthetic pesticides during the fruit bearing stage is rather difficult as the fruits are harvested at frequent intervals, so there every possibility to retain toxic residues that may cause health hazards. Effective non-pesticide pest management and Integrated Pest Management exist and are being practiced by farmers. The integrated pest management system, in combination with good farming practices are the only solution to good crops. Eco-friendly and environmentally safe pesticides may be recommended to control of this notorious pest. In view of the harmful effects of chemical pest control, several alternatives have been explored to control the insect pests.

In more recent times, there is a renewed interest in eco-friendly approaches to pest management and the rationale for biological approaches is irrefutable. In a broader sense, bio-pesticides include pesticides of biological origin. The insecticides evaluated in the field for *L. orbonalis* control on eggplant revealed that avermectin (Vertimec 1.9 EC; 0.5ml/l) was the most effective in suppressing dead heart caused by the pest, closely followed by *Beauveria bassiana* (Biorin 107 conidia/ml; 1ml/l) and Bacillus thuringiensis Berliner (Biolep 5 × 107 spores/ml; 1g/l). Significantly lower levels of fruit damage were recorded after avermectin treatment, closely followed by DDVP (0.05%) (Nuvan 76 SL; 2ml/3l) when compared with the untreated control.

The other insecticides tested, including a neem formulation (Neemactin 0.15 EC; 2.5 ml/l) and malathion (0.05%) (Malathion 50 EC; 1.0 ml/l) were less effective. None of the insecticides evaluated produced satisfactory results against L. orbonalis. However, avermectin, besides being environmentally safe, was effective for a longer duration and could thus be recommended for Integrated Pest Management programmes on eggplant.

Key words: *Leucinodes orbonalis*, incidence, Vegetable IPM, biopesticides, organic farming.

INTRODUCTION

Population explosion in India, occupying the second place among the nations of the world poses a challenge especially to agricultural scientists in proportionate increase in the production of cereals, pulses, vegetables and fruits despite constraints. Though our country has made substantial progress in the 'green revolution' in respect of self sufficient in production of cereals, it is quite evident that the minimum dietary needs of the common man have not meet so far. Balanced feeding is essential for a healthy life. Vegetables play an important role in our diet as a potential rich source of nutrients which are often deficient in our food materials. At present, the diet of an average Indian is ill-balanced. While the daily consumption per head of vegetables in the advanced countries is 316 g, in India it is only 30 g. According to dietitians, an individual should consume about 115g each of leafy and other vegetables and 70 g root vegetables daily for a balanced diet.

India is gifted with varied agro-climatic conditions for growing an array of vegetable crops to combat the present ill-balanced diet. Vegetables rank next to cereals and occupy a very important place in human diet and serve as supplementary source of nutrients like carbohydrates, proteins, vitamins, minerals and energy for all (N.R.C., 1978). Besides nutrition, vegetables act as an important source of dietary fiber comprised of inassimilable cellulose, hemicelluloses, protein and lignin. These dietary fibers provide the roughage and have an important effect on gut functioning due to their bulk, their ability to absorb water and their being substrates for normal bacterial flora of the gut (Jones, 1978).

The brinjal (also known as eggplant) is said to have originated in India and is known to have been cultivated for over 4000 years. Second only to the potato in terms of total quantity produced, the brinjal continues to be an important domestic crop cultivated across the country accounting for 9% of total vegetable production and covering 8.14% of the land under vegetable cultivation. It is an economically important vegetable grown over 1.7 million hectare world wide with a production of 29.46 million tones with an average productivity of 17.43 tones per hectare during 2004-5 (Anon., 2006a). In India, eggplant occupies an area of 0.51 million hectares with an estimated annual production of 8.20 million tones and the productivity stands at 16.08 tones per hectare during 2005-6 (anon., 2006b).

The brinjal belongs to the family Solanaceous and to the genus Solanum, species melongena. The egg plant, Guinea squash are some synonyms to brinjal. Brinjal is a native to India. It shows the secondary diversity in China and South East Asia (Nath *et al.*, 1987). The brinjal was known to India since ancient time (Decando Le, 1986). The centre of origin for brinjal is India with China as a secondary centre (Thompson and Kelly, 1957). However, it is widely cultivated in both temperate and tropical regions of the globe (Rai *et al.*, 1995).

It is grown year round throughout most part of India and Bangladesh (Singh, 1967). The leading brinjal countries of the world in order of importance are India, China, Japan, Turkey, Italy, Egypt, Iraq, USA and France (Kochhar, 1981). It is a hardy crop and does best in worm and moist climate. The crop is generally grown twice or thrice in a year. The edible part, fruit is of high nutritive value and can well be compared with tomatoes (Chowdhury, 1976). The unripe fruits are consumed after being boiled, cocked, fried or roasted and as pickles as well (Kochar, 1981). The fruits contain 4-6% carbohydrates, 1.4% protein, 0.3% fat and a large amount of minerals including calcium, phosphorus and iron (Aykroyd, 1963, Chowdhury, 1983). The fruits are also quite rich in vitamin A, thiamin, riboflavin, nicotinic acid and vitamin C (Aykroyd, 1963, Chowdhury, 1983). Brinjal is an excellent remedy for those suffering from liver complaints, and it is also said to be good for patients suffering from diabetes (Chowdhury, 1967).

It has been an established fact that any attempt at improvement of agricultural production by using new cultivars with the recommended package of agronomic practices has invariably resulted in the increase in activity and damage by pest and diseases. Though brinjal is being grown throughout the year, it is subjected to attack by a number of insect and non-insect pests.

It is, therefore, considered necessary to focus the attention of scientists, extension workers enlightened cultivars to the pest problems which are causing economic losses even under the present conditions. Similarly, other pests which are of minor importance at present are likely to become serious, once efforts are intensified to produce more, using improved technology.

Congenial climate, presence of alternate hosts like other solanaceous crops and weeds make certain pest to emerge as devastating ones. Insect pest constitute the major limiting factors in the successful production of brinjal. Successful cultivation of the crops calls for an adequate knowledge of insect pest. Least work has been done, and many spending in preparing land, manuring, transplantation and buying good seeds may all be undone by the ravages of insect pest. The damage of crop is done by direct feeding on some parts of the plants or by dissemination of harmful organisms from diseased to healthy plants. The crop is attacked by a number of serious pests.

Among the various insect pests causing limitations, shoot and fruit borer, *Leucinodes orbonalis* Guen. has become an alarming pest in brinjal growing areas including West Bengal (Banerjee and Basu, 1955 & 1956) and ranks first as a pest directly affecting the crop yield as well as its quality. During the first few decades this crop has been increasingly ravaged by *Leucinodes orbonalis* Guen., the larvae of which bore inside eggplant fruit. Farmers have resorted to frequent sprays of pesticides to kill the larva before it enters the fruit. Such extensive use of pesticides cuts into profitability of eggplant production makes more expensive to consumers, poses health hazards, and causes environmental pollution and resource degradation. Socio-economic studies of current control practice in Coochbehar District, West Bengal indicated that 98% of farmers relied exclusively on the use of pesticides and more than 60% farmers sprayed their crop 84 times or more in the 6-7 month cropping season.

Common Name	Scientific Name	Systematic Position	Attacked Plant Parts
Shoot & fruit borer	*Leucinides orbonalis* (Guen.)	Family: Pyralidae Order: Lepidoptera	Shoot & fruit
Hadda or spotted leaf beetle	*Henosepilachna vigintioctopunctata* Fabr.	Fam.: Coccinellidae Order: Coleoptera	Leaf
Brinjal leaf roller	*Eublema olivacea* Walk.	Fam.: Noctuidae Order: Lepidoptera	Leaf
Brinjal stem borer	*Euzophera particella* Rag.	Fam.: Phycitidae Order: Lepidoptera	Shoot
Lace-wing bug	*Urentius sentis* Dist.	Fam.: Tingidae Order: Hemiptera	Leaf
Aphid	*Aphis gossypii* Glov.	Fam. Aphididae Order: Hemiptera	Leaf
Jassid	*Amrasca biguttula biguttula* Ishida	Fam. Cicadellidae Order: Hemiptera	Leaf
Thrips	*Thrips tabaci* Lin.	Fam. Thripidae Order: Thysanoptera	Leaf
Whitefly	*Bemisia tabaci* Genn.	Fam. Aleyrodidae Order: Hemiptera	Leaf
Flea beetle	*Phyllotreta* spp.	Fam.: Chrysomelidae Order: Coleoptera	Leaf
Mite	*Tetranychus cinnabarinus* Boisd. *T. neocaledonicus* Andre	Fam.: Tetranychidae Order: Acarina	Leaf
Root-knot nematode	*Meloydogyne incognita* White	Fam.: Heteroderidae Order: Tylenchida	Root

Biology of *Leucinodes orbonalis* Guen

Eggplant shoot and fruit borer was first described as *Leucinodes orbonalis* by Guenee in 1854. This insect belongs to family Pyralidae of the insect order Lepidoptera.

Egg: Oviposition takes place during the night and adult females lay eggs 80-250 singly on the foliage like lower surface of young leaves, green stems, flower buds, and calyces of the fruits. Eggs are flattened, elliptical and measuring 0.4-0.5 mm in diameter. They are creamy –white soon after they are laid, but change to red before hatching. Eggs hatch in 3 to 6 days.

Larva: Soon after hatching from eggs, young caterpillars search for and bore into tender shoot near the growing point, into flower buds, or into the fruits. Caterpillars prefer fruits over other plant parts. Larvae go through 5-6 instars (Atwal, 1976). Larval period lasts 12-15 days in the summer and up to 22 days in winter. Larval feeding in fruit and shoot is responsible for the damage to eggplant crop. During heavy winter the pest goes hibernation in larval stage.

Pupa: Mature larvae come out of their feeding tunnels and pupate in tough silken cocoons among the fallen leaves and other plant debris on the soil surface near the base of brinjal plants. The colour and texture of the cocoon matches the surroundings making it difficult to detect. Some studies indicate the presence of cocoons at soil depth of 1-3 cm. The pupa period lasts 6 to 17 days depending upon temperature.

Adult: Moths come out of pupa cocoons at night. Females are slightly bigger than males. The abdomen of the female moth tends to be pointed and curl upwards, whereas the male moth possesses a blunt abdomen. The moth is white but has pale brown or black spots on the dorsum of thorax and abdomen. Wings are white with a pinkish or bluish tinge and are ringed with small hairs along the apical and anal margin. The forewings are ornamented with a number of black, pale, and light brown spots. The moth measures 20-22 mm across the spread of wings. Longevity of adults was 1.5-2.4 days for males and 2.0-3.9 days for females. The pre-oviposition and oviposition periods were 1.2-2.1 and 1.4-2.9 days, respectively (Mehto *et al.*, 1983).

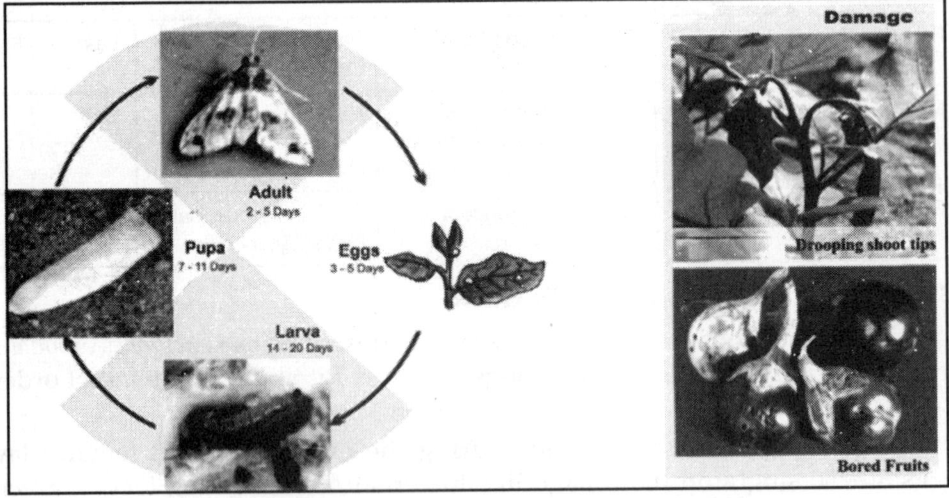

Shoot and Fruit Borer of Brinjal

Nature of Symptoms and Damage

Just after hatching, larva bores into the nearest tender shoot, flower, or fruit. Soon after boring into shoots or fruits, they plug the entrance hole with excreta. In young plants, caterpillars are reported to bore inside petioles and midribs of large leaves. As a result, the affected leaves may drop off (Butani and Jotwani, 1984).

Larval feeding inside shoots results in wilting of the young shoots. Presence of wilted shoots in an eggplant field is the surest sign of damage by this pest. The damaged shoots ultimately wither and drop off. This reduces plant growth, which in turn, reduce fruit numbers and size. Larval feeding in flowers- a relatively rare occurrence-results in failure to form fruit from damaged flowers. Larval feeding inside the fruit results in destruction of fruit tissue. This makes even slightly damaged fruit unfit for marketing. The yield loss varies from season to season and from location to location. Damage to the fruits in India, particularly in autumn, is very severe and the whole crop can be destroyed (Atwal, 1976).

During the early stage of the plant, the caterpillar bores the growing shoots resulting withering symptom eventually causing interference with its normal growth. La‹er on, as soon as the fruit appear they are also attacked. *L. orbonalis* is cosmopolitan in distribution and is reported as a major pest of brinjal in India (Banerjee and Basu, 1055; Lefroy, 1909; Srinivasan and Gowder, 1959) and abrosd, Germany (Marstall, 1013); Myanmar and Sri Lanka (Flecher, 1919); Ghana (Fremponr and Buahin, 1977); China (Zhu *et al.*, 1987); Bangladesh (Kabir and Rahaman, 1971).

As to the extent of damage to the brinjal plant by the shoot and fruit borer, various workers have estimated the loss variously from different brinjal growing tracts of the world. Nighut and Taley (1979) estimated the losses to fruits between 28-85%. Lal (1991) reported that infestation on brinjal by *L. orbonalis* can be as high as 70%. The severity of damage ranged as high as 30-80% in Bihar (Singh and Singh, 1963-64). As to the qualitative loss of crop Hami (1955) reported that the content of vitamin (ascorbic acid) in fruits is reduced by 68% as a result of attack by the pest to fruits. In the sub-Himalayan region of N-E India eggplant (*Solanum melongena* L.) is cultivated all year round on a commercial scale but insect pest damage is limiting factor for its successful production (Ghosh, 1999). During the fruit bearing stage, this key pest feeds internally in the fruit and is very difficult to control, and any loss at this time cannot be recovered and the damaged fruits become unfit for human consumption. Verma (1986) reported that yield loss of eggplant due to attack of *L. orbonalis* was as high as 95.2% in Haryana during June. In the Khasi hills (Meghalaya), *L. orbonalis* damaged 26.3% to 62.5% of fruits (Gangwar and Sachan, 1981). Rao and Rai (1988) recorded 75% infestation of shoots and 87.5% of fruits.

Host Range

The pest is practically monophagus, feeding principally on eggplant; however, other plants belonging to family Solanaceae are reported to be host of this pest. They include tomato (*Lycopersicon esculentum*), potato (*Solanum tuberosum*), selected nightsheds (*S. nigrum* and *S. indicum*) and turkey berry (*S. torvum*). Apart from brinjal *L. orbonalis* also infest potatoes at Ranchi, Bihar, Mysore and Bangalore (Mishra and Chand, 1975) and tomato at Bhubanaswar (Dash and Patnaik, 1970).

Seasonal Incidence of *Leucinodes orbonalis* Guen

The activity of the pest varies with different agro-climatic situations. Patel *et al.*, (1988) observed that little difference between maximum and minimum temperature, high relative humidity and heavy rain are favorable for the outbreak of the pest. Atwal and Verma (1972) reported that development was quicker and the survival rate was greater at higher temperature and humidity, leading to greater abundance during the monsoon period.

An experiment on seasonal incidence was conducted at the instructional farm of UBKV at Pundibari, Cooch Behar, West Bengal, India for the two years (1996-8) study. Eggplant variety 'Pusa Purple Long' was grown year-round during 1996-1998 under standard recommended fertilizer levels (130:65:65 Kg NPK/ha) and cultural practices in 4.8m × 4.5m plots with six replications, without adopting any plant protection measures. During the fruit bearing stage the fruits were harvested at frequent intervals, as and when they attained marketable size. After each harvest, damaged and healthy fruits and their number and weight were recorded. From these results, the percentages of damaged fruits obtained from the different harvests were calculated for each week of the year. These pest infestation data were correlated with corresponding meteorological data for ambient temperature, relative humidity and rainfall, collected throughout the study period.

Analysis of the pooled mean data on borer infestation revealed that the borer was active throughout the year. However, during January-February borer infestation was very low and thereafter increased gradually with the rise of temperature until October. Again, with the onset of winter (*i.e.* from November) infestation declined. Peak borer infestation (80.9%) was recorded in the middle of June (22nd standard week), when the average temperature, relative humidity and weekly rainfall were 22.8 °C, 74.2% and 81.2 mm, respectively. However, the borer was most active and infestation was highest (more than 50% damage) during May-August (Fig. 6.1).

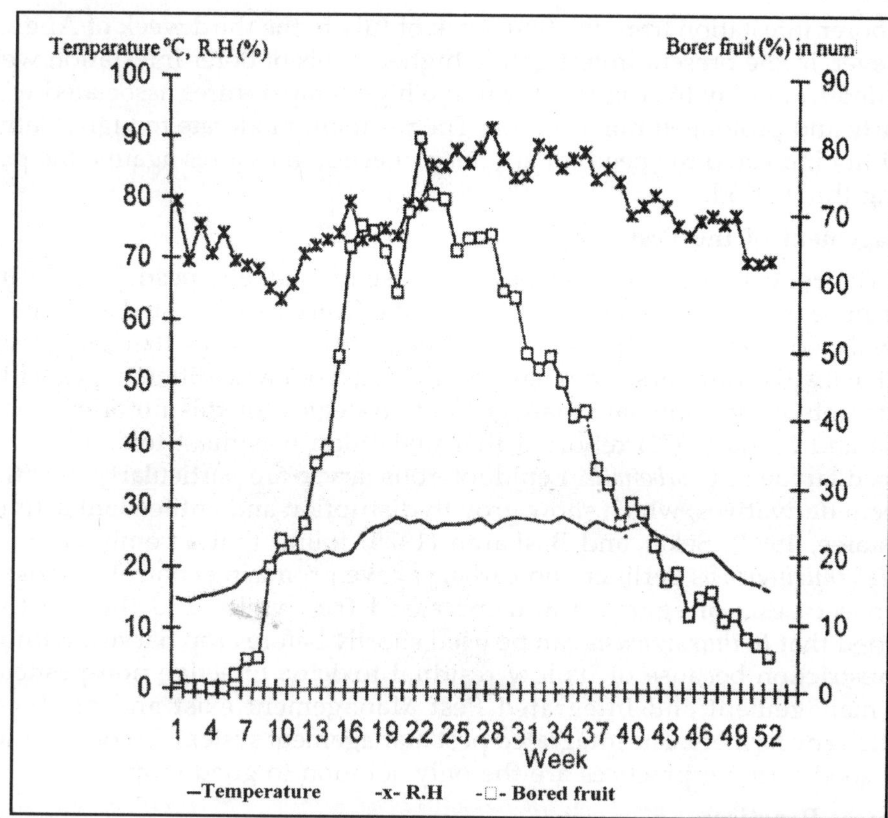

Fig. 6.1: **Incidence of *L. orbonalis*, % of Infested Fruit in Number as Influence by Temperature and RH**

Table 6.1: Correlation Co-efficients Between Weather Parameters and Incidence of *Leucinodes orbonalis* Guen

Infested fruit (%) in number	Temperature				Relative Humidity			Total Rainfall
	Maximum	Minimum	Difference	Average	Maximum	Minimum	Average	
	0.804*	0.837*	(-)0.634*	0.845*	(-)0.226	0.687*	0.580*	0.611*

* Significant

Correlation between borer infestations with important weather parameters (Table 6.1) showed that infestation was positively and significantly correlated with temperature, relative humidity (minimum and average) and weekly rainfall but negatively and significantly with temperature gradient. Non-significant but negative correlation was recorded between borer infestation and maximum relative humidity. The findings of the present investigation conform to those of Patel *et al.*, (1988), where low temperature gradient, high relative humidity and heavy rainfall favored outbreak of shoot and fruit borer. Similarly Shukla (1989) found higher levels of shoot and fruit borer infestation from the first week of July to the third week of August. However, in the present investigation higher levels of borer infestation were recorded from May to August, due to the high temperatures associated with an early and prolonged rainy season. The resultant moderate to high relative humidity indicated the need for special protection measures against the pest during this period.

Management of the Pest

The control of this pest through the use of synthetic pesticides during the fruit bearing stage is rather difficult as the fruits are harvested at frequent intervals, so there every possibility to retain toxic residues that may cause health hazards. Various studies have been carried out with different pesticides in attempts to develop safe management strategies for this notorious pest. Teotia and Sinha (1972) reported that malathion was most toxic to newly hatched larvae of *L. orbonalis*. Lepidopterous larvae are particularly sensitive to neem derivatives, which show growth disruption and antifeedant activity (Mustafee, 1997). Sekar and Baskaran (1976) found that a combination of *Bacillus thuringiensis* Berliner and carbaryl gave promising control of most of the insect pests of eggplant and increased fruit yield, and they further reported that *B. thuringiensis* can be used shortly before crop harvest without any restriction because of its low residual toxicity. Effective non-pesticide pest management and Integrated Pest Management exist and are being practiced by farmers. The integrated pest management system, in combination with good farming practices are the only solution to good crops.

Cultural Practices

- Crop rotation is beneficial as the insect survives only on brinjal. Crop should be rotated so rationalized that most of the pests of brinjal do not get alternate host plant. In the crop rotation programme Solanaceous crops should be avoided as most of the pests are common to them.
- Intercropping brinjal with other crops as each crop has a characteristic odour, the adult moths are confused by various odors and that results in decreased infestation. Intercropping cowpea, maize, coriander improves the natural habitat for natural enemies (like spiders, lace wings, ladybirds etc) against the pest.
- The small and stout fruits are more susceptible to the pest attack compared to long and slender varieties. It is better to go for the long and slender ones in the areas that are highly infested with the pest.
- Collection, destruction of dried shoot tips and bored fruits is beneficial to reduce the pest population. This is an efficient method because the larvae tend to pupate (transform into pupa and takes rest) in the plant residues itself. Burning of the infested parts and composting the crop remains is useful in preventing the build up of the moth populations in a given area.

Mechanical Control

Mechanical control techniques give immediate and tangible results, even though they are time consuming. Some of the common practices include: handpicking of larvae and adults; erecting mechanical barriers; cleaning of planted areas prior to, during or after the cropping season (also termed sanitation) and denying pests alternate sources of food. The combination of mechanical barriers and prompt destruction of freshly wilted shoots harboring pest larvae has potential in controlling the pest effectively. Without a barrier, even if one removed damaged shoots promptly, the source of insects flying in from other fields to the experimental area remains unchecked. The use of barriers combined with prompt destruction of pest-damaged shoots may reduce damage to shoots by an average of 62.7%. Suitable barrier can reduce migration of pest and lower the infestation of the crop. That is why the combination of barrier and sanitation gave greater reduction in pest damage to shoots.

Biological Control

Most insect pests have natural enemies, which can be other arthropods, or entomopathogens such as fungi, bacteria, viruses, or nematodes. Under natural conditions these natural enemies keep the pest populations under reasonable control. As many as sixteen parasitoids, three predators, and three species of entomopathogens have been reported as natural enemies of brinjal shoot and fruit borer from all over the world (Khorsheduzzaman *et al.*, 1998). However, they do not seem to play any significant role in keeping damage under reasonable control (Srivastava and Butani, 1998), especially in South Asia.

Natural Enemied Against *L. orbonalis* reported in India

Predators: *Campyloneura sp (a bug), Cheilomenes sexmaculata (a ladybird beetle),* ***Coccinella septempunctata*** *(seven spotted ladybird beetle),* ***Brumoides suturalis*** (three striped ladybird).

Parasitoids: *Diadegma apostata, Pseudoperichaeta sp, Phanerotoma sp, Itamoplex sp, Eriborus argenteopilosus.*

Entomopathogens: Fungus *(Bipolaris tetramera)*, Baculovirus, Nuclear polyhedrosis virus.

The sole exception is a study from Sri Lanka were Sandanayake and Edirisinghe (1992) reported a high level of parasitism of brinjal shoot and fruit borer larvae by a parasitoid, *Trathala flavor-orbitalis* Cameron (Hymenoptera: Ichneumonidae). This parasitoid has been reported to be present in India (Naresh *et al.*, 1986) and Bangladesh (Alam and Sana, 1964), however, its contribution to pest control was rarely documented and does not appear to be significant. Since biological control is an important component in IPM and very little information is available on the role of biological control agents in combating brinjal shoot and fruit borer.

Sex Pheromones

Sex pheromone chemicals are increasingly used to control insect pests of vegetables and fruits. Zhu *et al.*, (1987) working in China identified (E)-11- hexadecenyl acetate (E 11-16:Ac) as the major component of the female sex pheromone of brinjal shoot and fruit borer and suggested that it was attracting male moths in the field. Subsequently, Attygalle *et al.*, (1988) in Sri Lanka confirmed the presence of E 11-16: Ac in virgin females and found trace amounts of (E)-11-hexadecen-1-01 (E 11-16: OH). High concentration of E 11-16: Ac alone or low concentrations of mixtures of E 11-16: Ac and E 11-16: OH (10:0.5 or 10:1) attract large numbers of male moths to pheromone-baited traps (AVRDC, 1996; Praveen Kumar and Sundara Babu, 1997; Srinivasan and Sundara Babu, 2000). These results formed the basis for inclusion of sex pheromone as one of the components of IPM of brinjal shoot and fruit borer. *Leucinodes* being a monophagous (completes its life cycle on one single host) pest the female moths are obligated to lay eggs on brinjal plants. Understanding this behaviour, using pheromone traps in big numbers across brinjal fields is very efficient method to control the pest besides monitoring its population. Pheromones can be used in low-cost water-trough traps @ 40-60 traps per acre is very efficient in avoiding the pest in the first place. The pheromones traps trap the adult male moths (and not female ones) which reduces the fertilizing the eggs of female moths.

Pesticide Control

Brinjal cultivation involves huge amounts of pesticide. 60% of plant protection cost is for controlling shoot and fruit borer. Small and marginal farmers use 25-80 sprays of pesticides in brinjal cultivation. In spite of the extensive use of chemical pesticides, the pest is difficult to control by the application of pesticides as the larvae are often hidden in the fruit and do not come in contact with the insecticides.

Harmful Effect of Chemical Insecticides

Since the discovery of DDT as an insecticide in 1939 by Dr. Paul Muller, there has been a great expansion in the use of chemicals for pest control. Pesticides during manufacturing, transportation, storage and actual use enter in the abiotic and biotic components of the environment through air, water and soil and disturb the ecosystem, causing great disaster sometimes. Miss Rachel Carson published an epoch-making book "Silent Spring" in the year 1962 awakened the people referring the forceful account of the danger of pesticides. These days the pollution of the environment is a problem of great importance and is of everybody's concern. The pesticides may accumulate in the environment and contaminate all the systems i.e. air, water, soil, plants animals etc. by being transported from one system to another. Although they are protecting the crops from pests for boosting up the agricultural produce but bring out ecological disturbance and environmental pollution.

A variety of insecticides like BHC, aldrin, dieldrin, heptachlor, chlordane, toxaphene, methyl parathion, phorate etc. are being used in our country for the control of termite, white grub, cutworm, root borer etc. It is found that the pesticides disturb the microbial activity of the soil, adverse effect on the earth worm and may harm the predatory mites and carabid beetles. They may have adverse effect on some invertebrates that were responsible soil fertility. The uptake of insecticide residues by some crops adversely affects our health. The people around vicinity of pesticide factories even upto 5-7 km area badly feel off flavor and such suffocated environment ultimately results in different kind of diseases among the residents. The contamination of air during application of pesticides may also take place which could pose serious health hazards, if the concentration in air raised above the thresh hold values. Different doses of pesticides at different dose levels are being used on the different types of crops against noxious pest all over the country for the last four decades. Saxena et al., (1990) reported that the residue of malathion was found more than the permissible limits in tomato, okra, cauliflower, brinjal and beans. Gupta et al., (1987-88) reported that above 60% samples of potato, brinjal, cabbage, cauliflower okra and cucurbits were containing the residues of organophosphatic insecticides more than the permissible level. Water has been found contaminated with pesticides by different ways. Many great rivers of the world have been found to contain large amount of insecticide residues which killed the fishes and other aquatic animals living there (Srivastava and Saxena, 1989). In order to destroy unwanted plants, insects and fishes etc. the deliberate use of pesticide is being done due to which water is contaminated. Water has also been found to be contaminated with pesticides through run off from fields, through sewage disposal, through the effluents of industries using pesticides, through dead and decayed plants treated with pesticides. In UK the presence of insecticides was reported in rain water. Fresh rain water on the mountain top of the Himalaya was found possessing pesticide residues. Commonly cultivated crops, vegetables and fruit plants have been found to be affected with injudicious use of pesticides right from germination through growth to harvest. The application of pesticides may bring the resurgence of the target pests against which the chemicals are applied, the outbreak of some unimportant pests. The pesticides are also harmful to beneficial fauna such as honey bees and natural enemies like parasites, predators and pathogens of the pests etc. As a result of pesticide pollution several diseases may develop in human beings and domestic animals.

Importance of Bio-pesticides for Pest Control in Vegetable Field

In view of the harmful effects of chemical pest control, several alternatives have been explored to control the insect pests. In more recent times, there is a renewed interest in eco-friendly approaches to pest management and the rationale for biological approaches is irrefutable. In a broader sense, bio-pesticides include pesticides of biological origin.

Botanical Extracts

Botanical pesticides are either naturally occurring plant materials or products derived rather simply from such plant materials. They are water extracts or organic solvent extracts of insecticide components of plants. Plant substances are produced as byproducts of major biochemical pathways and chemically, they include alkaloids, terpenoids and phenols as well as a number of other compounds. These chemicals repel approaching insects, deter feeding and oviposition on the plants, disrupt behaviour and physiology of insects in various ways and even prove toxic to different developmental stages of many insects (Dhaliwal and Arora, 2001). The use of plants as pesticides has been practiced since times immemorial. The Hindu book, the 'Rig Veda' written in India in 2000 BC, makes a mention of the use of poisonous plants for pest control. Crude botanical pesticides have been used for several countries and were known in tribal or traditional indigenous technologies around the world before being introduced to Europe. Those with long histories of traditional use include neem in India, rotenone in East Asia and South America, pyrethrum in Persia, and sabadilla in Central and South America. Neem (*Azadirachta indica)* tree is indigenous to India and is a storehouse of large number of pesticidally active tetranortriterpenes, commonly called limonoids, among which azadirachtin, salanin and nimbin are the most active. Although neem seeds and leaves have been used as traditional insecticides for centuries, modern interest in neem as an insecticide dates back to the work of Pradhan *et al.* (1962) who reported that dilute aqueous kernel extracts prevented feeding of the desert locust, *Schistocerca gregaria*. The most abundant neem constituent, azadirachtin is considered an excellent botanical pesticide because of its biodegradability, demonstrated low toxicity to vertebrates, environmental safety, and safety to non-target organisms (Jacobson, 1989; Rembold, 1989). Its multi-pronged effects against insects including repellent, antifeedant, oviposition deterrent, molting or growth disruption, sterilant, ovicidal and oviposition deterrent, etc. help to an effective control of a variety of farm and household insect pests and pathogens infesting agricultural plantation and cash crops. Several commercial formulations of neem like Neem Gold, Neemazal, Econeem, Neemark, Neemcure and Azatin among now available in many countries including the United States, India, Germany and several Latin American countries. Inadequate stability, problems in large-scale production, lack of effective delivery system, poor self life, diminished residual toxicity under field condition, non-availability of reliable standards and inadequate availability of the raw material are some impediments in successful commercialization of neem pesticides. *Polygonum* and *Pongamia* are such type of plants having insecticidal properties needed to be conservation. *Polygonum hydropiper*, a well known weed in northeast India especially in the foot hill of the Himalaya, locally known as "biskanthali" is widely used indigenously in different tribal areas for pest control in vegetable field. *Pongamia pinnata*, a medium sized tree is well known in terai region of West Bengal having humid and subtropical climate. It is one of the few nitrogen fixing trees often planted as an ornamental and shade tree. *Pongamia* oil and leaf extract is useful for pest control in vegetable field.

More than 1000 species of plants have been reported to have chemicals in leaves, stems, flowers, seeds and roots which have insecticidal properties. Various scientists direct their attention to discover such type of plant toxicant which are eco-friendly and play a better role in the control of pest. Their limited persistence in the environment helps to minimize their adverse effects (Weinzierl, 2000). It is an important component of IPM. Plant origin insecticides offer a great advantage by being compatible with other low risk options such as pheromones, biopesticides and bioagents such as entomopathogenic fungi and nematodes, predators and parasitoids, etc. which can be integrated in IPM programmes.

Microbial Pesticides

Microbial pesticides consist of disease causing microorganisms, which are disseminated in the pest populations in large quantities in a manner similar to application of chemical pesticides. Insects are susceptible to a variety of diseases caused by different groups of microorganisms including viruses, bacteria, fungi, micoplasma, protozoa, rickettisae and nematodes. Pathogens may exert controlling effect by means of their invasive properties, toxins, enzymes and other substances (Arora *et al.*, 2000; Lewis, 2006). Over 3000 microorganisms have been reported to cause diseases in insects. Problems with the use of chemical insecticides and emphasis on low-input sustainable agriculture have pushed the microbial agents to the fore-front for use in IPM systems. The major advantage of exploitation microorganisms for pest control is their environmental safety primarily due to their host specificity of these pathogens. Many insect pathogens are compatible with other control methods including the chemical insecticides and parasitoids. There is minimum effect on non-target organisms. Interaction of insect pathogens with other methods of pest control should be thoroughly studued to develop better IPM strategies. The self-perpetuating nature of most of the pathogens in both space and time would certainly prove to be an asset in sustainable agriculture.

Field Efficacy of Bio-pesticides Against *Leucinodes orbonalis*

An experiment on bio-pesticides against *Leucinodes orbonalis* was conducted at the instructional farm of UBKV at Pundibari, Cooch Behar, West Bengal, India for the two years (1996-8) study.

The seedlings of eggplant variety Pusa Purple Long were transplanted in the middle of February in both years, with recommended fertilizer doses (130:65:65 kg NPK/ha) and usual cultural practices, at a spacing of 75 cm × 60 cm in plots of 4.5m × 1.8m arranged in a randomized block design with three replications.

Four bio-pesticides, namely azadiractin (Neemactin 0.15 EC) @ 2.5 ml/l, *Bacillus thuringiensis* var. kurstaki Berliner (Biolep, 5 × 107 spores/mg) @ 1.0 g/l, *Beauveria bassiana* (Bals) Vuillemin (Biorin, 107 conidia/ml) @ 1.0 ml/l, and avermectin (Vertimec 1.9 EC) @ 0.5 ml/l, were evaluated and compared with synthetic organic chemicals, malathion (0.05%) (malathion 50 EC, 1.0ml/l) and DDVP (0.05%) (Nuvan 76SL, 2ml/3l), both used as recommended standards against *Leucinodes orbonalis*. Four sprayings at intervals of 15 days were made, starting at the initiation of infestation.

Observations on dead heart due to attack by *L. orbonalis* were recorded at 3, 8 and 14 days after each spraying. The total dead hearts per plant from five randomly selected plants per replicate were recorded. The data thus obtained were used to compute the percentages of dead hearts and analyzed statistically.

The fruits were harvested at frequent intervals, as and when they attained marketable size. The infested and healthy fruits from each plot were individually sorted and their numbers and weights were recorded separately at each harvest. The percentages of infested fruit based on numbers and weights from the cumulative data of all harvests were computed and analyzed. The yield of marketable produce was calculated for the different years on the basis of fruit yield per plot and converted to tons per hectare.

Among the six insecticides evaluated (Table 6.2) avermectin caused the greatest suppression of dead heart of eggplant caused by L. orbonalis (57.8% suppression), closely followed by Beauveria bassiana (55.9% suppression) and Bacillus thuringiensis var. kurstaki (53.4% suppression), which were at par with each other. The least suppression was recorded from neem (38.0% suppression), followed by malathion (43.2% suppression).

Three days after spraying, avermectin was found the most effective (59.6% suppression) against dead heart, closely followed by DDVP (56.4% suppression); there was no significant difference in the efficacy of these two insecticedes. Malathion was the least effective (45.8% suppression). At 8 days after spraying, Bacillus thuriengiensis var. kurstaki was the most effective (69.8% suppression) followed by Beauveria bassiana (69.0% suppression), the least effective being neem (41.0% suppression). At 14 days after spraying, avermectin was best (50.4% suppression), and the least effective was neem (23.1% suppression).

None of the insecticides evaluated (Table 6.3) produced satisfactory results against fruit borer. However, significantly fewer damaged fruit were obtained with avermectin (damaged fruits 45.2% in number and 40.2% in weight), closely followed by DDVP (48.8% in number and 43.3% in weight); there was no significant difference between these two products. The performance of all insecticides was poor but they gave significantly better results than the untreated control (damaged fruits 72.9% in number and 67.6% in weight).

Table 6.2: Field Efficacy of Insecticides Against Dead Heart Caused by *Leucinodes orbonalis* Guen

Insecticides	Suppression of Dead Heart (%)											
	3 DAS			8 DAS			14 DAS			Grand mean		
	1997	1998	Mean	1997	1998	Mean	1997	1998	Mean	1997	1998	Mean
Malathion (0.05%)	53.79 (47.22)	38.55 (38.24)	**45.83 (42.77)**	54.45 (47.64)	36.83 (37.27)	**47.31 (43.44)**	44.25 (41.66)	28.43 (32.08)	**36.34 (36.98)**	50.83 (45.51)	34.60 (35.86)	**43.16 (41.06)**
DDVP (0.05%)	75.56 (60.61)	37.24 (37.54)	**56.39 (48.71)**	59.03 (50.29)	50.37 (45.22)	**54.70 (47.74)**	41.11 (39.86)	24.32 (29.47)	**32.71 (34.85)**	58.57 (50.25)	37.31 (37.41)	**47.93 (43.77)**
Neem (2.5 ml/l.)	64.23 (53.34)	30.40 (33.31)	**49.91 (43.44)**	51.03 (45.60)	30.88 (33.63)	**40.95 (39.74)**	30.95 (33.72)	15.15 (22.82)	**23.05 (28.60)**	48.74 (44.22)	25.48 (29.92)	**37.97 (37.26)**
Bacillus thuringiensis (1.0 g/l.)	41.19 (39.86)	53.59 (47.08)	**47.39 (43.49)**	80.92 (65.00)	58.62 (50.00)	**69.77 (56.83)**	49.65 (44.80)	36.53 (37.15)	**43.09 (41.00)**	57.25 (49.89)	49.58 (44.74)	**53.42 (47.11)**
Beauveria bassiana (1.0 ml/l.)	62.39 (52.23)	50.33 (45.13)	**56.30 (48.64)**	77.25 (62.02)	60.66 (51.22)	**68.95 (56.32)**	45.99 (42.67)	38.73 (38.47)	**42.36 (40.57)**	61.88 (52.31)	49.91 (44.94)	**55.87 (48.51)**
Avermectin (0.5 ml/l.)	64.07 (53.25)	55.07 (47.92)	**59.57 (50.55)**	66.11 (54.52)	60.78 (51.26)	**63.44 (52.86)**	55.56 (48.22)	45.34 (42.31)	**50.44 (45.26)**	61.91 (52.00)	53.73 (47.17)	**57.82 (49.56)**
Control	–	–	–	–	–	–	–	–	–	–	–	–
Mean	60.20 **(51.08)**	44.20 **(41.54)**	52.56 **(46.27)**	64.80 **(54.18)**	49.69 **(44.77)**	57.52 **(49.49)**	44.58 **(41.82)**	31.42 **(33.72)**	38.00 **(37.88)**	– –	– –	– –

* Figures in parentheses indicate angular transformed values; ** DAS = Days after spraying.

Table 6.3:

S.E.M. (±) CD at 5%	1997			1998			Mean		
	A	B	A x B	A	B	A x B	A	B	A x B
	1.209	1.710	2.962	0.887	1.254	2.172	1.010	1.422	2.463
	3.478	4.919	8.520	2.551	3.607	N.S.	2.905	4.090	7.085

A = Days after spraying; B = Insecticides; AxB = Interaction of DAS with insecticides.

Yield is directly related to the efficacy of insecticides. The best yield was obtained from avermectin treatment (31.0 t/ha), closely followed by DDVP (30.8 t/ha) (Table 6.3). Considering its moderate to higher efficacy and the fact that it is less harmful to natural enemies and humans, avermectin can be incorporated in future IPM programmes.

Bt brinjal

Bt brinjal is the first Genetically Modified food crop in India that has reached the approval stage for commercialization. Bt brinjal would reduce the pesticide usage in cultivation by 80%.

Bt brinjal is a transgenic brinjal created by inserting a gene *cry 1 Ac* from the soil bacterium *Bacillus thurigiensis* into brinjal. This is said to give the brinjal plant registance against lapidopteran insects like brinjal shoot and fruit borer, *Leucinodes orbonalis*. It is a genetically modified brinjal developed by the Maharastra Hybrid Seed company Ltd. (Mahyco) in India.

When brinjal shoot and fruit borer larvae feed on Bt brinjal plants, they ingest the Bt protein *Cry 1 Ac* along with plant tissue. In the insect gut which is alkaline with a pH> 9.5, the protein is solubilized and activated by gut proteases crystallizing into fine needle-like shards that pierce the insect gut lining making holes in it. This leads to disruption of digestive processes, paralysis and subsequent death of the larvae.

Bt brinjal has generated much debate in India. The promoters say that Bt brinjal will be beneficial to small farmers because it is insect resistant, increases yields, is more cost-effective and will have minimal environmental impact. On the other hand, concerns about Bt brinjal relate to its possible adverse impact on human health and bio-safety, livelihoods and biodiversity.

REFERENCES

Alam, A.Z. and Sana, D.L. (1964): Biology of *Leucinodes orbonalis* Guenee in East Pakistan. In: *Review of research, Division of Entomology*, 1947-64. Dhaka: Agriculture Information Service, Department of Agriculture. pp. 192-200.

Anonymus, (2006a): Improvement of Bt brinjal in India. *Agriculture and Industry Survey*, 33: 19.

Anonymus, (2006b): www.indiacrop.in (Agriculture Statistics, Ministry of Agriculture, India).

Arora, R., Battu, G.S. and Ramakrishan, N. (2000): Microbial Pesticides: Current Status and Future Outlook. In: G.S. Dhaliwal and B. Singh (eds) *Pesticides and Environment*. Commonwealth Publishers, New Delhi, pp. 344-395.

Attygalle, A.B., Schwarz,J. and Gunawardena, N.E. (1988): Sex Pheromone of Brinjal Shoot and Pod Borer, *Leucinodes orbonalis* Guen. (Lepidoptera: Pyralidar) *Zeitschrift fuer Naturforschung* 43c: 790-792.

Atwal, A.S. (1976): Agricultural Pests of Indian and South East Asia. New Delhi: Kalyani Publishers. 529 pp.

Atwal, A.S. and Verma, N.D. (1972): Development of *Leucinodes orbonalis* Guen. (Lepidoptera: Pyraustidae) in Relation to Different Levels of Temperature and Humidity. *Indian J. Agric. Sci.* 42 (9): 49-54.

AVRDC. 1996. AVRDC 1995 Report AVRDC Publication No. 96-449. Shanhua, Taiwan: Asian Vegetable Research and Development Centre. 187 pp.

Aykroyd, W.R. (1963): Indian Council of Medical Res. Special Report, 42.

Banerjee, S.N. and Basu, A.N. (1955): On the Control of Brinjal Stem and Fruit Borer, *Leucinodes orbonalis* Guen. In West Bengal. *Sci. Cult.* 20(7): 350-351.

Banerjee, S.N. and Basu, A.N. (1956): Evaluation of Insecticides Against the Brinjal Shoot and Fruit Borer, *Leucinodes orbonalis* Guen. In West Bengal, F.A.O. *Pl. Prot. Bull.* 5(1):7-8.

Butani, D.K. and Jotwani, M.G. (1984): Insects in Vegetables. New Delhi: Periodical Expert Book Agency. 356 pp.

Chowdhury, B. (1967): Vegetables. National Book Trust, New Delhi, p. 198.

Chowdhury, B. ed.(1976): Vegetables. National Book Trust, New Delhi, p. 214.

Chowdhury, B. ed.(1983): Vegetables. National Book Trust, New Delhi, p. 214.

Dash, M.S. and Patnaik, B.H. (1970): A New Host of the Brinjal Shoot and Fruit Borer, *Leucinodes orbonalis* Guen. And its Biology. *J. Bomb. Nat. Hist. Soc.* 67(3): 601-603.

Decando Le, A. (1986): Origin of Cultivated Plants. *Int. Nat. Sci. Ser. Lond.* (2nd Ed.). 48(8): 468.

Dhaliwal, G.S. Arora, R. (2001): Role of Phytochemicals in Integrated Pest Management. In: O.Kaul and G.S. Dhaliwal (eds) *Phytochemical Biopesticides*. Harwood Academic Publishers, Amsterdam, The Netherlands, pp. 97-117.

Flecher, T.B. (1919): Annotate List of Indian Crop Pest. *Third. Ent. Meet. Pusa*. p. 132.

Frem Pong, E. and Buahin, G.K.A. (1977): Studies on the Insect Pests of Eggplant, *Solanum melongena* L in Ghana. Bulletin del 'Institute Fundamental d' Afrique Noire, Series A 39(3): 627-641.

Gangwar, S.K. and J.N. Sachin (1981): Seasonal Incidence and Control of Insect Pests of Brinjal with Special Reference to Shoot and Fruit Borer, *Leucinodes orbonalis* Guen. in Meghalaya. *J Res. Assam Agric. Univ.* 2(2): 187-192.

Ghosh, S.K. (1999): Studies on the Pest Constraints of Brinjal and Their Management under Terai Region of West Bengal. A Thesis Sunmitted to the B.C.K.V., Mohanpur, Nadia, West Bengal for the Award of Ph.D Degree.

Gupta, H.C.L., Jain, K.L. and Kumar, A. (1987-88): Monitoring of Insecticide Residues in Marketed Vegetables and Fruits, *Reports of Zone* 1V-A, RAU, Udaipur.

Hami, M.A. (1955): Effect of Borer Attack on Vitamin-c Content of Brinjal. *Pakist. J.* 4: 223-224.

Jacobson, M. (1989): Pharmacology and Toxicology of Neem. In: *Phytochemical Pesticides*, Vol. 1. *The Neem Tree*, M. Jacobson (ed.) CRC Press, Boca Raton, FL, pp. 133-153.

Jones, F.A. (1978): Diet and Intestinal Disease. Pages 109-126. In: ed. J. Yudkin, Diet of man: Needs and wants, Applied Science Publoshers, London.

Kabir,S.M.H. and Rahman, A.K.M.M. (1971): Field Tests of Insecticides Against the Eggplant Pest Complex. *J. Econ. Ent.* 64(3): 758-759.

Khorsheduzzaman, A.K.M., Ali, M.I., Mannan, M.A. and Karim, M.A. (1988): Component Technologies of IPM Package for Brinjal Shoot and Fruit Borer for Bangladesh: A Review, *Bangladesh Journal of Agricultural Research,* 23: 593-606.

Kochhar, S.L. ed. (1981): Economic Botany in the Tropics. The Mac Millen Press. New Delhi, pp. 476.

Lal, O.P. (1991): Varietal Resistance in the Eggplant, *Solanum melongena* L. Against the Brinjal Shoot and Fruit Borer, *Leucinodes orbonalis* Guen. *Zeitschrift fupfla Zenkrankheiten Pflamxenschulz* 98(4): 405-410.

Lefroy, H.M. (1909): Indian Insect Life. pp. 1-518.

Lewis, L.C. (2006): Ecological Considerations for the Use of Entomopathogens in Integrated Pest Management. In: O. Kaul and G. W. Cuperus (eds) *Ecologically Based Integrated Pest Management*. CAB International, Wallingford, UK, pp. 249-268.

Marstall, H. (1913): List Schadlicher Insekton (List of Noxious Insects) (In German) *Der. Pflanzer Dares Salam* 9 (6) cf. 1913 R.A.E. (A) 1: 413.

Mehto, D.N., Singh, K.M., Singh, R.N. and Prasad, D. (1983): Biology of Brinjal Shoot and Fruit Borer, *Leucinodes orbonalis* Guen. Bulletin of Entomology, 24(2): 112-115.

Mishra, U.K. and Chand, P. (1975): *Leucinodes orbonalis* Guen. As a Pest of Potato. *Entomologists' News* l. 5(4):24-25.

Mustafee, T.P. (1997): Need for Efficient Pesticidal Management in Changing Agricultural Scenario. Proc. Symp. on Pest Management in Changing Agricultural Situation, March 15-16, Viswa Bharati.

Naresh, J.S., Malik,V.S. and Balan, J.S.(1986): Estimation of Fruit Damage and Larval Population of Brinjal Fruit Borer, *Leucinodes orbonalis* Guen. And its Parasitization by Trathala sp on Brinjal. *Bulletin of Entomology,* (India) 27: 44-47.

Nath, P., Velayudhan, S. and Singh, D.P. (1987): Vegetables for the Tropical Region. ICAR, New Delhi, India. pp.120

National Research Council (1978): Post Harvest Food Losses in Developing Countries. *Nat. Acad. Sci. Washington,* D.C. pp. 206.

Nighut, V.S. and Taley, Y.M. (1979): Chemical Control of Brinjal Tissue Borer. *Pesticides.* 13(12): 12-14.

Patel, J.R., Korat D.M. and Patel, V. B. (1988): Incidence of Shoot and Fruit Borer (*Leucinodes orbonalis* Guen.) and its Effect on Yield in Brinjal. *Indian. J. Pl. Prot.* 16(2): 143-145.

Pradhan, S., Jotwani, M.G. and Rai, B.K. (1962): The Neem Seed Deterent to Locusts. *Indian Fmg.*12: 7-11.

Praveen Kumar, S. and Sundara Babu, P.C. (1997): Evaluation of Sex pheromone Componrnts of *Leucinodes Orbonalis* Guen. To Monitor the Pest Population in Field Through Water Trough Trap. *Journal of Entomological Research.* 21: 85-88.

Rai, M., Gupta, P.L. and Agarwal, R.C. (1995): Catalogue on Eggplant (*Solanum melongena* L.), *Germplasm Plant-1.*

Rao, K.V. and S. Rai (1988): Spatial Dispersion of Shoot and Fruit Infestation on Brinjal Crop. *Ann. Agric. Res.* 9 (1): 32-36.

Rembold, H. (1989): Azadirachtins. Their Structure and Mode of Action. In: *Insecticides of Plant Origin,* J.T. Arnason, B.J.R. Philogene and P. Morand (eds) *Am. Chem. Soc. Symp. Ser 387,* Washington, DC, pp. 150-163.

Sandanayake, W.R.M. and Edirisinghe, J.P. (1992): Trathala Flavoorbitalis: Parasitization and Development in Relation to Host-stage Attacked. *Insect Science and its application.* 13(3): 287-292.

Saxena, R.C., Srivastava, R.P., Singh,R. and Srivastava, A.K. (1990): Studies on Residues of Insecticides on Locally Marketed Fruits and Vegetables. *Indian J. Ent.* 53: 258-264.

Sekar,P. and Baskaran, P. (1976): Investigation on Dipel- Organic Insecticide Combinations Against Insect Pest of Brinjal. *Madras Agric. J.* 63: 542-544.

Singh, H. (1967): Vegetables. Chapter-7. pp. 387-406 in cd. C.G. Raghava Kurup. Hand Book of Agriculture, Indian Council Agric. Res., New Delhi, pp. 877.

Singh, M.P. and Singh, M.M. (1963-64): Control Schedule for *Leucinodes orbonalis* Guen. of Brinjal (*Leucinodes orbonalis* Guen.). *Proc. Bihar Acad. Agric. Sci.* pp. 26-30.

Srinivasan, P.M. and Gowder, R.B. (1959): A Note on the Control of the Brinjal Shoot and Fruit Borer, *Leucinodes orbonalis* Guen. *Indian J. Agric. Sci.* 29: 71-73.

Srinivasan, G. and Sundara Babu, P.C. (2000): Sex Pheromone for Brinjal Shoot and Fruit Borer, *Leucinodes orbonalis* Guen. *Indian Journal of Entomology*. 62: 94-95.

Srivastava, K.P. and Butani, D.K. (1998): Pest Management in Vegetables, Part 1. Houston, USA: Research Periodical and Book Publishing House. 294 pp.

Srivastava, R.P. and Saxena, R.C. (1989): *A Text Book of Insect Toxicology.* Himanshu Publications, Udaipur. 165 pp.

Teotia, T.P.S. and Sinha, S.N. (1972): Relative Toxicity of Some Insecticides to the Larvae of Brinjal Shoot and Fruit Borer, *Leucinodes orbonalis* Guen. *Indian J. Ent.* 33: 217-219.

Thompson, C.H. and Kelly, C.W. (1957): Vegetable Crops. Mc Graw Hill Book Co. Inc. USA. pp. 611.

Verma, T.S. (1986): Picking Behaviour and Population of Diapaused Pupae of Shoot and Fruit Borer in Relation to its Resistance in Brinjal. *Himachal J Agric. Res.* 12: 63-65.

Weinzierl, R.A. (2000): Botanical Insecticides, Soaps and Oils. In: J.E. Rachcigl and N.A. Rachcigl (eds) *Biological and Biotechnological Control of Insect Pests.* Lewis Publishers, Boca Raton, Florida, pp. 101-121.

Zhu, P., Kong, F. and Xu, J. (1987): Identification of the Sex Pheromone of Eggplant Borer *Leucinodes orbonalis* Guen. (Lepidoptera: Pyralidae). *Zeitschrift fuer Naturforschung* 42c: 1347-1348.

Eradication of Lantana by Under Planting with Bamboo

Deepak Kholiya

ABSTRACT

The initiation of the biological control programme against the invasive weed *Lantana camara* L. in Punjab, several biological control agents have been introduced, yet the problem remains still. Bamboo a natural regenerating, fast growing species would be an effective biological control agent against *Lantana camara* infested areas to stop its further invasion in forest ecosystem, which is presently has been declared as forest ecosystem terrorist.

Lantana is widely grown as an ornamental shrub throughout the tropics and temperate environment in about more than 50 countries. The general ill impacts of *Lantana* towards land are: Decreased productivity in pastures. Poisons for cattle, Non fodder species, Invades disturbed natural ecosystems, establishing in open situation creek, river banks and roadsides, Excludes understorey species, Changes floral & faunal makeup by providing perch sites and cover. Creates allelo-chemical effects in soil by providing allopathic compounds through leaf decomposition, Understorey competitors for forestry.

Department of Environmental Science, Graphic Era Hill University, Bhimtal Campus, Nainital (Uttarakhand), India.

Thus the most serious effect of invading *Lantana* shrub plants occur when they alter the forest/pastures environment. However, the most dramatic changes produced by invading species occur when they alter the disturbance regime of the land ecosystem. Thus, *Lantana* species has been nominated as among 100 of the "World worst invaders". For eradication of *Lantana*, Bamboo two species (*Dendrocalamus strictus* and *Bambusa bambos*) were planted as a biological weed control agent for the noxious weed *Lantana camara* L. from infested forest areas which showed positive results.

Key Words: Biological weed control; *Lantana* & Bamboo; invasive weed; fast growing; forest ecosystem terrorists; world worst invaders.

INTRODUCTION

Lantana is an exotic weed, introduced in India as a flowering shrub. However, it found the Indian climate suitable for its growth grew aggressively and has already covered large areas in open forests. Since it forms thick patches, it inhibits natural regeneration of the local vegetation. The species is not of much economic value. Even the cattle do not feed on its foliage. Hence, all the areas covered by *Lantana* are economically non-productive scrubs. Many efrorts have been made in the past for the eradication of this weed, but no satisfactory method is yet available.

Bamboos are a large and diverse group of woody plants belonging to family: Poaceae. They are economically most important plants hence known as "Green Gold". To rural people it provides food, wood for home, mat to sleep, chopsticks to eat with, cup to drink from, hat to shade his eyes and umbrella to shelter him from rain. Though called "Poor man's timber" it is no cheaper. Its use in paper and pulp industry is well known. Due to over utilization in paper and pulp, there is acute shortage of its supply. The short supply is further compounded with the problems of gregarious flowering resulting in death of entire clumps. Propagation through seeds is restricted to their non-availability as most of the economic species flower from 30-60 years of age.

National Mission on Bamboo Technology and Trade Development, India has concluded that bamboo has a very important role in socio-ecological development, employment generation and poverty elimination in India. It is estimated that the size of bamboo industry will grow from Rs. 2042.5 crores in 2001 to Rs. 26,840 crore in 2015, bamboo sector will create gainful employment for 6.61 million persons and raise 5.01 million families above poverty line by the end of 10th Plan (NMBTTD, 2003). But there are several hurdles that must be crossed for realizing this potential of bamboo. One such hurdle is non-availability of quality raw material in sufficient quantities. The current industrial demand of bamboo is 26.69 million tonnes but total supply is only 13.47 million tonnes (NMBTTDI, 2003). With spurt in growth of bamboo industry, the demand will increase many folds whereas the production of raw bamboo in India is on the decline. To overcome this problem, the National Mission on Bamboo Trade and Technology Development has recommended that work should immediately be taken up on selection of high yielding clones of the preferred species of bamboo viz., *Bambusa balcooa, B. tulda, B. nutans, Dendrocalamus hamiltonii* etc. and development of suitable clonal technologies for their rapid, mass multiplication.

Increase industrial production of value added bamboo products will place higher demands of superior quality raw material of selected species of bamboo. This call us for selection of high yielding clones of selected species of bamboo and their mass clonal propagation for bulk production of superior quality planting stock.

Bamboo tolerates shade in initial stages of growth. However, the subsequent growth once full-grown culm formation is much faster in bamboo than the growth of *Lantana*. This indicates that bamboo has a competitive advantage over *Lantana*, and if bamboo is planted in stands covered with *Lantana*, it may successfully eradicate the latter species. The main objectives of the conducted research project study are:

1. To develop a silvicultural method of *Lantana* eradication by evaluating competitive advantage of bamboo over *Lantana* in a mixed stand.
2. To study the growth behaviour of bamboo in competition with *Lantana* species.

LITERATURE REVIEW

Sharma (1989), reviewed the literature on *Lantana camara* in India. Under certain conditions, *Lantana* can be beneficial as it readily invades and covers up the barren sites of deforested areas and checks soil erosion. However, these beneficial effects of *Lantana* are far outweighed by its evil effects. Various methods i.e. mechanical, chemical, biological and silvicultural have been tried to check the spread of *Lantana*. However, these methods have not been found applicable on large scale.

Mechanical Control

The known methods viz. uprooting are of no avail. In parts of Tamil Nadu and Kerala, elephants were earlier trained to pull up *Lantana*. The use of elephant was possible only on a limited scale and was restricted to Tamil Nadu and Kerala on teak plantation sites. *Lantana* regrows very fast even after physical weeding.

Chemical Control

The use of chemicals to control *Lantana* has shown some promise. The investigations done at Forest Research Institute (FRI) concluded that amongst various weedicides, Tordon formulations were more effective in killing

Lantana as comparison to other weedicide tried (Ghose, 1980). At times stump cutting method of *Lantana* is recommended before herbicide can be applied to the new growth (Selander and Chomba 1989). Rana and Singh (1999), has tried eradication of *Lantana* by chemicals in the Kandi region of Himachal Pradesh and estimated the increased green grass yield from *Lantana* control areas. But the use of chemicals to control Lantana spread is neither environment friendly nor economical.

Biological Control

Possibility of destroying *Lantana* by biological agents has for long been under investigation. The problem is far from having been solved either in India or abroad. The foremost important biological control agents, insect species, which feeds on Lantana leaves, are:

1. Sap Sucking bug *(Teleonemia Scrupulosa)*
2. Leaf Mining beetle *(Uroplata girardi)*
3. Leaf Mining beetle *(Qctotoma scabripennis)*.
4. Seed Feeding fly *(Ophiomyia lantanae)*

Rao (1920), recorded 148 species in India and Burma (Now Myanmar) frequenting various parts of *Lantana*. Of these plume moths *Lantanophaga pusillidactyla* was considered to some extent. The seed fly *Ophiomyia lantanae*, which was imported in 1921 also failed to control *Lantana*. In 1941, the *Lantana* lace bug *Teleonemia scrupulosa* stal was imported by Forest Research Institute from Australia. Later on whole lot was destroyed as it was found to breed on some other plants of economic importance, particularly verbenaceous trees. Again in 1971 and 1977 four more species *Octotoma scabripennis, Uroplata girardi, Plagiohammus spinipennis* and *Leptobyrsa deora* were imported from Australia. The later two were declared unsafe and destroyed (Thakur et al, 1992).

Julien and Griffiths (1998) noted 19 agents (including four which were already present in South Africa prior to deliberate introduction); Baars and Neser (1999) added another two agents to the list (*Falconis intermedia* (Distant) and *Cremastobombycia lantanelle* (Busek), a species that was never intentionally introduced, but that is established on L. camara in South Africa); and Simelane (2002) reported on the release of *Ophiomya camarae* Spencer, bringing the number of agents, whether or not intentionally released, to 22 insect species. Despite the establishment of 9 of the agents (Julien and Griffith, 1998), (not taking into account the recently introduced *F. intermedia* and *O. camarae*), the biological programme has had limited success (Cilliers and Neser, 1991; Baars and Neser, 1999). *Lantana camara* is the result of hybridization between several *Lantana* species, forming a complex of hybridizing varieties in the field (Stirton, 1977; Spies, 1984). None of the naturally occurring *Lantana* species matches any of the *Lantana* varieties occurring in South Africa or any other country (L. S. Smith, unpubl. Data in Day and Neser, 2000). This means that the varieties introduced insects bio-control agents encounter in the field, are genetically so far removed from the naturally occurring *Lantana* species, that the interactions between imported biocontrol agents and the *Lantana* varieties are difficult to predict (Baars and Neser, 1999).

Many of the insect species introduced for bio-control of *L. camara* show a preference for certain varieties and perform better on these than on other varieties (Radunz, 1971; Cilliers and Neser, 1991; Baars and Neser, 1999), although contradictory evidence shows that varietal preferences do not occur in certain species, while it does occur in others (Broughton, 1999, 2000; Day and Neser, 2000). Another factor that may have contributed to the limited success of the bio-control programme is the wide range of climatic conditions under which *L. camara* infestations occur. Again, most of the released bio-control agents established and performed better in some areas than others (Baars and Neser, 1999; Day and Neser, 2000; Broughton, 2000). Day and Neser (2000) state that most agents established in Australia and South Africa is found in discrete areas and that climate is considered the principal contributing factor to their distribution, as many areas contain more than on *L. camara* variety. Therefore, to control *L. camara sensu lato*, a suit of natural enemy insect species, is required (Cilliers and Neser, 1991; Baars and Neser, 1999).

The tortoise beetle, *Charidotis pygmaea* Klug, was evaluated as a potential bio-control agent for *L. camara* in Australia and at a later stage for *L. camara* in South Africa. Day *et al.* (1999) reported that during host specificity testing, the insect performed better on the invasive creeping *Lantana, L. montevidensis* (Spreng.) Briq., than on any of the naturalized Australian *L. camara* varieties and the insect consequently was released as a bio-control agent for *L. montevidensis* only. *Lantana montevidensis* is sterile in South Africa and therefore not invasive. However, as the naturalized *L. camara* varieties in South Africa most likely differ from their counterparts in Australia, probably as a result of different progenitors (Day *et al.* 1999), evaluating the performance of *C. pygmaea* on selected South African naturalized *L. camara* varieties was considered necessary.

Silvicultural Control

Lantana is known to be a high light-demander. Underplanting of *Lantana* scrub with heavy foliage species under which the light demanding *Lantana* can not thrive has been tried from time to time. The castor oil plant (*Ricinus cumminis)* was found to check its growth but did not kill it. *Ficus elastica* was tried in Tamil Nadu but could not be established successfully.

Considerable success has been achieved in parts of Tamil Nadu and Kerala by underplanting *Lantana* with fast growing species like bamboo, *Bambusa arundinacea* and *Dendrocalamus strictus*. Raghavan (1944), in his experiments in Wynaad (Kerala) has shown that *Bambusa arundinacea* can be successfully established in dense *Lantana* areas in mixed deciduous forests. In Indonesia, planting of *Lecaena leucocephala* has been tried to suppress *Lantana*, while in Sri Lanka *Tithonia diversfoilia* is reported to have given good results (Annon, 1992).

PROJECT PRACTICAL UTILITY

1. Bamboo is a fast growing, multiuse forest produce which is currently rated high for socio-economic and environmentally compatible development of weaker rural societies of tropical and subtropical world.
2. Development of an effective method for the eradication of *Lantana* and simultaneously covering the area with a more useful species will certainly help in boosting local economy.
3. The findings was likely to be of great value in raising plantations of economically important bamboo species in Kandi areas of Punjab, which are currently scrub forests/wastelands because of thick growth of *Lantana*, which looks impossible to eradicate.
4. Initial discussions made with the villagers living around the project area showed that the villagers were eager to plant bamboo on their lands.

DESCRIPTION OF THE STUDY SITES

Project Area

The project covers the Kandi Tract of the State of Punjab in the north-west of India. The tract includes the low range of Shivalik Hills, forming the base of the Himalayan foothills, and also the undulating sub montane plain immediately below the hills. In the natural state the area supports a scrub forest with *Acacia* species. Predominating and a certain amount of commercially valuable bhabbar grass and fair to poor quality fodder grass. The existing vegetation cover varies widely from near climax level in some protected or unpopulated watersheds to severely denude in some pockets where pressure is high. In the later areas, which are normally associated with population centers, there is a notable absence of any mature trees, grass is sparse and of poor quality and hardy shrubs of little value like *Lantana camara* predominate. Overall the cover is moderate but not sufficient to prevent erosion occurring at an estimated rate at least doubles that of the undisturbed natural state.

The village economy is heavily dependent on livestock but commercial exploitation of the bhabbar grass and Khair (*Acacia catechu*) is also important. The terrain range from relatively flat to strong undulating and even rugged in places; the former areas have generally very deep, well drained to excessively drained low fertility sandy to loamy sand soils while in the later areas the soil are more sandy loam to silt loam texture, particularly on the more elevated land, easily workable but with rather low inherent fertility.

Depth to water table varies from a few meters to more than 40 meters in Bheet area at Balachaur Forest Division, but is generally in the range of 10-30 meters over much of the area in Kharkan at Hoshiarpur Forest Division and Tibba Tappariyan of Ropar Forest Division (Punjab). A programme of plantation, strict resource management and livestock control can substantially increase the output of commercially valuable forest products such as bamboo, from the hill area.

Study Sites

The Kandi area (Shivaliks) of Punjab experiences Koeppen's Cwg category climate based on annual and monthly means of temperature and rainfall. This is characterized by humid and tropical summer, rainy season and dry winter, extreme seasonal temperatures, long dry-short wet seasons and potential evaporation exceeding precipitation which varies from 800 to 1200 mm annually.

Kharkan, Hoshiarpur Forest Division

The study site is located in Hoshiarpur Forest Division at Latitude 31° 32′ N, Longitude 75° 57′ E and 260 meters above mean sea level. The land is almost level with gentle slope. Scattered trees mainly of Dalbergia sissoo, *Acacia catechu, Morus alba* and *Ziziphus jujube* were found on the site. Lantana camara was the main shrub species and the main herbs were *Parthenium hysterophorous, Canabis sativa* etc. Mean annual rainfall received at the site is about 750 mm. Mean maximum summer temperature reaches 39.3°C while the mean minimum winter temperature is 0.7° C. The soil is light grey to light brownish grey in colour and it is sandy upto 138 cm. it was interesting to observe a clay rich horizon between 138 and 157 cm depth which was moist and showed distinct mottles of brown colour which indicates that water table rises up to 138 cm and remains there for a considerable time. The soil up to 138 cm depth was structure less due to sandy texture and little amount of organic matter. However, fine week blocky structure was noted below 138 cm depth. The consistency was dry loose in upper three layers and moist firm in two lower layers.

Bheet, Balachaur Forest Division

The study site Bheet is located within Balachaur Forest Division at Latitiude 31° 13′ N, Longitude 76° 11′ E and 290 meters above mean sea level. The mean maximum summer temperature is 40° C and minimum winter temperature is 6° C. The average annual rainfall is about 1100 mm. It is surrounded by forest area in all its four side with in steep foothills of Shiwalik range. The site is located near village Pindiara Pindoria. Vegetation comprises of scattered trees mainly of *Dalbergia sissoo, Acacia catechu, Ziziphus mummularia* and Atylosia scarabaeoides shrubs mainly *Lantana camara, Murraya koenigii* and herb like *Desmodium triflorum, Desmodium gangetium.* The area is under severing biological pressure due to grazing by Neelgai and other villagers livestock. This is a bouldary tract in Bheet Area. The area is upland with moderate to gentle slopes and garlanded with seasonal Nalahs. Presence of assorted boulders and stones on the surface and beneath the soil is common. The stones of 20 cm circumference are proportionately more than 75 cm size few stones of 95 cm size are also found. In general, the soil is about 10 cm deep followed by the layers very rich in gravels and stones. However at certain places, normally in the middle slopes area, the surface soil is deeper due to deposition from the upper slopes. The soil is yellowish red or reddish brown in colour. The texture is fine near the surface and turns sandy with increasing depth. The surface is dry hard with coarse strong and blocky structure. The soil is dry up to 160 cm depth and moist below this layer. The stone and gravels are about 85% between 60 and 160 cm depth and their quantity decreases to about 40% below 160 cm depth.

Tibba Tappariyan, Ropar Forest Division

The study site Tibba Tappariyan is located within Ropar Forest Division at latitude 30° 58′ N, Longitude 760 3′ E and 290 meters above mean sea level. The maximum summer temperature may reach 45° C and minimum winter 20 C. The site receives about 700 mm rainfall per year. It lies on Ropar–Una Road and surrounded by forests. The site is undulating and sloping with thick vegetation. The main tree species are *Acacia catechu*, *Dalbergia sissoo* and *Ziziphus mummularia*. The major shrubs species besides *Lantana camara* are *Anisomeles indica, Clerodendrum inerme, Duranta plumeri*. The ground flora has a variety of herbs including *Parthenium hysterophorus*. The soil is yellowish red in colour and loam in texture. The boundary between surface (0-6 cm) and next lower horizon (6-18 cm) is diffuse because the surface has been enriched with organic matter by the vegetation but the process of mineralization and eluviations is in initial phase. The soil structure is granular upto 18 cm due to adequate amount of organic matter but the lower layers are blocky in structure. The upper layer of the soil (0-18) cm is friable but the lower layers are firm and hard. The gravels and stones appear at a depth of 30 cm however, plenty of big boulders and stones were found below 90 cm depth.

METHODOLOGY

Two bamboo species namely *Dendrocalamus* strictus and *Bambusa bambos* were selected for the study. Bamboo seedlings were raised in F. R. I. Dehradun nursery and planted in the month of August 2003 at the three selected experimental locations.

Experimental Design- Randomized Block Design (R.B.D.)

Bamboo species: Two

1. *Dendrocalamus strictus*
2. *Bambusa bambos.*

Treatments: Five

T_1 = Control (Only *Lantana*)

T_2 = No *Lantana* removal + *Dendrocalamus strictus.*

T_3 = *Lantana* removal + *Dendrocalamus strictus.*

T_4 = No *Lantana* removal + *Bambusa bambos.*

T_5 = *Lantana* removal + *Bambusa bambos.*

Treatment Plot Size: 20m × 20m

Spacing for planting bamboo: 2.5m × 2.5m

Number of bamboo plants in each treatment plot: 64

Number of replications: 4

Experimental Sites: **Three (3)**

1. Karkan in Hoshiarpur;
2. Pandiyara Pindori (Bheet area) in Balachaur; and
3. Tibba Tappariyan of Ropar Forest Division.

OBSERVATIONS

Observations on survival, height, culm diameter and number of culms will be recorded at quarterly intervals. Data on photosynthesis, canopy covered area etc. will be recorded once a year. Following parameters of Bamboo growth were measured:

Culm Height

Height of longest Culm was measured using a meter scale with marking down to 1 mm. Data on height of the tallest culm is given in Table-1. In general, culm height was more in *Bambusa bambos* than in *Dendrocalamus strictus*. It was maximum on Kharkan (Hoshiarpur) followed by Tibba Tappariyan (Ropar) and minimum at Bheet area, Balachaur (Table 7.1). The height growth of each species of bamboo was generally higher in bamboo alone plantation as compared with bamboo + *Lantana*.

Number of Culms per Clump

Data on number of all the culms produced in each clump were recorded and is given in Table 7.2. More culms per clump were produced by *Dendrocalamus strictus* than *Bambusa bambos*. However, site had a strong effect on regeneration of culms. The number was maximum at Kharkan (Hoshiarpur) followed by Tibba Tappariyan (Ropar) and minimum at Bheet area, Balachaur (Table 7.2). Presence of *Lantana* slightly decreased the number of culms produced on per clump.

Table 7.1: Culm Height (cm)

Sites	Treatments	Months of Observation (Year 2003-04)						
		October 2003	January 2004	April 2004	July 2004	August 2004	October 2004	December 2004
	Control – Only *Lantana*	NA	NA	NA	NA	NA	NA	NA
KHARKAN	*Lantana + D. strictus*	81.40	69.57	65.19	78.79	87.97	98.52	111.48
	D. strictus	68.07	67.45	75.27	88.92	89.25	107.26	119.25
	Lantana + B. Bambos	106.30	86.96	103.27	106.3	109.90	129.09	134.25
	B. Bambos	106.40	91.27	111.01	116	118.04	134.40	149.34
	Average	**90.54**	**78.81**	**88.69**	**97.51**	**101.29**	**117.32**	**128.58**
	Control – Only *Lantana*	NA	NA	NA	NA	NA	NA	NA
BHEET	*Lantana + D. strictus*	69.57	66.42	43.63	50.60	60.69	80.96	98.46
	D. strictus	67.45	64.51	46.66	65.66	72.66	92.36	104.63
	Lantana + B. Bambos	86.96	87.33	78.79	88.52	98.52	100.25	113.23
	B. Bambos	91.27	94.64	81.34	99.96	111.01	121.10	132.26
	Average	**78.81**	**78.23**	**62.61**	**76.19**	**85.72**	**98.67**	**112.15**
	Control – Only *Lantana*	NA	NA	NA	NA	NA	NA	NA
TIBBA TAPPARIYAN	*Lantana + D. strictus*	65.19	76.63	50.6	64.51	74.5	97.45	108.46
	D. strictus	75.27	87.31	70.37	86.96	96.69	106.96	116.37
	Lantana + B. Bambos	103.27	96.41	88.52	91.27	101.72	121.27	134.78
	B. Bambos	98.44	107.14	99.96	103.3	106.7	126.77	148.92
	Average	**85.54**	**91.87**	**77.36**	**86.50**	**94.90**	**113.11**	**127.13**

Significance Treatment*
Month*
Interaction N.S. (Non-Significant)

Table 7.2: Number of Clumps per Clump

Sites	Treatments	Months of Observation (Year 2003-04)						
		October 2003	January 2004	April 2004	July 2004	August 2004	October 2004	December 2004
	Control – Only *Lantana*	NA	NA	NA	NA	NA	NA	NA
KHARKAN	*Lantana + D. strictus*	4.30	4.38	4.88	5.97	6.79	7.97	8.79
	D. strictus	4.50	4.67	5.6	6.97	7.81	8.18	8.81
	Lantana + B. Bambos	3.79	4.23	4.89	5.69	6.76	7.67	8.76
	B. Bambos	3.82	4.85	5.57	6.89	7.98	8.89	9.09
	Average	**4.10**						
	Control – Only *Lantana*	NA	NA	NA	NA	NA	NA	NA
BHEET	*Lantana + D. strictus*	3.69	5.97	2.97	3.79	4.97	5.79	6.74
	D. strictus	3.59	5.12	3.88	4.47	5.74	6.47	7.04
	Lantana + B. Bambos	3.24	4.16	3.54	5.97	6.79	7.69	7.96
	B. Bambos	3.11	3.97	3.47	4.89	5.98	6.89	7.88
	Average	**3.41**	**4.81**	**3.47**	**4.78**	**5.87**	**6.71**	**7.41**
	Control – Only *Lantana*	NA	NA	NA	NA	NA	NA	NA
TIBBA TAPPARIYAN	*Lantana + D. strictus*	4.80	5.97	4.19	5.57	5.75	6.57	7.77
	D. strictus	5.71	4.44	4.93	5.97	5.98	6.89	6.98
	Lantana + B. Bambos	3.82	3.79	3.07	4.89	6.08	7.8	7.04
	B. Bambos	4.80	5.62	4.47	5.62	6.72	7.27	8.72
	Average	**4.78**	**4.96**	**4.17**	**5.51**	**6.13**	**7.13**	**7.63**

Significance Treatment*
Month*
Interaction N.S. (Non-Significant)

Culm Diameter

Basal diameter of culms was recorded using digital Vernier Caliper. Data on culm diameter are presented in Table 7.3. Culms of *Bambusa bambos* had larger diameter than those of *Dendrocalamus strictus*. *Lantana* caused a reduction of culm diameter in both species. As site had a strong effect on growth of culm diameter. Culm diameter was observed maximum at Kharkan (Hoshiarpur) followed by Tibba Tappariyan (Ropar) and minimum at Bheet area (Balachaur) (Table 7.3).

Percent Survival of Bamboos

All the surviving bamboo seedlings in each treatment were counted, periodically and percent survival was calculated. Data on percentage of survival are presented in Table 7.4. Presence or absence of *Lantana* did not have much effect on percent survival of bamboo. Percent survival varied with site and the lowest values of percent survival of bamboo were observed at Bheet (Balachaur) (Table 7.4).

Photosynthetic Efficiency

Photosynthetic efficiency of bamboo and Lantana species was measured as ratio of Fv/Fm with a portable Hansatech Photosynthetic Analyzer (Hansatech, King's Lynn, U.K.) which gives direct digital units in Fv/Fm ratio where Fv=variable fluorescence and Fm=Maximum fluorescence, using the method as described by Kumar *et al.* (2003).

Data on photosynthetic efficiency are presented in Table 7.5. The presence or absence of *Lantana* shrubs did not have much effect on photosynthetic efficiency of bamboo. However, the lower values of photosynthetic efficiency were observed in *Bambusa bambos* species than in *Dendrocalamus strictus*. Photosynthetic efficiency was also the lowest at (Balachaur) Bheet area (Table 7.5).

Lantana Growth

Growth of Lantana was assessed by measuring the size of gaps in its canopy layer. The data is presented in Table 7.6. Practically no gaps were observed in the canopy layer of treatment plots where only *Lantana* grew (T_1). Gaps were created in the canopy layer of *Lantana* in July 2003 in the treatment plots where *D. strictus* or *B. bambos* seedlings were planted under existing *Lantana* bushes or after removing *Lantana* i.e. treatments T_2 to T_5. By October, 2004, *Lantana* grew again in treatments T_2 to T_5 also gaps of about 50.0 cm diameter remained in its canopy layer. The size of these gaps did not differ significantly among treatments from T_2 to T_5.

Table 7.3: Culm Diameter (cm)

Sites	Treatments	Months of Observation (Year 2003-04)						
		October 2003	January 2004	April 2004	July 2004	August 2004	October 2004	December 2004
	Control – Only *Lantana*	NA	NA	NA	NA	NA	NA	NA
KHARKAN	*Lantana + D. strictus*	0.52	0.57	0.63	0.79	0.94	1.28	1.84
	D. strictus	0.55	0.68	0.68	0.76	0.89	1.21	1.44
	Lantana + B. Bambos	0.70	0.68	0.69	0.81	0.97	1.39	1.54
	B. Bambos	0.76	0.81	0.91	0.92	0.98	1.34	1.68
	Average	**0.63**	**0.69**	**0.73**	**0.82**	**0.95**	**1.31**	**1.63**
	Control – Only *Lantana*	NA	NA	NA	NA	NA	NA	NA
BHEET	*Lantana + D. strictus*	0.40	0.40	0.35	0.33	0.35	0.82	1.02
	D. strictus	0.36	0.37	0.36	0.42	0.88	1.11	1.25
	Lantana + B. Bambos	0.64	0.66	0.63	0.79	0.85	1.34	1.56
	B. Bambos	0.63	0.68	0.68	0.81	0.88	1.39	1.44
	Average	**0.51**	**0.52**	**0.50**	**0.59**	**0.86**	**1.22**	**1.40**
	Control – Only *Lantana*	NA	NA	NA	NA	NA	NA	NA
TIBBA TAPPARIYAN	*Lantana + D. strictus*	0.35	0.42	0.34	0.36	0.68	1.48	1.64
	D. strictus	0.52	0.46	0.52	0.63	0.76	1.15	1.29
	Lantana + B. Bambos	0.59	0.65	0.57	0.66	0.81	1.62	1.86
	B. Bambos	0.70	0.86	0.79	0.81	0.92	1.87	1.97
	Average	**0.54**	**0.60**	**0.56**	**0.62**	**0.79**	**1.53**	**1.69**

Significance Treatment *
Month*
Interaction N.S. (Non-Significant)

Table 7.4: Bamboo Survival (%)

Sites	Treatments	Months of Observation (Year 2003-04)						
		October 2003	January 2004	April 2004	July 2004	August 2004	October 2004	December 2004
	Control – Only *Lantana*	NA	NA	NA	NA	NA	NA	NA
KHARKAN	*Lantana + D. strictus*	98.05	96.09	94.92	90.92	92.92	94.29	94.29
	D. strictus	98.44	96.88	94.53	92.56	94.58	93.85	93.85
	Lantana + B. Bambos	96.48	92.58	92.97	94.14	96.14	97.41	97.41
	B. Bambos	96.88	95.7	94.92	94.53	98.53	95.35	95.35
	Average	**97.46**	**95.31**	**94.34**	**93.04**	**95.54**	**95.23**	**95.23**
	Control – Only *Lantana*	NA	NA	NA	NA	NA	NA	NA
BHEET	*Lantana + D. strictus*	91.80	89.45	25.00	26.00	29.00	28.54	28.54
	D. strictus	95.31	89.45	45.70	46.68	56.68	48.76	48.76
	Lantana + B. Bambos	95.70	94.14	84.38	89.48	89.04	90.4	90.4
	B. Bambos	94.53	92.58	79.69	82.07	90.03	90.3	90.3
	Average	**94.34**	**91.41**	**58.69**	**61.06**	**66.19**	**64.50**	**64.50**
	Control – Only *Lantana*	NA	NA	NA	NA	NA	NA	NA
TIBBA TAPPARIYAN	*Lantana + D. strictus*	96.88	94.53	71.88	79.69	80.96	82.69	82.69
	D. strictus	98.83	98.05	76.95	84.38	86.83	87.38	87.38
	Lantana + B. Bambos	98.83	94.53	82.03	89.45	90.04	90.40	90.40
	B. Bambos	98.44	98.83	92.97	94.53	94.58	95.85	95.85
	Average	**98.25**	**96.49**	**80.96**	**87.01**	**88.10**	**89.08**	**89.08**

Significance Treatment *
Month*
Interaction N.S. (Non-Significant)

Table 7.5: Bamboo Leaves Photosynthetic Efficiency Fv/Fm Ratio (μ mol/m²/sec.)

Sites	Treatments	Months of Observation (Year 2003-04)			
		October 2003	April 2004	October 2004	December 2004
	Control – Only *Lantana*	NA	NA	NA	NA
KHARKAN	*Lantana + D. strictus*	0.69	0.71	0.70	0.68
	D. strictus	0.67	0.71	0.68	0.66
	Lantana + B. Bambos	0.67	0.73	0.69	0.68
	B. Bambos	0.68	0.63	0.72	0.65
	Average	**0.68**	**0.70**	**0.70**	**0.67**
	Control – Only *Lantana*	NA	NA	NA	NA
BHEET	*Lantana + D. strictus*	0.68	0.66	0.69	0.71
	D. strictus	0.69	0.70	0.71	0.7
	Lantana + B. Bambos	0.65	0.61	0.68	0.66
	B. Bambos	0.70	0.67	0.72	0.69
	Average	**0.68**	**0.68**	**0.71**	**0.70**
	Control – Only *Lantana*	NA	NA	NA	NA
TIBBA TAPPARIYAN	*Lantana + D. strictus*	0.69	0.75	0.71	0.72
	D. strictus	0.70	0.68	0.72	0.69
	Lantana + B. Bambos	0.68	0.69	0.69	0.71
	B. Bambos	0.70	0.66	0.71	0.7
	Average	**0.69**	**0.69**	**0.71**	**0.71**

(Fv/Fm = Variation in florescence recorded)

Significance Treatment*
Month*
Interaction N.S. (Non-Significant)

General Problems

1. **Rodents Attack:** Seedlings of both species of bamboo were attacked by the rats, which were mainly of two types: Annah chuha and Wild rat. The rats damaged young culms as well as rhizomes of the seedlings. Interestingly, while seedlings of *Dendrocalamus strictus* were frequently found damaged by the rats. Very little or no damage was caused to the seedlings of *Bambusa bambos*. Maximum damage by rats was caused at Tibba Tappariyan site of Ropar Forest division while, practically no attack was observed at the other two sites.

Data on percent damage caused to bamboo seedlings by rats is given in Table 7.7. Significant damage was caused to bamboo seedlings by rats at Tibba Tappariyan site, while it was insignificant at the other two sites. Seedlings of *D. strictus* suffered more damage than seedlings of *Bambusa bambos*. Further treatments having lantana together with bamboo seedlings showed lesser damage than treatments where *Lantana* was removed. Again bamboo seedlings of both species suffered more damage by rats in April than in June, 2004.

Table 7.6: Size of Gaps in the Canopy Layer of *Lantana* (Diameter in cm)

Sites	Treatments	Months of Observation (Year 2003-04)
		(diameter in cm)
	Control – Only *Lantana*	Nil
KHARKAN	*Lantana + D. strictus*	47.60
	D. strictus	50.20
	Lantana + B. Bambos	48.80
	B. Bambos	54.40
	Average	**50.25**
	Control – Only *Lantana*	Nil
BHEET	*Lantana + D. strictus*	55.60
	D. strictus	64.40
	Lantana + B. Bambos	58.70
	B. Bambos	59.6
	Average	**59.58**
	Control – Only *Lantana*	Nil
TIBBA TAPPARIYAN	*Lantana + D. strictus*	39.80
	D. strictus	46.60
	Lantana + B. Bambos	52.40
	B. Bambos	59.20
	Average	**49.50**

Significance: N.S. (Non Significant)

Table 7.7: Percent Damage to Bamboo caused by Rodents Attack

Site	Treatments	Months of Observation (Year 2003-04)	
		April, 2004	July, 2004
	Control – Only *Lantana*	NA	NA
TIBBA TAPPARIYAN	*Lantana + D. strictus*	47.50	15.00
	D. strictus	32.50	9.00
	Lantana + B. Bambos	12.50	2.50
	B. Bambos	6.25	2.50
	Average	**24.69**	**7.25**

Significance Treatment *
Month*
Interaction N.S. (Non-Significant)

2. **Grazing by wild herbivore and livestocks:** Grazing by cattle damaged bamboo seedlings at all the three sites. Damage was more severe to the seedlings of *Dendrocalamus strictus* than to *Bambusa bambos* seedlings due to the thorns present below leaf base and on stem parts. Cattle damaged bamboo shoots and suppressed seedling growth. Damage of bamboo seedlings by cattle was observed on all the three sites. Wild grazing animals like, Neel Gai, Cheetal, Shambar and other wild herbivores grazed on bamboo seedlings after six months of their transplantation. Attack by Neel Gai was more frequent than by other animals and incidences of such attack were higher at Pandiyara Pindori (Bheet area), in Balachaur and Tibba Tappariyan in Ropar Forest division while, negligible at Kharkan in (Hoshiarpur).

Data on percent damage caused to bamboo seedlings due to grazing is given in Table 7.8. Thus grazing animals, both domestic as well as wild, caused considerable damage to bamboo seedlings. The damage varied with the site, season and the species of bamboo. In general maximum damage to bamboo due to grazing was caused at Bheet, during summer (April, 2004), and *Dendrocalamus strictus* seedlings. Damage due to grazing was less in *Lantana* + bamboo treatments.

Table 7.8: Percent Damage to Bamboo due to Grazing

Sites	Treatments	Months of Observation (Year 2004)	
		April, 2004	July, 2004
	Control – Only *Lantana*	**NA**	**NA**
KHARKAN	*Lantana + D. strictus*	20.50	7.50
	D. strictus	35.00	12.50
	Lantana + B. Bambos	6.50	5.00
	B. Bambos	5.50	5.00
	Average	**16.88**	**7.50**
	Control – Only *Lantana*	NA	NA
BHEET	*Lantana + D. strictus*	32.50	12.50
	D. strictus	45.00	18.25
	Lantana + B. Bambos	12.50	9.75
	B. Bambos	10.25	6.50
	Average	**25.06**	**11.75**
	Control – Only *Lantana*	NA	NA
TIBBA TAPPARIYAN	*Lantana + D. strictus*	25.50	20.25
	D. strictus	30.25	15.00
	Lantana + B. Bambos	6.25	10.25
	B. Bambos	2.50	7.50
	Average	**16.13**	**13.25**

Significance Treatment *
Month*
Interaction N.S. (Non-Significant).

3. **Damage by porcupines and Wild Boar:** Porcupines damaged the seedlings of bamboo by uprooting them. The attack was more severe during the post harvest seasons when porcupine does not get enough food in agricultural lands. It caused maximum damage to the seedlings of *Dendrocalamus strictus* while, only insignificant damage to the seedling of *Bambusa bambos.* Maximum attack of porcupine on bamboo seedlings was observed in Pandiyara Pindori (Bheet area) Balachaur.

Wild boar attacked rhizomes as well as young culms of seedlings of both species of bamboo. The damage by wild boar was observed mainly in Pandiyara Pindori (Bheet area) Balachaur. Wild boar attack was more severe in winter and summer than in the other seasons.

Data on percent damage to bamboo seedlings caused by wild boar and porcupine is given in Table 7.9. Significant damage to bamboo seedlings by wild boar and porcupine was observed only at Bheet. The percent damage values differed significantly with treatment but month of observation did not cause any significant effect. Seedlings of *D. strictus* suffered more damage than those of *Bambusa bambos,* and in each species the percent damage values were higher in treatments having bamboo seedlings alone than bamboo seedlings+*Lantana.*

Table 7.9: Percent Damage to Bamboo caused by Porcupine and Wild Boar

Site	Treatments	Months of Observation (Year 2004)	
		April, 2004	July, 2004
	Control – Only *Lantana*	NA	NA
BHEETBALACHAUR	*Lantana + D. strictus*	36.15	34.25
	D. strictus	48.3	46.11
	Lantana + B. Bambos	11.01	10.20
	B. Bambos	14.12	12.50
	Average	**27.40**	**25.77**

Significance Treatment*
Month*
Interaction N.S. (Non-Significant)

RESULTS AND DISCUSSION

Although the available data is for limited period only, some interesting trends are already visible which have a strong bearing on management of forest areas infested with *Lantana camara.*

Growth Differences in Bamboos

Both species of bamboo differ in their growth. *B. bambos* grew taller with large culms then *D. strictus* at all the three sites, but *D. strictus* produced more culms per clump. The site also had a strong effect on growth and survival of both species of bamboo; Kharkan (Hoshiarpur) was better site than the other two sites in this regard. Variation in growth and survival of bamboo due to species and site has already been reported from Western Ghat areas of Karnataka (Devar, 2000).

One interesting feature about these two species of bamboo is that while *B. bambos* has larger culms and wider leaves than *D. strictus,* which may provide competitive advantage in a mixed stand. *D. strictus* is known to tolerate water stress better than *B. bambos* which may be of great advantage as large part of Kandi area of Punjab witness severs water stress during pre-monsoon season. Hence, the trend of growth performance of these two species may change the next 2-3 years.

Response of Bamboo to Biotic Pressure

Besides *Lantana camara* and other weeds, rodents, wild boar and grazing animals were the major factors causing biotic pressure and affecting growth and survival of bamboo. Rats cut the culms of young seedlings while grazing animals ate away the top portion of seedlings. Most of bamboo seedlings tolerated it and new culms grew from the rhizome. Porcupine and wild boar uprooted bamboo seedlings and the damage was irreversible. It is interesting to note that different sites had different type of biotic pressure, and these grazing animals and rodents differed in their preference for bamboo. In general, all these animals indicated a preference for *D. strictus* over *B. bambos.* As a result, damage caused to *D. strictus* was sever while it was mild in case of *B. bambos.* Further, maximum damage due to grazing was recorded at Bheet; rats caused maximum damage at Tibba Tappariyan while porcupine and wild boar caused severe damage at Bheet only. Hence, site specific strategies must be adopted to contain the biotic pressures which may have a determinative role in a successful establishment of bamboo in *Lantana* infested areas. Proper selection of bamboo species may be of great advantage in this regard.

Growth of *Lantana camara*

Lantana camara grew well on all the sites and its crown covered practically entire ground area of the experimental plots. Biotic factors seemingly had little effect on the growth and survival of this species.

Competition Between *Bamboo* and *Lantana*

There was no significant effect of bamboo and *Lantana camara* on each other's growth during the first year. Even there was no effect of pressure of *Lantana* bushes on photosynthetic activity and nutrient uptake in bamboo seedlings. It is well known fact that bamboo can withstand shade at the initial stage of its growth (Troup, 1921). Competition for growth between *Lantana* and bamboo became evident after one year as bamboo seedlings had put lesser growth in *Lantana* + Bamboo treatments than in bamboo alone.

But by this time some plants of bamboo had already grown above the crown layer of *Lantana*. During next 3-4 years, the growth of bamboo culms is expected to be faster, as it is well known that the rate of bamboo Culm growth increases each year until full growth is achieved. This will provide a great competitive advantage to bamboo over *Lantana*.

Lantana bushes appear to protect bamboo seedlings from damage by grazing animals, porcupine and wild boar. Damage caused by these animals was less in Bamboo + *Lantana* treatments plots than in bamboo alone. Rats caused more damage in Bamboo + *Lantana* treatment plots than in bamboo alone; perhaps *Lantana* bushes provide rats a safe hide out. But bamboo seedlings almost recovered from the damage caused by rats, while porcupine, wild boars and grazing animals had a very severe affect on growth and survival of bamboo. The protection to bamboo seedlings by *Lantana* bushes may play a significant beneficial role in survival of bamboo under conditions of severe biotic stress, as exists in Kandi area of Punjab.

CONCLUSIONS

Both species of bamboo (*Bambusa bambos* + *Dendrocalamus strictus*) tolerate the presence of *Lantana* as is evident from the data on percent survival and growth of bamboo seedlings planted alongwith *Lantana*. Grazing cattle, wild herbivores, porcupines, wild boar, rodents, and adverse site conditions affect survival of bamboo strongly. These may alter the interaction between *Lantana* and bamboo. The preference of rodents, mainly rats, for bamboo appears to vary with bamboo species. Hence, it may be possible to overcome this problem by proper selection of bamboo species (*Bambusa bambos*) which was found best suited in these conditions.

Justification of work/Project outcome: The favourable bamboo growth results/findings are likely to be of great value for areas infested with *Lantana*, and for forest officials in raising plantations of economically important fast growing bamboo species in Kandi (Punjab) and other areas, which are currently scrub forest / wastelands because of thick growth of *Lantana* which looks otherwise impossible to eradicate. It was a suitable trail for maintaining the forest floral &, faunal biodiversity, forest ecology and management.

REFERENCES

1. Annon, 1992. Troup's Silviculture of Indian Trees. Vol.–VII. Revised and Enlarged by Editorial Board, Forest Research Institute, Dehradun.
2. Baars, J.R., Neser, S., 1999. Past and Present Initiatives on the Biological Control of *Lantana camara* (Venenaceae) in South Africa. *Afri. Ent. Mem.* 1, 21-33.
3. Broughton, S., 1999. Evaluation of Some Insects Species Introduced for the Biological Control of *Lantana camara* L. in South – East Queensland, Australia, Ph.D. Thesis, The University of Queensland, Brisbane, Australia.
4. Broughton, S., 2000. Commentary. Review and Evaluation of *Lantana* Biocontrol Programmes. *Biol. Contr.* 17, 272-286.

5. Cilliers, C.J., Neser, S., 1991. Biological Control of *Lantana camara* (Verbenaceae) in South Africa. *Agric. Ecosyst. Environ.* 37, 57-75.

6. Day, M.D., Neser, S., 2000. Factors Influencing the Biological Control of *Lantana camara* in Australia and South Africa. In: N.R. Spencer (ed.), *Proceedings of the Xth International Symposium on Biological Control of Weeds,* July 4-14, 1999. Montana State University, Bozeman, Montana, USA. 897-908.

7. Day, M.D., Wilson, B.W., Nahrung, H.F., 1999. The Life History and Host Range of *Charidotis pygmaea* (Col.: Chrysomelidae), a Biological Control Agent for Lantana Montevidensis (Verbenaceae). *Biocontrol Sci. Technol.* 9, 347-354.

8. Devar, K.V., 2000. Improvement Studies in Bamboo. Final Report of RGF (ICFRE) Project No. 38-85/97 – ICFRE (R), 199.

9. Ghose, R.C., 1980. Chemical Control of *Lantana camara* and *Imperata cylendrica;* Two Major Weeds in Forest in India. Paper Presented at XI Silvicultural Conference, Trinidad and Tobago and Jamaica, Common Wealth Forestry Review. 59, 182.

10. Julien, Griffiths, 1998. *Biological Control of Weeds: A World Catalogue of Agents and Their Targets Weeds,* 4th edn. CABI Publishing, UK.

11. NMBTTDI, 2003. National Mission on Bamboo Technology and Trade Development, Planning Commission, Annon, 2003. Govt. of India, New Delhi, 181.

12. Radunz, L. A. J., 1971. Some Aspects of the Preferential Behaviour of *Teleonemia scrupulosa* Stal, Towards Its Host Plant *Lantana camara*. Hons. Thesis, University of Queensland.

13. Raghavan M. S., 1944. Recommendation for the Closure of Experimental Plot No. 32 Wynaad Division (Central Silviculturists Ledger Files) FRI, Dehradun.

14. Rana, R.S., Singh, L. N., 1999. Eradication of *Lantana camara* and Wasteland Utilization in Kandi Region of Himanchal Pradesh.

15. Rao, Y.R., 1920. *Lantana* Insects in India. Mem. Deptt. Agri. India (Ent Series) Calcutta. 5 (6), 239-314.

16. Selander, J., Chomba, B. M., 1989. Control of *Lantana camara* in Forest Plantations. A Research Note: Division of Forest Research, Kitwe No. 44, Forest Deptt. Zambia.

17. Sharma, O.P., 1989. How to Control Lantana (*Lantana camara*) menance? A Current Perspective.

18. Simelane, D.O., 2002. Biology and Host Range of *Ophiomyia camarae,* a Biological Control Agent for *Lantana camara* in South Africa. *Bio Control*. 47, 575-585.

19. Spies, J.J., 1984. A Cytotaxonomic Study of *Lantana camara* (Verbenaceae) from South Africa. *S. Afr. J. Bot.* 3, 231-250.

20. Stirton, C.H., 1977. Some Thoughts on the Polyploid Complex *Lantana camara* L. (Verbenaceae). *Proceedings of the Second National Weeds Conference of South Africa.* A. A. Balkema, Cape Town. 321-344.

21. Thakur, M.L., Ahmand, M., Thakur, R. K., 1992. Lantana Weed (*Lantana camara* var. *L. aculeate* Linn.) and its Possible Management Through Natural Insects Pest in India. *Indian Forester*. 118 (8), 466-488.

22. Troup, R.S., 1921. The Silviculture of Indian Trees. 3, 977-1013, Clarendon Press, Oxford.

Accumulation of Some Heavy Metals in Hair Plasma and Milk of Cattle and Buffaloes Grazing Berseem or Reed Plants in Egypt

H.M.A. Gaafar

SUMMARY

Twenty four dairy cows and buffaloes were divided in two locations with 6 dairy cows and 6 dairy buffaloes in each. The animals in the first location were fed on berseem irrigated with Nile water, while in the second location (Burullus Lake) they were kept on reed plants. The obtained results showed that increasing the concentrations of heavy metals (lead, cadmium, copper, nikel, aluminum, arsenic and mercury) in lake water compared to nile water led to higher heavy metals contents in reed plants than in berseem.

The concentrations of heavy metals in hair, plasma and milk of cattle and buffaloes grazing on reed plants were significantly higher ($P<0.01$) than of those fed berseem. Moreover, the concentrations of heavy metals in hair were significantly higher ($P<0.05$) in cattle than buffaloes, while the concentrations of heavy metals in plasma and milk were significantly higher ($P<0.05$) in buffaloes than cattle.

It could be concluded that grazing cattle and buffaloes on reed plants in Burullus Lake led to higher accumulation of heavy metals in their hair, plasma and milk, causing possible hazardous effect on human health.

Keywords: Heavy metals, reed plants, cattle, buffaloes, hair, plasma, milk.

Animal Production Research Institute, Agricultural Research Center, Dokki, Egypt.

INTRODUCTION

Heavy metal concentration has increased in the air, soil and waters, especially in the cities and industrial areas. According to predictions based on research monitoring the changes of heavy metal concentrations in the soil and plants, heavy metals will probably become important environmental stress factors over the next decades (Pais, 1992). Heavy metal deposition in rural areas is sometimes a problem because of industrial and sewage sludge contamination and as a consequence, grazing animals are particularly exposed to pollutants deposited on pastures (Smith *et al.*, 1991 and Pittia, 1992).

Mechanism of collecting, distribution, concentration and effects of heavy metals in plants cannot be generalized for the reason that they are exposed to heavy metals from air, water and soil (Webber, 1981; Fergusson, 1990; Ure and Berrow, 1982). High contents of heavy metals in soil can lead to their accumulation in plant tissues, inhibit or block their physiological functions or make them unusable for nutrition (Ure and Berrow, 1982). Mammary glands in cows are the most physiologically active part and therefore the input and output of heavy metals in their organisms are clearly reflected through milk. Monitoring the route of heavy metals in relation soil-fodder-milk is important since the consequences of their activity have a great impact on both environment and people's health (Sharma, 1980; Markert and Friese, 2000 and Vidovic *et al.*, 2003).

Hair has been increasingly used as an index of exposure to heavy metals and has some advantages over blood tests since it is non-invasive, stressless and the concentration of elements in hair tissue is much higher than in body fluids, which simplifies analytical procedures and reduces the possibility of contamination (Krejpcio and Gawêcki, 2002). Recently, trace elements including rare earth elements have begun to be used in large amounts for advanced industries. These are expected to be discharged into surface waters or drainaged (industrial, agricultural and human) into lakes causing harmful effects on aquatic life. Burullus Lake has a great importance based on the different uses of the lake and its surroundings, namely recreation, tourism, fisheries, industrial water source, etc (Diab *et al.*, 2006).

The aim of the present study was to examine the accumulation of heavy metals (lead, cadmium, copper, nikel, aluminum, arsenic and mercury) in hair, plasma and milk of dairy cattle and buffaloes grazing reed plants at Burullus Lake, North Delta, Egypt.

MATERIALS AND METHODS

Experimental Animals

The current work was carried out at North Delta of Egypt. Twenty four dairy cows and buffaloes were divided in two locations with 6 dairy cows and 6 dairy buffaloes in each. The animals in the first location were fed berseem (*Trifolium Alexandrinum*) irrigated by Nile water, while in the second location (Burullus Lake) they grazed reed plants.

Hair, Plasma and Milk Samples

Hair, plasma and milk samples were taken from the experimental animals at Burullus Lake to study the effect of grazing reed plants on the content of heavy metals (lead, cadmium, copper, nickel, aluminum, arsenic and mercury) in comparison with those fed berseem from the land irrigated with fresh Nile water. Samples of berseem, reed plants, hair, plasma and milk were prepared for heavy metals determination according to the methods of AOAC (1995) as follows:

Hair samples were collected from the upper right or left cage for each animal by a clean shaving tackle close to the skin surface of the animal in clean nylon bag. Each sample was thoroughly washed by tap water, and then rinsed with distilled and boiled distilled water until both the filter and filtrate appeared clear. Hair samples were dried in the oven at 60 °C for 72 hours, then weighed into crucibles and ashed for 5 hours at 500 °C. Ten ml HCL (10%) was added to ash and diluted by 15 ml distilled water and then placed on hot plate until the solution completely evaporated. Thereafter, 10 ml HCL (10%) was added and the solution was heated to observe ascending vapors (about 80-90 °C), following filtration in volumetric flask (50 ml), transferred into bottles and kept for heavy metals determination.

Blood samples were taken from the jugular vein by clean sterile needle in clean dry plastic tubes using heparin as an anticoagulant. Then centrifuged at 4000 rotations per minute for 15 minute to obtain plasma. One ml of each plasma sample was wet ashed by using 5 ml pure sulphuric acid and 2.5 ml of pure nitric acid, diluted to 50 ml by distilled water and kept for heavy metals determination.

Milk samples from the evening and morning milkings for each animal were thoroughly mixed. After that, a 5 ml sample was wet ashed in a similar manner to blood plasma samples and kept for heavy metals determination.

Water, Berseem and Reed Plants Samples

Nile and lake water samples were taken for heavy metals determination. The samples of berseem and reed plants were dried at 60 °C for 72 hours and ground, then ashed for 5 hours at 500 °C and solubilized as previously described in hair and kept for heavy metals determination.

Determination of Heavy Metals

Heavy metals in berseem, reed plants, hair, plasma and milk samples were determined by Atomic Absorption Spectrophotometer (Perkin Elmer 2380).

Statistical Analysis

The data of heavy metals content was statistically analyzed using general liner models procedure adapted by SPSS (2004) for user's guide with one-way ANOVA. Duncan test within programme SPSS was used to determine the degree of significance between the means.

RESULTS AND DISCUSSION

Heavy Metals Contents in Water, Berseem and Reed Plants

Data in Table (8.1) showed that increasing the concentrations of heavy metals (lead, cadmium, copper, nikel, aluminum, arsenic and mercury) in lake water compared to nile water led to higher heavy metals contents in reed plants than berseem. The concentrations of heavy metals in lake water increased by 56.60, 71.43, 65.85, 56.25, 62.02, 78.82 and 65.45% for Pb, Cd, Cu, Ni, Al, Ar and Hg compared to nile, respectively. The contents of heavy metals in reed plants increased by 48.35, 51.35, 44.86, 34.93, 49.40, 46.49 and 45.71% for Pb, Cd, Cu, Ni, Al, Ar and Hg compared with berseem, respectively. The higher contents of heavy metals in reed plants could be attributed to the sewage sludge presented in water of Burullus Lake. The contents of Cd and Hg in reed plants were higher than the maximum tolerable levels of these elements by cattle being 0.5 and 2 ppm, respectively (NRC, 1980). The contents of Pb, Cu, Ni, Al and Ar in reed plants are within the maximum tolerable levels of these elements by cattle being 30, 100, 50, 1000 and 50 ppm, respectively (NRC, 1980). These results are within the magnitude of values obtained by Parkpian *et al.* (2003). When sewage sludge is surface-applied to grassland, herbage may become contaminated with heavy metals from adhering solids, posing a risk to the health of grazing livestock and possibly increasing the entry of heavy metals into food products (Klessa and Desira-Buttigieg, 1992). Diab *et al.* (2006) found higher contents of heavy metals (Cd, Cr, Co, Cu, Mn, Ni, Pb and Zn) in water and sediment samples taken from Burullus Lake.

Table 8.1: The Contents of Heavy Metals in Nile and Lake Water, Berseem and Reed Plants

Item	Pb	Cd	Cu	Ni	Al	Ar	Hg
Water	(ppm on fresh basis)						
Nile	2.65	0.21	0.82	0.32	84.23	0.85	0.055
Lake	4.15	0.36	1.36	0.50	136.47	1.52	0.091
Feeds	(ppm on DM basis)						
Berseem	4.55	0.37	10.70	1.46	4.15	5.70	1.75
Reed plants	6.75	0.56	15.50	1.97	6.20	8.35	2.55

Heavy Metals Contents in Hair

The contents of heavy metals in hair of cattle and buffaloes fed berseem and reed plants are presented in Table (8.2). The contents of heavy metals in hair of cattle and buffaloes grazed reed plants were significantly higher (P<0.01) than in hair of those fed berseem. The contents of heavy metals in hair increased by 61.57% for Pb, 61.59% for Cd; 63.81% for Cu, 53.13% for Ni, 59.80% for Al, 57.22% for Ar and 65.55% for Hg when animals were grazed reed plants compared with those fed berseem. The high positive correlations between the contents of Pb, Cd, Cu, Ni, Al, Ar and Hg in berseem and reed plants and its contents in hair were 0.86, 0.85, 0.94, 0.82, 0.84, 0.85 and 0.81, respectively. These results are in accordance with those obtained by Rashed and Soltan (2005) who found that heavy metal concentrations in hair reflect the presence of these metals in the surrounding forage and soil and vary from one area to another, and give knowledge about pollution in the area. Correlation statistics analysis and cluster analysis showed good and significant values between metals concentrations in hair and plants. Draghici *et al.* (2002) concluded that hair can be used as biological marker of pollution and that regular chemical tests of hair can provide information on the level of heavy metals in the body tissues.

Table 8.2: Effect of Feeding Berseem and Reed Plants on Heavy Metals Contents (ppm on DM basis) in Hair of Cattle and Buffaloes

Item	Pb	Cd	Cu	Ni	Al	Ar	Hg
Feeding							
Berseem	24.20	2.76	8.51	4.16	4.08	1.94	5.95
Reed plants	39.10	4.46	13.94	6.37	6.52	3.05	9.85
SEM	1.51	0.16	0.46	0.26	0.20	0.10	0.37
P value	0.01	0.01	0.01	0.01	0.01	0.01	0.01
Animals							
Cattle	34.90	3.96	12.18	5.81	5.73	2.70	8.68
Buffaloes	28.40	3.26	10.27	4.72	4.87	2.29	7.12
SEM	3.37	0.38	1.23	0.50	0.55	0.25	0.89
P value	0.05	0.05	0.05	0.05	0.05	0.05	0.05

Moreover, the contents of heavy metals were significantly higher (P<0.05) in the hair of cattle compared with buffaloes (Table 2). The contents of heavy metals in hair of cattle increased by 22.89% for Pb, 21.47% for Cd, 18.60% for Cu, 23.09% for Ni, 17.66% for Al, 17.90% for Ar and 21.91% for Hg compared with buffaloes. These results may be attributed to the minerals content in hair, which were closely related with the content of melanin black pigment of hair. These results are within the values obtained by Patrashkov *et al.*

(2003) and agreed with those obtained by Gaafar (1994) and Abdel-Raouf *et al.* (1994) who reported that minerals contents were higher in black hair of Friesian cows than buffaloes.

Heavy Metals Concentrations in Plasma

The concentrations of heavy metals in plasma of cattle and buffaloes are presented in Table (8.3). The concentrations of heavy metals in plasma of cattle and buffaloes grazed reed plants were significantly higher (P<0.01) than of feeding berseem. The concentrations in heavy metals in plasma of cattle and buffaloes grazed reed plants increased by 47.75% for Pb, 48.41% for Cd, 48.17% for Cu, 38.12% for Ni, 43.30% for Al, 49.01% for Ar and 42.31% for Hg than in those fed berseem. The high positive correlations between the contents of Pb, Cd, Cu, Ni, Al, Ar and Hg in berseem and reed plants and its concentrations in plasma were 0.87, 0.76, 0.88, 0.86, 0.85, 0.88 and 0.87, respectively. Similar results were obtained by Gaafar *et al.* (2005) who found that the concentrations of heavy metals in plasma of Friesian calves increased with increasing their contents in ration.

Moreover, the concentrations of heavy metals in plasma of buffaloes were significantly higher (P<0.05) than cattle (Table 8.3). The concentrations of heavy metals in plasma of buffaloes increased by 28.11% for Pb, 25.17% for Cd, 23.81% for Cu, 19.13% for Ni, 22.76% for Al, 26.94% for Ar and 21.98% for Hg than cattle. These results agreed with those obtained by Gaafar (1994) and Abdel-Raouf *et al.* (1994) who reported that minerals concentrations in plasma of buffaloes were higher than in cows.

Table 8.3: Effect of Feeding Berseem and Reed Plants on Heavy Metals Concentrations (ug/ 100 ml) in Plasma of Cattle and Buffaloes

Item	Pb	Cd	Cu	Ni	Al	Ar	Hg
Feeding							
Berseem	5.11	1.26	81.8	4.04	18.87	5.04	5.27
Reed plants	7.55	1.87	121.20	5.58	27.04	7.51	7.58
SEM	0.78	0.18	10.80	0.42	2.35	0.75	0.48
P value	0.01	0.01	0.01	0.01	0.01	0.01	0.01
Animals							
Cattle	5.55	1.39	90.70	4.39	20.61	5.53	5.93
Buffaloes	7.11	1.74	112.30	5.23	25.30	7.02	6.92
SEM	1.22	0.31	19.70	0.77	4.09	1.24	1.17
P value	0.05	0.05	0.05	0.05	0.05	0.05	0.05

Heavy Metals Contents in Milk

The contents of heavy metals in milk of cattle and buffaloes are shown in Table (8.4). The contents of heavy metals in milk of cattle and buffaloes grazing reed plants were significantly higher (P<0.01) than those animals, which were fed berseem. The contents in heavy metals in milk of cattle and buffaloes grazing reed plants increased by 48.72% for Pb, 46.15% for Cd, 45.96% for Cu, 46.81% for Ni, 44.88% for Al, 45.71% for Ar and 44.00% for Hg than those fed berseem. The high positive correlations between the contents of Pb, Cd, Cu, Ni, Al, Ar and Hg in berseem and reed plants and its contents in milk were 0.88, 0.84, 0.85, 0.85, 0.80, 0.88 and 0.87, respectively. These results are in agreement with those obtained by Sharma *et al.* (1982) who found that low dietary intake of heavy metals do not produce an appreciable rise of these metals in edible products, e.g., milk. Parkpian *et al.* (2003) reported that improvements of farm management give significant reduction in elevated levels of Pb and Cd in soil and plants, and however leads to minimize the amount of Pb and Cd in produced milk. El-Gazaly and Sallam (2002) indicated higher heavy metals contents in milk of cows and buffaloes in contaminated areas.

Moreover, the contents of heavy metals in milk of buffaloes were significantly higher ($P<0.05$) than cattle (Table 8.4). The contents of heavy metals in milk of buffaloes increased by 25.58% for Pb, 28.57% for Cd, 24.90% for Cu, 27.45% for Ni, 24.11% for Al, 25.00% for Ar and 25.93% for Hg than cattle. The higher contents of heavy metals in buffalo's milk could be attributed to its higher ash content compared with cow's milk. In this connection, El-Gazaly and Sallam (2002) reported that the contents of heavy metals were higher in buffalo's milk than those of cow's milk.

Table 8.4: Effect of Feeding Berseem and Reed Plants on Heavy Metals Contents (ppm on Fresh Basis) in Milk of Cattle and Buffaloes

Item	Pb	Cd	Cu	Ni	Al	Ar	Hg
Feeding							
Berseem	0.39	0.26	2.35	0.47	2.05	0.70	0.50
Reed plants	0.58	0.38	3.43	0.69	2.97	1.02	0.72
SEM	0.06	0.04	0.32	0.07	0.27	0.10	0.07
P value	0.01	0.01	0.01	0.01	0.01	0.01	0.01
Animals							
Cattle	0.43	0.28	2.57	0.51	2.24	0.76	0.54
Buffaloes	0.54	0.36	3.21	0.65	2.78	0.96	0.68
SEM	0.10	0.06	0.54	0.11	0.46	0.16	0.11
P value	0.05	0.05	0.05	0.05	0.05	0.05	0.05

CONCLUSION

From these results it could be concluded that grazing cattle and buffaloes on reed plants in Burullus Lake led to higher accumulation of heavy metals in their hair, blood plasma and milk, causing possible hazardous effect on human health.

REFERENCES

Abdel-Raouf, E.M., M.K. Mohsen, S.A. Mahmoud and H.M.A. Gaafar, 1994. Hair and Blood Plasma as Indicators of Mineral Status in Cattle and Buffaloes. J. Agric. Sci. Mansoura Univ., 19: 103.

AOAC, 1995. Official Methods of Analysis (16th Ed.). Association of Official Analytical Chemists, Arlington, USA.

Diab, H.M., A.B. Ramadan and M.H.E. Monged, 2006. Assessment of Natural Radioactivity and Heavy Metals in Burullus Lake, Egypt. International J. of Low Radiation, 3: 273.

Draghici, C., D. Crisan, S. Eftimie and V. Pop, 2002. The Presence and Persistence of Heavy Metals in the Hair of Cattle Raised within the Industrially Polluted Area of Baia Mare. Seria Medicina Veterinara, 58: 185.

El-Gazaly, F.M. and M.T. Sallam, 2002. Lead, Cadmium and Aluminum Concentration Levels in Raw Milk of Lactating Cows and Buffaloes Raised in Localities Under Different Ecological Conditions in Middle Egypt. 1st Ann. Sc. Conf. Anim. & Fish Prod. Mansoura, 24 & 25 Sep., p. 48.

Fergusson, E., 1990. The Heavy Elements: Chemistry, Environmental Impact and Health Effects. Pergamon Press, Oxford, p. 461.

Gaafar, H.M.A., 1994. Metabolism of Some Minerals in Cattle and Buffaloes. M. Sc. Thesis, Faculty of Agric., Kafr El-Shiekh, Tanta Univ.

Gaafar, H.M.A., R.M. Abou-Aiana, G.H.A. Ghanem and Mona A. Ali, 2005. Accumulation of Some Heavy Metals and Histological Aspects of Body Tissues of Growing Friesian Calves Fed Poultry Litter and Corn Silage. Egyptian J. Anim. Prod., 42: 95.

Klessa, D.A. and A. Desira-Buttigieg, 1992. The Adhesion to Leaf Surfaces of Heavy Metals from Sewage Sludge Applied to Grassland. Soil Use and Management, 8: 115.

Krejpcio, Z. and J. Gawêcki, 2002. Hair Lead and Body Lead Burden in Lead-intoxicated Rats Fed Diets Enriched with Dietary Fiber. Polish Journal of Environmental Studies, 11: 123.

Markert, B. and K. Friese, 2000. Trace Elements. Their Distribution and Effects in the Environment. (1st Ed.). Elsevier, Oxford.

NRC, 1980. Mineral Tolerance of Domestic Animals. National Academy Press. Washington, D.C.

Pais, I., 1992. Az általánosan létfontosságú mikroelemek (A mikroelemek korszaka) (Essencially microelements). Biokémia, p. 352.

Parkpian, P., S.T. Leong, P. Laortanakul and N. Thunthaisong, 2003. Regional Monitoring of Lead and Cadmium Contamination in a Tropical Grazing Land Site, Thailand. Environmental Monitoring and Assessment, 85: 157.

Patrashkov, S.A., V.L. Petukhov, O.S. Korotkevich and I.V. Petukhov, 2003. Content of Heavy Metals in the Hair. J. Phys. IV France, 107: 1025.

Pittia, P., 1992. Indagine sul contenuto in piombo in latte della Provincia di Udine (The content of lead in milk from the Province of Udine). Scienza e Tecnica Lattiero Casearia, 43: 201.

Rashed, M. and M. Soltan, 2005. Animal Hair as Biological Indicator for Heavy Metal Pollution in Urban and Rural Areas. Environmental Monitoring and Assessment, 110: 41.

Sharma, R.P., 1980. Soil-plant-animal Distribution of Cadmium in the Environment. In "Cadmium in the Environment". (J. O. Nriagu, Ed.), pp. 587-605. Wiley, New York.

Sharma, R.P., J.C. Street, J.L. Shupe and D.R. Bourcier, 1982. Accumulation and Depletion of Cadmium and Lead in Tissues and Milk of Lactating Cows Fed Small Amounts of These Metals. J. Dairy Sci., 65: 972.

Smith, R.M., R.M. Leach, L.D. Mulles, L.C. Griel, Jr. and D.E. Bakefi, 1991. Effects of Long-term Dietary Cadmium Chloride on Tissue, Milk, and Urine Mineral Concentrations of Lactating Dairy Cows. J. Anim. Sci., 69: 4088.

SPSS for Windows, 2004. Statistical Package for the Social Sciences, Release 13, SPSS INC, Chicago, USA.

Ure, A.M. and M.L. Berrow 1982. Berrow: The Elemental Constituents of Soil. In" Reporter, Environmental Chemistry. (H.J.M. Bowen, Ed.), Roy. Soc., 1: 142.

Vidovic, M.M., U.M. Vidovic and N.M. Rodic, 2003. Heavy Metals in Relation to Soil-fodder-milk. http://www.Prague 2003.fsu. edu/content/pdf/606.pdf

Webber, J., 1981. Trace Metals in Agriculture. In "Effect of Heavy Metal Pollution on Plants". (N. W. Lepp, Ed.), Appl. Sci. Publ., 2: 159.

9

Effect of Polluted Irrigation Water on Accumulation of Some Heavy Metals in Clay Soil, Berseem and Milk of Cows and Buffaloes

Gaafar H.M.A.[1]; G.H.A. Ghanem[1]; M.M. Bendary[1]
F.I. Zein[2]; A.A.I. Atwa[2]; Hamida M.A. El-Sanafawy[2]

SUMMARY

The current work was carried out at Kafr El-Sheikh Governorate during 2007/2008 season to investigate the effect of using three water quality; Nile water (Abou-Omar, W_1), mixed Nile and polluted drainage water (El-Bana, W_2) and polluted drainage water (Kafr Dokhmeis, W_3) in irrigation of agricultural land on accumulation of some heavy metals in clay soil and berseem grown thereon and subsequently in milk of cows and buffaloes fed on this berseem.

Results showed that W_3 recorded significantly ($P<0.05$) the highest electrical conductivity (EC) value, cations (Ca^{2+}, Mg^{2+}, Na^+ and K^+) and anions (HCo_3^-, Cl^- and So_4) concentrations followed by W_2, while W_1 had the lowest values. Moreover, soil irrigated with W_3 recorded significantly ($P<0.05$) the highest EC, cations and anions concentrations followed by this irrigated with W_2, but this irrigated with W_1 had the lowest values. Polluted drainage water (W_3) recorded significantly ($P<0.05$) the highest concentrations of heavy metals (Mn, Cu, Pb, Cd and Ni) followed by W_2, while W_1 had the lowest concentrations. Moreover, soil irrigated with

1. Animal Production Research Institute, Agricultural Research Center, Dokki, Egypt.
2. Soil, Water and Environment Research Institute, Agricultural Research Center, Giza, Egypt.

W_3 recorded significantly (P<0.05) the highest contents of Mn, Cu, Pb, Cd and Ni followed by soi; irrigated with W_2, while soil irrigated with W_1 had the lowest contents. Berseem samples grown in soil irrigated with W_3 showed significantly (P<0.05) the highest heavy metals contents followed by berseem grown in soil irrigated with W_2, while berseem grown in soil irrigated with W_1 had the lowest contents. The highest contents of Mn, Cu, Pb, Cd and Ni in milk of cows and buffaloes were found with feeding berseem grown in soil irrigated with W_3 following with feeding berseem grown in soil irrigated with W_2, but the lowest content noticed with feeding berseem grown in soil irrigated with W_1 (P<0.05).

It could be concluded that using polluted drainage water alone or mixed with Nile water in irrigation of agricultural land led to increasing the accumulation of heavy metals in clay soil, berseem and milk of cows and buffaloes causing possible hazardous effect in animal and human health.

Keywords: Polluted drainage water, heavy metals, soil, berseem, cows and buffaloes milk.

INTRODUCTION

In fact, agriculture expansion in Egypt depends mainly on irrigation. Water supply from irrigation canals is not sufficient enough, especially in the areas located at the terminals of these canals. Therefore, farmers are obliged to reuse drainage water for irrigation in some governorates, for instance in Kafr El-Sheikh. In addition, mixing fresh and drainage water is officially done in order to cover the shortage of fresh water and meet their demands for more food production (Zein *et al.*, 2002c). In north Delta region, using drainage water polluted by waste water effluent of some factories higher in heavy metals content for irrigation, it will contaminate and enrich soils and crops which may be risky for human food and animal fooder (Zein *et al.*, 1998).

After sewage sludge compost had been applied on the land, heavy metals might be taken up from soil by plants, ingested by grazing animals or leached into ground water and surface water bodies. Mobility of heavy metals as well as their bioavailability in soil depend on soil texture, clay and organic matter content, acidity, their decomposing ability, also on the nature and specific properties of heavy metal ions (Sahibin *et al.*, 2002). Matloub and Mehana (1998) showed that the use of sewage effluent from Ismailiya treated plant or mixed with Nile water for irrigation increased the levels of extractable heavy metals (Cu, Pb and Ni) compared to the Nile water. However, the obtained levels were lower than the maximum permissible limits and the normal ranges. Abdel Aziz (1992) reported that the average content of total Mn, Cu, Pb and Cd in the soil surface layers irrigated with sewage water reached 3.3, 9.6, 6.9 and 3.2 times that of soil irrigated with Nile water. Khalil (1990) reported that the prolonged period of irrigation with sewage water has markedly increased the amount of Mn, Cu, Pb and Ni in grown plants.

The sewage effluents are considered not only a rich source of organic matter and many other plant food nutrients (Ibrahim *et al*., 1998) but they also contain heavy metals like Mn, Cu, Pb and Ni. However, continuous use of such effluents for crop production can result in accumulation of such metals in concentrations that may become toxic (Kirkham, 1983; Ghafoor *et al*., 1999). Brady (1984) and Underwood (1981) reported that the most toxic elements to plants when present in excess are Cd, Cu and Pb but damage may also be caused by Mn and Ni.

The aim of the present study was to investigate the effect of reuse of polluted drainage water in irrigation of agricultural land in North Delta on the accumulation of heavy metals in clay soil, berseem and milk of cows and buffaloes.

MATERIALS AND METHODS

The current work was carried out at Kafr El-Sheikh Governorate during 2007/2008 season to investigate the effect of using three water quality; Nile water (Abou-Omar, W_1), mixed Nile and polluted drainage water (El-Bana, W_2) and polluted drainage water (Kafr Dokhmeis, W_3) in irrigation of agricultural land on accumulation of some heavy metals in clay soil and berseem grown thereon and subsequently in milk of cows and buffaloes fed on this berseem.

Representing samples of water, soil, berseem and milk of cows and buffaloes were collected from the studied areas for heavy metals determination. Soil samples were collected, air dried, separated to pass the 2 mm sieve and the fine fractions less than 2 mm were used for chemical analysis, ECe, soluble cations and anions in the soil paste extract (Richards, 1969). Soil heavy metals (Mn, Cu, Pb, Cd and Ni) were analyzed using aqua reiga (Lindsay and Norvell, 1978). Also, water samples were collected and analyzed by the same way using aqua regia method described by Cottenie *et al*. (1982).

Berseem and milk samples were prepared for minerals determination according to AOAC (1990). Berseem samples were dried at 60 ºC for 72 hours and ground, then about 2 g was ashed for 5 hours at 500 ºC. Ten ml HCL (10%) was added to the ash and diluted by 15 ml of distilled water and then placed on hot plate until the solution completely evaporated. Thereafter, 10 ml HCL (10%) was added and the solution was heated to observe ascending vapors (about 80-90 ºC), following filtration in volumetric flask (50 ml), transferred into bottles and kept for heavy metals determination. Milk samples from the evening and morning milkings for each animal were thoroughly mixed. After that, a 5 ml sample was wet ashed by using 5 ml pure sulphuric acid and 2.5 ml of pure nitric acid, diluted to 50 ml by distilled water and kept for heavy metals determination. Heavy metals in water, soil, berseem and milk were determined by atomic absorption spectrophotometer, Perken Elmer 3300.

The layout of the experiment was completely randomize blocks design with four replicates were statistically analyzed using general liner models procedure adapted by SPSS (2004) for user's guide with one way ANOVA. Duncan test within programme SPSS was used to determine the degree of significance between the means.

RESULTS AND DISCUSSION

Data presented in Table (9.1) showed significant difference ($P<0.05$) between electrical conductivity (EC) values of the different types of water, where polluted drainage water (W_3) showed the highest mean value followed by mixed water (W_2), while Nile water (W_1) had the lowest mean value. The EC values of W_2 and W_3 were 2.47 and 4.58 times that of W_1. Generally EC values of water samples are in the permissible level for using water in irrigation ranged from 0 to 3 (Shahinasi and Kashuta, 2008). According to EC criteria of irrigation water adapted by Bauder *et al.* (2008), Nile water was good (0.25-0.75), mixed water was permissible (0.76-2.00) and drainage water was doubtful (2.01-3.00).

Table 9.1: Electrical Conductivity (dS/m), Soluble Cations and Anions Concentrations (meq/l) of Different Kinds of Water

Item	Water Quality		
	W_1	W_2	W_3
EC	0.53^c	1.31^b	2.43^a
Cations			
Ca^{2+}	1.80^c	3.30^b	4.60^a
Mg^{2+}	1.70^c	2.20^b	3.40^a
Na^+	1.60^c	4.50^b	6.00^a
K^+	0.20^b	0.25^{ab}	0.30^a
Anions			
HCo_3^-	3.23^b	3.70^{ab}	4.20^a
Cl^-	1.45^c	4.00^b	7.60^a
So_4	0.52^c	1.90^b	3.00^a

a, b, c: Values in the same row with different superscripts differ significantly ($P<0.05$).

The soluble cations (Ca^{2+}, Mg^{2+}, Na^+ and K^+) and anions (HCo_3^-, Cl^- and So_4) concentrations differ significantly ($P<0.05$) among the different types of water, where W_3 showed the highest concentrations followed by W_2, but W_1 had the lowest concentrations (Table 9.1). The concentrations of Ca^{2+}, Mg^{2+}, Na^+, K^+, HCo_3^-, Cl^- and So_4^- in mixed water were 1.83, 1.29, 2.81, 1.25, 1.15, 2.76 and 3.65 times that in Nile water, respectively. The corresponding values in polluted drainage water were 2.56, 2.00, 3.75, 1.50, 1.30, 5.24 and 5.77, respectively. The concentrations of cations and anions of different types of water normal ranking in irrigation water adapted by Shahinasi and Kashuta (2008) being 20, 5, 40, 2, 10, 30 and 20 mg/l for Ca^{2+}, Mg^{2+}, Na^+, K^+, HCo_3^-, Cl^- and So_4^-, respectively. Also, results revealed that Na^+ was the predominant cation and Cl^- was the predominant anion in mixed and polluted drainage water, while Ca^{2+} was the predominant cation and HCo_3^- was the predominant anion in Nile water, revealing the salinity of polluted drainage water. Similar results obtained by Abd El-Hady (2007).

Results of clay soil characteristics are shown in Table (9.2), the irrigation water had significant effect ($P<0.05$) on soil electrical conductivity (ECe), soluble cations (Ca^{2+}, Mg^{2+}, Na^+ and K^+) and anions (HCo_3^-, Cl^- and So_4) concentrations. Soil irrigated with W_3 recorded significantly ($P<0.05$) the highest ECe, cations (Ca^{2+}, Mg^{2+}, Na^+ and K^+) and anions (HCo_3^-, Cl^- and So_4) concentrations followed by this irrigated with W_2, but that irrigated with W_1 had the lowest means. The ECe values and concentrations of Ca^{2+}, Mg^{2+}, Na^+, K^+, HCo_3^-, Cl^- and So_4^- in soil irrigated with W_2 were 1.67, 1.82, 1.31, 1.54, 1.18, 1.13, 1.63 and 1.84 times that of soil irrigated with W_1, respectively. The corresponding values in soil irrigated with W_3 were 2.11, 2.49, 1.60, 2.16, 1.33, 1.19, 2.04 and 2.43, respectively. Soil irrigated with W_1 was suitable for salt moderately tolerant crops (ECe, 3-6), however those irrigated by W_2 and W_3 were suitable for salt tolerant crops (ECe, 6-10) according to Maas and Chapman (2005). It was obviously from the results that Na^+ was the predominant cation and Cl^- was the predominant anion in soil indicating that it was salinity soil. These results are in agreement with those obtained by El-Arby and Elbordiny (2006) who reported that the ECe of soil samples irrigated with waste water are approximately twice those irrigated by Nile water. This may be attributed to the secondary and/or annually addition of soluble salts as a result of irrigation with mixed water. On the other hand, the highest soluble cation was Na^+ while Cl^- was the highest soluble anions. Zein *et al.* (2002a) reported that using poor water for irrigation increased ECe, soluble Na^+, Mg^{2+}, So_4^- and Cl^- in soil paste extract.

The concentrations of heavy metals in different types of water are shown in Table (9.3) and Fig. (9.1). There were significant differences ($P<0.05$) in the concentrations of heavy metals among the different water types, where W_3 recorded the highest concentrations followed by W_2, while W_1 had the lowest concentrations. The concentrations of Mn, Cu, Pb, Cd and Ni in W_2 were 2.00, 1.50, 2.12, 3.00 and 2.40 times that in W_1, respectively. The corresponding values in W_3 were 3.23, 2.00, 3.56, 4.40 and 3.33, respectively.

The concentrations of Mn, Cu, Cd and Ni in W_2 and W_3 and Pb concentration in W_3 were higher than the normal level of heavy metals recommended in irrigation water being 0.2, 0.2, 5, 0.01 and 0.2 mg/l for Mn, Cu, Pb, Cd and Ni, respectively (FAO, 1976 and WHO, 1993). Zein *et al*. (2002a,b) found that heavy metals content were higher in drainage water than Nile water.

Table 9.2: Effect of Water on Electrical Conductivity (dS/m), Soluble Cations and Anions Concentrations (meq/l) of Soil

Item	Water Quality		
	W_1	W_2	W_3
ECe	4.08[c]	6.82[b]	8.60[a]
Cations			
Ca^{2+}	8.40[c]	15.30[b]	20.90[a]
Mg^{2+}	7.70[c]	10.10[b]	12.30[a]
Na^{+}	24.10[c]	37.20[b]	52.00[a]
K^{+}	0.60[b]	0.71[ab]	0.80[a]
Anions			
HCo_3^-	3.20[b]	3.60[ab]	3.80[a]
Cl^-	23.60[c]	38.40[b]	48.25[a]
So_4	14.00[c]	25.80[b]	33.95[a]

a, b, c: Values in the same row with different superscripts differ significantly ($P<0.05$)

Table 9.3: Heavy Metals Concentrations (ppm) in Different Kinds of Water

Item	Water Quality		
	W_1	W_2	W_3
Manganese (Mn)	0.13[c]	0.26[b]	0.42[a]
Copper (Cu)	0.18[c]	0.27[b]	0.36[a]
Lead (Pb)	1.53[c]	3.25[b]	5.45[a]
Cadmium (Cd)	0.005[c]	0.015[b]	0.022[a]
Nickel (Ni)	0.15[c]	0.36[b]	0.50[a]

a, b, c: Values in the same row with different superscripts differ significantly ($P<0.05$).

Results in Table (9.4) and Fig. (9.1) showed the effect of heavy metals concentrations in irrigation water on their contents on clay soil. Soil irrigated with W_3 recorded significantly ($P<0.05$) the highest contents of Mn, Cu, Pb, Cd and Ni followed by this irrigated with W_2, while this irrigated with W_1 had the lowest contents. The concentrations of Mn, Cu, Pb, Cd and Ni in soil irrigated with W_2 were 1.52, 1.12, 1.18, 1.50 and 1.79 fold that in soil irrigated with W_1, respectively. The corresponding values in soil irrigated with W_3

were 2.05, 1.39, 1.40, 2.17 and 2.66, respectively. The concentrations of heavy metals in soil presented in this study are within the normal range adapted by Alloway (1995) and He *et al.* (2005) being 2-300 ppm for Pb, 2-250 ppm for Cu, 0.01-2.00 ppm for Cd. The long term accumulation of heavy metals in agricultural soils has the potential to reduce soil productivity by inhibiting soil microbial (Birch *et al.*, 1995) and fauna (Georgieva *et al.*, 2002) populations. Abd El-Hady (2007) found that the highest content of trace elements (Mn, Cu, Ni, Pb and Cd) was found in soil irrigated by draimage water compared to that of irrigated by Nile water. Zein *et al.* (2002 a, b, c) reported that using poor water for irrigation increased heavy metals content in soil than that of using mixed or good quality water.

Table 9.4: Effect of Water Irrigation on Heavy Metals Contents (ppm) in Clay Soil

Item	Water Quality		
	W_1	W_2	W_3
Manganese (Mn)	8.96^{c}	13.60^{b}	18.40^{a}
Copper (Cu)	4.76^{c}	5.32^{b}	6.60^{a}
Lead (Pb)	2.12^{b}	2.50^{ab}	2.96^{a}
Cadmium (Cd)	0.12^{b}	0.18^{ab}	0.26^{a}
Nickel (Ni)	0.67^{c}	1.20^{b}	1.78^{a}

a, b, c: Values in the same row with different superscripts differ significantly (P<0.05).

Data in Table (9.5) and Fig. (9.1) showed the contents of heavy metals in berseem as affected by their contents in water and soil. There were significant differences (P<0.05) on heavy metals contents in berseem samples from the different locations, which reflect similar trend to their contents in water and soil. Berseem samples grown in soil irrigated with W_3 showed significantly (P<0.05) the highest heavy metals contents followed by those grown in soil irrigated with W_2, while berseem grown in soil irrigated with W_1 had the lowest contents. The contents of Mn, Cu, Pb, Cd and Ni in berseem grown in soil irrigated with W_2 were 1.24, 1.44, 6.67, 1.35 and 1.44 fold than that of berseem grown in soil irrigated with W_1, respectively. The corresponding values in berseem grown in soil irrigated with W_3 were 1.71, 1.94, 10.33, 1.97 and 1.93, respectively. These results agreed with those obtained by Rusan *et al.* (2006) who found that plant Cu, Mn, Pb and Cd increased with wastewater irrigation. Heavy metals such as Cu, Cd and Pb are potential bioaccumulative toxins of the dairy production system as soils tend to act as long term sinks for these metals (Alloway, 1995) via sorption onto metal oxides, particularly iron and manganese oxides (Brown and Parks, 2001). Abd El-Hady (2007) noticed that much higher Mn, Cu, Ni, Pb and Cd in plant grown in drainage water irrigated lands compared to plant grown in Nile irrigated lands. The contents of Mn, Cu, Pb, Cd and Ni in berseem are within the maximum tolerable levels of these elements by cattle being 1000, 100, 30, 0.5 and 50 ppm (NRC, 1980). Zein *et al.* (2002a) reported that the contents of heavy metals in wheat straw were greater when poor water quality was used for irrigation than that of the mixed or good water quality.

Table 9.5: Effect of Water Irrigation on Heavy Metals Contents (ppm on DM basis) in Berseem

Item	Water Quality		
	W_1	W_2	W_3
Manganese (Mn)	11.46[c]	14.17[b]	19.60[a]
Copper (Cu)	7.81[c]	11.24[b]	15.17[a]
Lead (Pb)	2.27[c]	15.15[b]	23.44[a]
Cadmium (Cd)	0.21[c]	0.32[b]	0.44[a]
Nickel (Ni)	4.78[c]	6.86[b]	9.23[a]

a, b, c: Values in the same row with different superscripts differ significantly (P<0.05).

Heavy metals accumulation in milk of cows and buffaloes are shown in Table (9.6) and Fig. (9.1). The highest contents of Mn, Cu, Pb, Cd and Ni in milk of cows and buffaloes were found with feeding berseem grown in soil irrigated with W_3 following with feeding berseem grown in soil irrigated with W_2, but the lowest content noticed with feeding berseem grown in soil irrigated with W_1 ($P<0.05$). The contents of Mn, Cu, Pb, Cd and Ni in milk of cows and buffaloes fed berseem grown in soil irrigated with W_2 were 2.12, 2.69, 1.39, 2.30 and 1.49 fold that of those fed berseem grown in soil irrigated with W_1, respectively. The corresponding values in milk of cows and buffaloes fed berseem grown in soil irrigated with W_3 were 2.88, 4.24, 1.98, 3.71 and 2.13, respectively. These results are in the similar manner of heavy metals contents in berseem. Moreover, the contents of heavy metals in buffaloes milk was higher significantly ($P<0.05$) than in cows milk, due to the higher ash content in milk of buffaloes than cows. The contents of Mn, Cu, Pb, Cd and Ni in buffaloes milk were 1.23, 1.26, 1.20, 1.22 and 1.32 fold than that in cows milk. The long-term accumulation of heavy metals in agricultural soils may pose a risk to animal, human, and ecosystem health (Alloway, 1995). Gaafar (2008) and Enb *et al.* (2009) found that heavy metals contents concentrated in buffalo's milk at higher levels comparing to cow's milk. The permissible limits for Cu, Cd and Pb are 0.4, 0.1 and 0.02 mg kg^{-1}, respectively according to (Anonymous, 1998). Tripathi *et al.* (1999) reported that Cu, Pb and Cd were detected in cow's and buffalo's milk samples at levels ranged between 0.043 to 0.195 mg/l, 1.70 to 3.35 ug/l and 0.07 to 0.10 ug/l, respectively. However, Onianwa *et al.* (1999) found that normal levels of Cu, Pb, Cd and Ni in milk ranged from 0.07 to 0.67, 0.03 to 0.18, 0.004 to 0.009 and 0.04 to 0.09 mg/l, respectively.

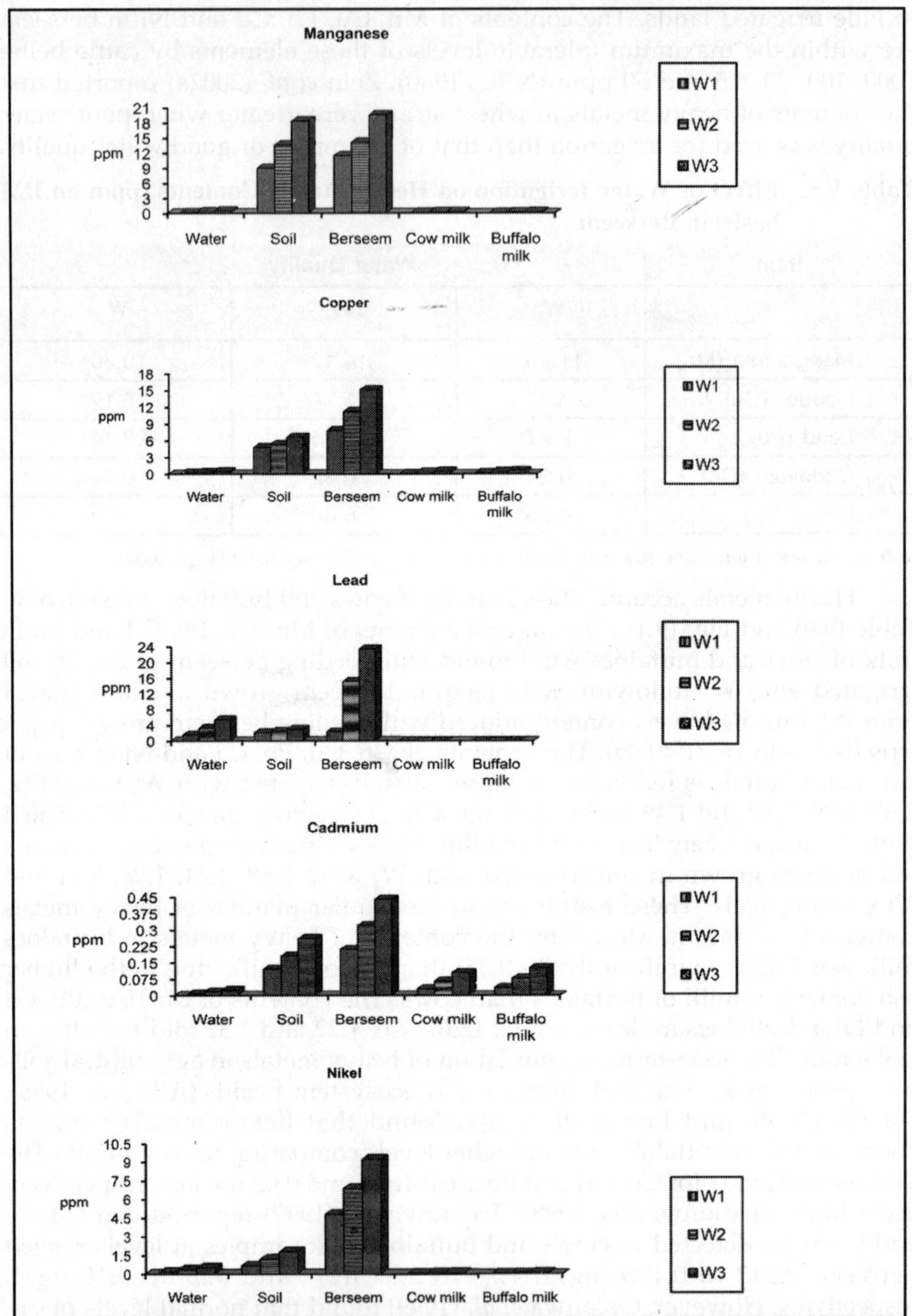

Fig. 9.1: **Heavy Metals Concentrations in Water, Clay Soil, Berseem, Cow Milk and Buffalo Milk**

From these results it could be concluded that using polluted drainage water alone or mixed with Nile water in irrigation of agriculture land led to increasing the accumulation of heavy metals in soil, berseem and milk of cows and buffaloes causing possible hazardous effect in animal and human health.

Table 9.6: Effect of Water on Heavy Metals Contents (ppm on wet basis) in Cow and Buffalo Milk

Item	Cows			Buffaloes		
	W_1	W_2	W_3	W_1	W_2	W_3
Manganese (Mn)	0.076^{d}	0.160^{c}	0.217^{b}	0.093^{d}	0.196^{b}	0.267^{a}
Copper (Cu)	0.104^{e}	0.281^{d}	0.442^{b}	0.132^{e}	0.355^{c}	0.558^{a}
Lead (Pb)	0.010^{e}	0.015^{cd}	0.021^{b}	0.013^{de}	0.017^{c}	0.025^{a}
Cadmium (Cd)	0.028^{d}	0.064^{c}	0.103^{b}	0.034^{d}	0.078^{c}	0.126^{a}
Nickel (Ni)	0.045^{d}	0.067^{c}	0.096^{b}	0.060^{cd}	0.089^{b}	0.127^{a}

a, b, c, d, e: Values in the same row with different superscripts differ significantly ($P<0.05$).

REFERENCES

Abd El-Hady, B.A. (2007). Compare the Effect of Polluted and River Nile Irrigation Water on Contents of Heavy Metals of Some Soils and Plants. Research Journal of Agriculture and Biological Sciences, 3: 287.

Abdel Aziz, W.H. (1992). Study on Soil Pollution in EL-Saff Region. M.Sc. Thesis, Fac. Agric., Ain Shams Univ., Egypt.

Alloway, B.J. (1995). Soil Processes and the Behaviour of Metals. Heavy Metals in Soils. 2nd ed. B.J. Alloway, ed. Kluwer Academic Publ., Dordrecht, The Netherlands. P. 11.

Anonymous (1998). General Standard for Contaminants and Toxins in Foods. Maximum Levels for Contaminants and Toxins in Foods. Finland, Decision No. 169/93 given by Ministry of Trafe and Industry, p. 4.

AOAC (1990). Association of Official Analytical Chemists. Official Methods of Analysis, 15th Ed., Washington, DC.

Bauder, T.A.; R.M. Waskom and J.G. Davis (2008). Irrigation Water Quality Criteria. http://www.ext.colostate.edu/PUBS/crops/00506.html.

Birch, L.D.; G. Geiger; H. Brandl; G. Furrer and R. Schulin (1995). The Influence of Heavy Metals on the Microbial Decomposition of Organic Substances. Bodenkundl. Ges. Schweiz. Dokument, 6: 13.

Brady, N. (1984). The Nature and Property of Soil (New York: Macmillan).

Brown, G.E. and G.A. Parks (2001). Sorption of Trace Elements on Mineral Surfaces: Modern Perspectives from Spectroscopic Studies, and Comments on Sorption in the Marine Environment. Int. Geol. Rev., 43: 963.

Cottenie, A.; M. Verloo; L. Kiekenes; G. Velghe and R. Camerlyuck (1982). Chemical Analytical of Plants and Soil. Lab. Anal. and Agrochem. State Univ. Gent. Belgium, Chapters 2, 3, pp. 14.

El-Arby, A.M. and M.M. Elbordiny (2006). Impact of Reused Wastewater for Irrigation on Availability of Heavy Metals in Sandy Soils and Their Uptake by Plants. Journal of Applied Sciences Research, 2: 106.

Enb, A.; M.A. Abou Donia; N.S. Abd-Rabou; A.A.K. Abou-Arab and M.H. El-Senaity (2009). Chemical Composition of Raw Milk and Heavy Metals Behaviour during Processing of Milk Products. Global Veterinaria, 3: 268.

FAO (1976). Soil Survey Investigations for Irrigation. Soil Bull. 42, Rome. Feachem, R.G., D.J. Bradley, H. Garelick and D.D. Mara. 1983. Sanitation and Disease-health Aspects of Excreta and Wastewater Management. John Wiley & Sons, Chicester, England.

Gaafar, H.M.A. (2008). Accumulation of Some Heavy Metals in Hair, Plasma and Milk of Cattle and Buffaloes Grazing Berseem and Reed Plants in Egypt. Egyptian J. Anim. Prod., 45: 71.

Georgieva, S.S.; S.P. McGrath; D.J. Hooper and B.S. Chambers (2002). Nematode Communities Under Stress: The Long-term Effects of Heavy Metals in Soil Treated with Sewage Sludge. Agric. Ecosyst. Environ., Appl. Soil Ecol., 20: 27.

Ghafoor, A.; S. Ahmad; M. Qadir; S.I. Hussain and G. Murtaza (1999). Formation and Leaching of Lead Species from a Sandy Loam Alluvial Soil as Related to pH and Cl: SO4 Ratio of Leachates. J. Int. Agri. Biol., 3: 82.

He, Z.L.; E.Y. Xiaoe and P.J. Stoffella (2005). Trace Elements in Agroecosystems and Impacts on the Environment. J. Trace Ele. Med. Bio., 19: 125.

Ibrahim, A.; N. Ahmad and S.A. Anwar (1998). Sewage Effluents and Soil Productivity, Intl. Seminar in Degraded Soils: Process, Management and Analysis. October 19-24, Univ. of Agric., Faisalabad, Pakistan.

Khalil, M.T. (1990). The Physical and Chemical Environment of Lake Manzala, Egypt. Hydrobiologia, 196: 193.

Kirkham, M.B. (1983). Study on Accumulation of Heavy Metals in Soils Receiving Sewage Water. Agri. Ecosystem Environ., 9: 251.

Lindsay, W.L. and W.A. Norvell (1978). Development of DTPA Test for Zinc, Iron, Manganese and Copper. Soil Sci. Soc. Am. J., 42: 421.

Maas, S. and V. Chapman (2005). Water & Soil Quality. http://www.nrw.qld.gov.au/rwue/factsheets.html#water_qual.

Matloub, M.A. and T.A. Mehana (1998). Utilization of Treated Sewage Effluent for Reclaiming a Salt-affected Soil. Egypt J. Appl. Sci., 13: 298.

NRC (1980). Mineral Tolerance of Domstic Animals. National Academy Press. Washington, D.C.

Onianwa, P.C.; I.G. Adetola; C.M.A. Iwegbue; M.F. Ojo and O.O. Tella (1999). Trace Heavy Metals Composition of Some Nigerian Beverages and Food Drinks. Food Chem., 66: 275.

Richards, L.A. (1969). Diagnosis and Improvement of Saline and Alkali Soils. U.S. Dept. Agric. Handbook No. 60.

Rusan, M.J.M.; S. Hinnawi and L. Rousan (2006). Long Term Effect of Waste Water Irrigation of Forage Crops on Soil and Plant Quality Parameters. Desalination, 215: 143.

Sahibin, A.R.; A.R. Zulfahmi; K.M. Lai; P. Errol and M.L. Talib (2002). Heavy Metals Content of Soil Under Vegetables Cultivation in Cameron Highland. Omar, R.; Z. Ali Rahman; M.T. Latif; T. Lihan and J.H. Adam (Eds.). Proceedings of the Regional Symposium on Environment and Natural Resources 10-11th April, Hotel Renaissance Kuala Lumpur, Malaysia. Vol. 1: 660.

Shahinasi, E. and V. Kashuta (2008). Irrigation Water Quality and its Effects Upon Soil. BALWOIS, Ohrid, Republic of Macedonia, 27-31 May.

SPSS (2004). Statistical Package for the Social Sciences. Release 13, SPSS INC, Chicago, USA.

Tripathi, R.M.; R. Raghunath; V.N. Sastry and T.M. Krishnamoorthy (1999). Daily Intake of Heavy Metals by Infants Throught Milk and Milk Products. Sci. Total Environ., 227: 229.

Underwood, E.J. (1981). The Mineral Nutrition of Livestock. 2nd Ed.. Slough, England: Commonwealth Agricultural Bureaux.

WHO (1993). World Health Organisation. Guidelines for Drinking-water Quality. Volume 1: Recommendations, 2nd ed. World Health Organisation, Geneva, Switzerland, p. 188.

Zein, F.I.; E.M. Omar; M.A.A. Abd-Allah and M.S. El-Yammani (2002c). Influence of Irrigation Water Quality on Heavy Metals Content of Soil, Water Table and some Crops at the Northern Nile Delta. Egypt. J. Soil Sci., 42: 739.

Zein, F.I.; M.S. El-Yammani; A.A. El-Leithy and A.T.A. Moustafa (2002b). Effect of Polluted Irrigation Water on Some Crops and Their Contents of Heavy Metals. 2- Sugar beet. Egypt. J. Soil Sci., 42: 307.

Zein, F.I.; Maani Z. Abou Amou; A.A. El-Leithi and M.M. El-Shami (2002a). Effect of Polluted Irrigation Water on Some Crops and Their Contents of Heavy Metals. 1- Wheat. Egypt. J. Soil Sci., 42: 139.

Zein, F.I.; O.A. Hegab and Hamida M.A. El-Sanafawy (1998). Geochemical Studies on Some Polluted Soils in Kafr El-Sheikh Governorate, Egypt. J. Agric. Sci. Mansours Univ., 23: 2557.

10

People's Biodiversity Register of Koti Village, District Chamba *Documenting Biodiversity for Natural Resource Management*

Pawan Kumar Attri

INTRODUCTION

We live in times of profound change, of unprecedented challenges and opportunities; we are in the midst of a biotechnology revolution, an information revolution and, alas an environmental crisis. We also live in a world that is becoming increasingly polarized with rich against poor nations; with the elite on one side and the disempowered on the other.

Humanity has responded to these changes in many ways; one is by accepting entirely new ways of managing living resources. These resources were till recently viewed as a common heritage of mankind. Now they are subject to two, somewhat conflicting systems of rights, embodied in the Convention on Biological Diversity and the General Agreement on Trade and Tariff. On the one hand they are viewed as sovereign property of nation states. On the other, they are being accepted as an intellectual property of enterprises which have manipulated or even simply discovered them. Intellectual property rights are also being established over the knowledge of many types of uses of these resources.

These are important challenges in all this for a country like India, rich as we are in biodiversity resources, and folk and traditional knowledge of properties and uses of these resources. Unfortunately, India is a poor country

Institute of Integrated Himalayan Studies, (UGC - Centre of Excellence), H.P. University Summerhill, Shimla - 5 (H.P.) India.

in terms of well-organized, well-substantiated, well-documented information. In the current information age, it is imperative that we overcome this weakness and establish sound systems of information on our biodiversity resources and their known uses. Such a system is especially needed to protect the interests of the ecosystem people of India, people who have played such a vital role in conserving the country's biodiversity, in augmenting it through evolving thousands of verities of cultivated plants and domesticated animals, and in developing a vast body of knowledge about their sustainable use.

BIODIVERSITY RESOURCES

Biodiversity is one of the most defining features of nature, vital for the ecological security of a region and livelihood security of millions of those who critically depend upon it for their daily sustenance. It provides the materials we need for food, clothing and shelter. It helps to ensure health, and contributes to human well being in many other ways. The present trend in biodiversity degradation is affecting one and all on this planet. Halting its degradation and loss, and ensuring the equitable use of genetic resources, will require a host of new and stronger actions at all levels.

Botany, a discipline that was the domain of the specialist biologist until the 1970's has gained importance and has grown to an extent that it has become the concern of people from all walks of life, from science to politics, encompassing almost all disciplines of acquiring knowledge.

Floristic diversity or plant diversity is the natural biotic capital of biodiversity, being a major provider of ecosystem services, meeting its basic livelihood needs. Humanity derives its supply of food, medicines, energy and a multitude of industrial products from the plants. Some of the products obtained from plants, without which life would be difficult, include timber, fuel, fodder, medicines, material for clothing and housing, etc. The very survival of mankind depends on these core ecological functions. The indirect ecosystem services provided through floristic- photosynthesis, pollination, and transpiration are nutrient cycling, climate regulation, maintaining the balance of atmospheric gases and hydrological cycles, etc.

The judicious management of floristic resources is therefore, paramount to ensure the conservation of biodiversity, its sustainable utilization and equitability in benefit sharing as ordained in the Convention on Biological Diversity. In this context the floristic inventories play a significant role in increasing our understanding and information level on the availability of resource and its relationship with mankind.

Biodiversity includes all species of plants, animals and microorganisms and the ecosystems of which they are parts. Biologists classify life on earth into a widely accepted hierarchical system that reflects evolutionary relationships among organisms. In ascending order, the main categories or taxa of living things are: Species, Genus, Family, Order, Class, Phylum and Kingdom. Species differ from one another in at least one characteristic and generally do not interbreed. In general, the higher the category ranking of an organism, the more ancient is the evolutionary divergence. Thus, with *Homo sapiens,* it was more recently that the species became established than the genus, and more recently that the genus evolved than did the family (Hominidiae), and so on up to the kingdom level. Most biologists recognize five kingdoms of organisms. Currently, approximately 100 phyla of organisms are recognized.

Biodiversity, besides its ecological and intrinsic values, represents a considerable socio-economic and monetary asset as well. Human society relies on biological resources and their diversity, and the ecosystems that sustain them to provide essential goods and services. Values attached to biodiversity can be classified into three categories: Productive use value; consumptive use value and indirect values. Productive use value is a value assigned to products that are commercially harvested from exchange in formal markets and is therefore the only value of biological resources that is reflected in national income accounts. Products such as fuel wood, timber, fish, animal skin, musk, fodder, fruits, cereals and medicines come under this category. On the other hand consumptive use value is the value placed on natural products that are consumed directly i.e., good do not enter the normal channels of trade. The value of such goods can be considerable. A significant number of such non-timber forest products such as soft broom grass and cane fall under this category. Indirect values are related primarily with the functions of ecosystems and do not normally appear in national accounting systems, but they may far out weigh consumptive and non-consumptive values. Maintenance of ecological balance and prevention of soil erosion are the examples of such indirect values (Negi, 1993).

Our economic, technological and biotechnological developments depend to a large extent on our natural resources including the biological resources. It is, therefore, considered absolutely essential and indispensable to have an in-depth knowledge of our biological wealth. It is also to ensure that the future growth and development of the country is not on the cost of faunal and floral resources. In order to be able to utilize this immense natural wealth we should first of all know the extent of richness of our biodiversity and should obtain information on their identity, distribution, interaction and population levels. The latter would certainly be of immense value in environment impact assessment, ecosystem maintenance, eco-regeneration, eco-restoration as well as in the sustainable utilization of these resources. Some of the efforts and studies could possibly lead to the development of newer biological technology in the fields of medicine, agriculture, etc., and livestock populations.

The theme of International Day for Biological Diversity, *"Biodiversity: Life Insurance for our Changing World"*, reminds us of central role of biodiversity in underpinning sustainable development, and in protecting society from the consequences of unexpected shocks such as water shortage, the emergence of infectious diseases, extreme weather events and the genetic vulnerability of crops and livestock.

> *"For millennia man has had an influence upon earth. The presence of humans can be traced back to approximately a few million years ago. From the beginning, man's influence irreversible changed the world. This war a relatively slow process compared with the modern mass eradication of land. As a result, it is becoming urgent to document the rich biodiversity so that informed choices on its management can be made"*.

Threats to Biodiversity

Plundering and unscrupulous exploitation of the forest resources by the local populace as well as pressure of production-oriented forestry system are said to be the main causes of forest loss in the region, and consequently a threat to the biodiversity. Recurrent natural calamities like forest fires, earthquake, landslides, floods and unconventional climatic behaviour, are also big threats to the floristic diversity in the Himachal Himalayas. Alongside multifarious destructive anthropogenic activities and natural calamities, some ecological changes like the constant anthropogenic pressures for agriculture and horticulture, building of hydro-electric projects, construction of roads, etc., and outbreak of diseases in the recent time also pose serious threats to the rich biodiversity of the state.

The following reasons have been identified as major threats to the floral diversity of the region:

- Population pressure, expansion of agricultural land, constructions of houses, roads, etc., and grazing by domestic animals.
- Unscrupulous harvesting of forest resources and insufficient measures to regenerate the resources.
- Indiscriminate use of chemical fertilizers and insecticides in orchards and adoption of unplanned agricultural practices.
- Lack of awareness among the people who matter most; the people living within or at the periphery of the forests.

Conservation Needs

Maintaining the biological integrity of the forest ecosystems, whose importance we often appreciate but do not as yet understand, presents difficulties to researchers developing a sustainable management system especially under current levels of natural and man made threat to the forests. It is estimated that a great number of species among plants are threatened with extinction for various reasons. Therefore, taking appropriate measures for conservation of biodiversity should be the highest priority. There is an urgent need for a holistic and integrated approach to biodiversity conservation involving *in situ* and *ex situ* strategies along with community participation and use of indigenous knowledge. We must preserve the biodiversity for the future generations to come.

India is quite rich in terms of biological diversity. It is recognized as one of the twelve mega-diversity countries of the world with two biodiversity hot spots, the North-East region and the Western ghats, of a total of 18 such sites identified throughout the globe. Our country possesses diversified ecosystems, varied climatic conditions and enormous eco and geo diversity. It is very rich in terms of not only species diversity but is blessed with an enormous variety and variability (genetic diversity) with in species along with the presence of a large number of endemic species.

The Himalayan ecosystem is unique and perhaps no other singly geographical feature had greater influence on the life, culture and history of the people of Indian subcontinent than these mountains. In additions, these are extremely rich repositories of natural resources and biological wealth. Though breath-taking beautiful, the Himalayan environment is largely inaccessible and hence for less degraded ecologically than the mainland but is rather extremely fragile and vulnerable to even small biophysical changes. The mountain ranges are approximately 2200 kms long with a total width varying between 40-400 kms. It is situated between latitudes 27° and 36° North and longitudes 70° and 96° East. Geographically, Himalaya is divisible in to east Himalaya, the central or Nepal Himalaya and northwest Himalaya which includes the state of Himachal Pradesh.

Himachal Pradesh: An Overview

Himachal Pradesh lies in the lap of the Himalayas. The Great Himalayas about which the first Prime Minister of independent India once said:

> *"Himalayas are not only bear to us, but also very dear, for they have always been a pat of our history and tradition, our thinking and poetry, our worship and devotion. They are not only physically present in India, dominating the vast Indian plains, but for every Indian they convey a deeper message".*
>
> –Jawahar Lal Nehru

Stretching in an area over 55,673 square kilometers, the state of Himachal Pradesh includes 12 districts. It is almost entirely mountainous with altitudes ranging from 450 meters to 7,025 meters above the mean sea level. Being located between latitude 30° 22 40 N to 33° 12 20 N and longitude 75° 45 55 E to 79° 04 20 E. The topography is deeply dissected with complex geological structure with a rich temperate flora in the sub-tropical altitudes. In the north it is bounded by Kashmir, in the south east by Uttranchal; In the south Haryana and in the west by Punjab. Towards north east it forms the Indian frontier with Tibet. The Physiography of the state is characterized with hilly terrain and reflects an mosaic of hills, valleys, splendid mountain ranges and snow clad peaks with altitude ranging between 450-7000 meters amsl. These snow-clad mountains are the most prominent physiographic features of Himachal Pradesh, being represented by the Dhauladhar, Pir Panjal, Shivaliks, greater Himalayas and the trans Himalaya ranges. Physiographically, the state can be divided into five zones viz.

1. **Wet sub-temperate zone** (*comprises Palampur and Dharamsala of Kangra District, Jogindernagar of Mandi district and Dalhousie area of Chamba district)*
2. **Humid sub-temperate zone** (*comprises the districts of Kullu, Shimla, parts of Mandi, Solan, Chamba, Kangra and Sirmour)*
3. **Dry temperate-alpine High lands** (*include major parts of Lahaul-Spiti. Pangi and Kinnaur)*
4. **Humid sub-tropical zone** (*consists district Sirmour, Bhattiyat Valley of district Chamba, Nalagarh area of district Solan. Dehragopibur and Nurpur areas of district Kangra)*
5. **Sub-humid and sub-tropical zone** (*Sirmour and Indora area of district Kangra)*

Climatically Himachal Pradesh can be divided into four zones:

(a) The outer Himalayas (Shivaliks)
(b) Lesser or lower Himalayas.
(c) The main or greater Himalayas, and
(d) Alpine zone or the trans-himalayas.

The outer Himalayas receive annual rainfall between 150 cms and 175 cms. For inner Himalayas it varies between 75 cms to 100 cms and the Alpine zone remains under permanent snow for about five to seven months. However, the average annual rainfall in the state is about ± 160 cms. The climate varies between hot and humid in the valley areas to freezing cold in the home of perpetual snow.

Soils of Himachal Pradesh can be divided into nine groups on the basis of their development and physio-chemical properties. These groups are alluvial soils, brown hill soils, brown earth, brown forests soils, grey woods or podozolic soils, grey brown podzolic soils, plansolic soils, humus and iron podzols and alpine humus mountain skeletal soils.

Rivers *Satluj, Beas, Ravi, Chenab* and *Yamuna* are the five perennial rivers flowing through the region. The utility of these rivers though restricted considerably by the rugged and undulating terrain of the state, nevertheless, these rivers possess immense potential for the generation of hydro-electricity.

The abrupt rise of the Himalayan Mountains from less than 500 meters to more than 8,000 meters results in a diversity of ecosystems that range, in only a couple of hundred kilometers, from alluvial grasslands (among the tallest in the world) and subtropical broadleaf forests along the foothills to temperate broadleaf forests in the mid hills, mixed conifer and conifer forests in the higher hills, and alpine meadows above the tree line.

Floristic Diversity of Himachal Pradesh

The biogeographically strategic location of Himachal Pradesh, coupled with varied phyto-climatic conditions met in its different physiographic divisions, makes it one of the hyper-biodiversity states of the North West Himalayas. The rich biodiversity of the state and its scenic grandeur have attracted the botanists, naturalists and the travellers, who all have contributed to our knowledge about its flora, since the early nineteenth century.

The floral analysis of Himachal Pradesh (3 Volumes) by Chowdhery and Wadhwa (1984) has been an excellent work, providing a comprehensive account of the flora of the state. The work being an outcome of a comprehensive survey of the floristic by botanists of the Botanical Survey of India, and the previous collections made by a number of eminent plant explorers like, William Moorcroft (1965-1825), Victor Jacquement (1801-1832), J. Royle (1800-1858), and the likes of Brandis, Hooker, Duthie, Lace, etc. Since, the publication of this flora (1984), many other comprehensive floristic studies have been undertaken, during the past 20 years. In order to provide a complete account of the flora of the state, and exhaustive enumeration of the plants has been undertaken. Prominent works include Flora of Lahaul Spiti (Aswal and Mehrotra, 1994), Flora of Sirmour (Kaur and Sharma, 2004). The Scrophulariaceae of the Western Himalayas (Pennel, 1997), Flora of Great Himalayan National Park (Singh and Rawat, 2000), Floristic composition of Chamba (Sharma and Singh, 1990,1996), Medicinal Wealth of Kinnaur (Singh, 1990a), Trees of Kinnaur (Singh, 1990b) and Medicinal and Aromatic Plants of Himachal Pradesh (Chauhan, 1999). Collett (1908) has made a comprehensive floristic survey of district Shimla and documented almost complete flora of the district in his book *Flora simlensis.*

Biodiversity resources may be defined as the variety of living organisms and their products of human utility other than as bulk material resources such as food for humans, fodder for domesticated animals, energy sources like fuel wood, nutrient sources like dung and leaf manure, and structural material such as bamboo, cane and timber. Biodiversity resources are biological materials used directly or in forms essentially derived there from as sources of special chemicals such as pharmaceuticals, fragrances, flavors, dyes and as genetic material underlying the production of such special chemicals as well as for enhancing the production of bulk material such as food or fiber through conferring on the concerned organisms such properties as higher growth rate, changed growth form or disease resistance. Biodiversity resources also include living organisms or their products used for purposes of scientific investigations.

People's Biodiversity Register is expected to serve:

(a) As a tool to document, monitor and provide information for sustainable management of local biodiversity resources;

(b) As a tool to promote biodiversity- friendly development in the emerging process of decentralized management of natural resources;

(c) As a tool to establish claims of individuals and local communities over knowledge of uses of biodiversity resources and to bring to them an equitable share of benefits flowing from the use of such knowledge and such resources;

(d) as a tool for teaching environment and biology; and finally

(e) As a tool to perpetuate and promote the development of practical ecological knowledge of local communities and of traditional "slow" sciences such as Ayurveda and Unani medicine.

PBR is a programme in tune with the objectives of the Convention on Biological Diversity, urging all parties, including India and some 150 other countries to:

- Respect, preserve and maintain the knowledge, innovations and practices of indigenous and local communities embodying traditional lifestyles relevant for the conservation and sustainable use of biological diversity;
- Promote the wider application of such knowledge, innovations and practices with approval and involvement of the holders;
- Encourage the equitable sharing of the benefits arising from the use of such knowledge, innovations and practices.

OBJECTIVES OF THE PBR

(a) Status of biodiversity resources such as populations of, cultivars of crops, fruit, trees, medicinal plants or faunal diversity.

(b) Various factors such as harvests from natural populations, changes in agricultural practices or discharge of industrial effluents, affecting the biodiversity resources.

(c) Ongoing involvement of local communities/individuals in sustainable use and conservation of biodiversity resources, such as systems of regulated grazing on pastures, maintenance of varieties of fruit plants, in sacred manners.

(d) Local knowledge, widely shared and publically disclosed of properties and uses of biodiversity resources e.g. Drought-resistance of a certain cultivar, methods of preservation of food or use of certain plants in treating human or livestock diseases.

(e) Local knowledge only partially disclosed; for instance, a claim that a particular medicine woman knows of a cure for asthma.

STUDY AREA

Physiographical, the mountainous region of India refer to Indian Himalaya, which starts in the North-western ranges (Jammu & Kashmir and Himachal Pradesh, Uttaranchal) and extends to Arunachal Pradesh. The Arunachal Pradesh portion of the eastern Himalaya (Sikkim and Arunachal Pradesh) further extends in northeast direction covering all north–eastern states (Assam, Tripura, Manipur, Nagaland, and Mizoram). It includes Indian states such as Jammu & Kashmir, Himachal Pradesh, Uttaranchal, hills of West Bengal, Sikkim and Arunachal Pradesh. Vertically it extends from Indian plains to Tibet high lands and has four parallel ranges from south to north. Attitudinally, the Indian Himalayan region can be divided into 4 distinct regions such as:

1. **Shivalik hills or outer Himalaya:** are low hills with altitude below 1000 m.
2. **Middle or lesser Himalaya:** is about 60 to 80 km width and has an altitude averaging 3500 m above msl.
3. **Inner or greater Himalaya ranges:** are high mountain ranges about 120 to 140 km in width.
4. **Trans-Himalayan region:** is about 40 km wide and includes arid, temperate areas of Ladakh, Lahual–Spiti, Pangi (Chamba).

Geographical Location: Nestling in the bosom of the Himalaya, Chamba district of Himachal Pradesh is unique in all aspects. Situated in the extreme north- west of the state of Himachal Pradesh, Chamba district is stretched between the upper Ravi (Vedic name-Purusni) valley and Chandra-Bhaga (Vedic name-Asikni) valley between North Latitude 32°10′ and 33°13′ and East Longitude 75°45′ and 77°33′ with an estimated area of 6,92,419 hectare. The district is surrounded on all sides by lofty hill ranges and the altitude in this entire mountainous territory ranges between 2,000 and 21,000 feet above sea level. The climate is warm, rainy season is well marked, the winter is mild and the snowfall is light.

Koti village is located in the catchment of the Seul River in Chamba tehsil of Chamba District of Himachal Pradesh. It is about 25 km. from Chamba town (district headquarter) toward Tissa. The area studied intensively lies roughly between N 32°39′ 52.77″ and 76°02′ 41.54″ E). The study area is situated near by Chamera Dam –I adjoining to Suel River. The forests around them are of a forestation of chir pine and some are natural. This village are part of Prahuni Panchayat of Chamba district in Himachal Pradesh.

The extent of the study area is roughly 472 hectares. There are four main approach routes to the study area. The easiest is from Chamba on the Chamba- Tissa main road. This route is oldest one. The other approach road is via Chamera Dam, which is accessible by road from the Banikhat to Sundla. Another one is From Chamba to Koti via Chakloo link road.

This entire document is centered on Koti village with the focus on the village, its five hamlets and land within its village boundaries. However, since local people from this village use part of the area adjoining the village boundary for their livelihood and sustenance, we have documented these areas as well.

Physical Features

The district is more or less oblong in shape contracted toward the north. The entire district is mountainous with an altitude ranging from 559 meters to about 6,162 meters above mean sea level but the habitation is found up to about 3,000 meters, there are three big valleys i.e. (1) Beas valley; (2) Ravi valley or Chamba valley; and (3) Chenab or Pangi-Chamba-Lahaul valleys.

Winter in Pangi is very severe and snowfall usually begins as early as October and entire valley remains under deep snow till March or April. The tract between the Ahthdhar and the Dhauladhar falls in the Beas valley and with the addition of small portion of the lower Ravi valley forms the Bhattiyat tehsil and Sihunta sub-tehsil. It is most populous and fertile valley of the district. Its vegetations are semi tropical and the bamboo, pepal and the mango flourish luxuriantly in the course or proximity of the fir, the barberry and the oak.

Climate

The district is wholly mountainous, with altitudes ranging from 1,834′ to 20,218′ above sea level and the climate is found varying from semi tropical to semi arctic. In lower part of Bhattiyat tehsil and Sihunta sub-tehsil, the climatic conditions are similar to those of Kangra and the Shiwalik area. In the higher portion the climate is temperate; the rainfall in this region is very heavy. In Ravi valley the climate conditions also vary with altitudes. Lower portions are semi tropical. The climate is warm, rainy season is well marked, the winter is mild and the snowfall is light. In the higher ranges semi arctic conditions prevail for several months in winter and the passes are blocked with snow. In Bharmour tehsil, the summer is mild and the winter is severe.

Geology

Chamba district covers an area of 6,528 Sq. Kms in the Shiwalik, lesser in central Himalayan region with typically rugged terrain with moderate to high cliff there are two important mountain ranges, the Pir-Panjab range divides water into two major rivers i. e. The Chenab in the north and the Ravi in the south. These rivers with their tributaries control the drainage of the area. The rocks exposed in the district have been classified into certain groups and encompass a period from Precambrian (over 600 million years) to recent times. These groups are Kalhel, Salooni, Manjir and Chamba-Basantpur. Mandi – Darla volcanoes, Murree and Shivalik. The rock types are generally sand stone, shale slate, limestone, conglomerates and quartzites.

Locally one comes across the indurated clays of Shiwalik group. The Kalhel, Salooni and Basantpur group contain fossils help in differentiating relative ages of the rock types. A huge granite body, named as Dhauladhar range, imparting it a rugged profile. In the Pangi valley of Chamba district apart from Chamba and Basantpur groups, older metamorphic and geneisasose, which may be over 600 million years old, are also exposed.

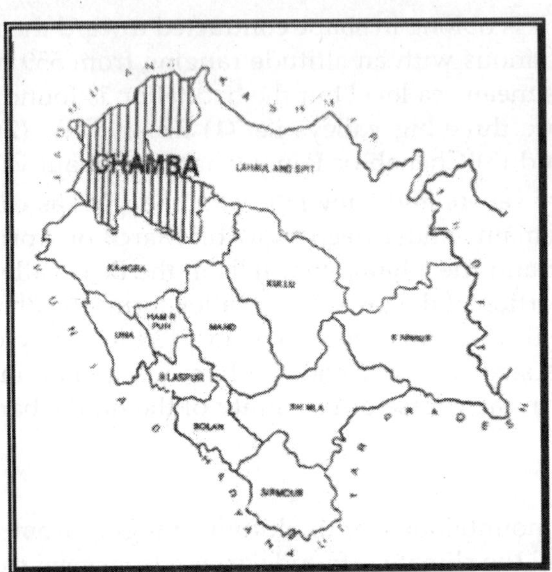

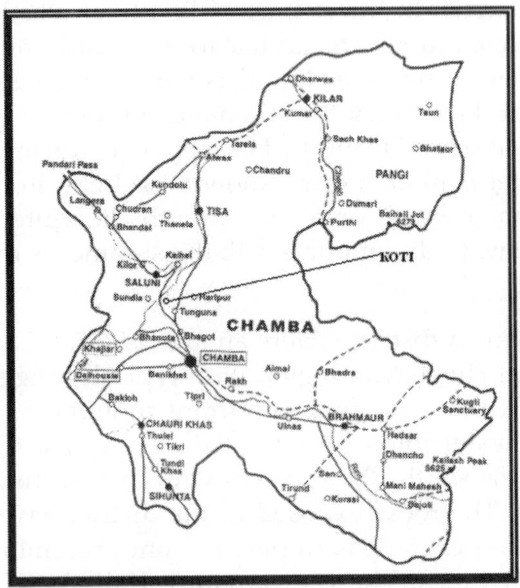

Map of Study Area

Methodology

Extensive field survey was conducted in village Koti of tehsil Chamba. The study was carried out on various communities and villager's dependence upon biodiversity for various purposes in day to day life. Keeping the objective in mind, intensive use explorations were undertaken in village. These villagers are dependent on the forests for timber, fuel wood, fodder, and other minor forest produce to a large extent. The society is largely agrarian. Wheat, maize and vegetable are the main crops. Different categories of people like family heads, healers, and old experienced and knowledgeable informants were repeatedly interviewed. Specific questions based upon performa designed by Madhav Gadgil, IISc, Bangalore were asked and the resultant information was recorded.

RESULT AND DISCUSSION

On the basis of the survey carried out in the village, different plant species and various uses of plants species are as follows:

Cultivated Plant Species

In view of heterogeneity in geographical condition, topography, temperature, moisture, elevation and soils, a large number of cereals, pseudocereals, pulses, oilseeds, vegetables, spices, condiments and horticultural crops are grown in the hills. Cereals, pulses, vegetable and oilseeds are grown in mixed in the same piece of land as a measure to ensure the food security. The details of the cultivated plant species grown in the village is given below:

Cereals and Psedocereals

Barley/Jao *(Hordeum vulgare* Linn.), Maize/Makki *(Zea mays* Linn.), Rice/ Chaval *(Oryza sativa* Linn.), Wheat/Kanak *(Triticum aestivum* Linn.), Amaranth/ Siyunl *(Amarantus paniculatus* Linn.), Amaranth/Kedari chllwa *(Amaranthus caudatus* Linn.), Buckwheat *(Fagopyrum esculentum* Linn.) and Chenopodium *(Chenopodium album* Linn.)

Mittets

Finger millet *(Eleusine coracana* Linn.), Proso millet *(Panicum miliaceum* Linn.), Kodo *(PaspalwlI serobiculatum* Linn.) and Sorghum *(Sorghum vulgare* Linn.)

Pulses

Rajmah *(Phaseolus vulgaris),* Maah *(Phaseolus radiatus),* French bean *(Phaseolus vulgaris* Linn.), Blackgram *(Vigna mungo* Linn.), Garden pea or Pea *(Pisum sativum* Linn.), Green gram *(Vigna radiata* Linn.), Soybean *(Glycine max* Linn.),

Oilseeds

Yellow sarson, Indian mustard (*Brassica juncea* Linn. cv. yellow sarson), Brown sarson (*B. juncea* Linn. cv. brown sarson), Toria (*B. campestris* Linn.), Sesame (*Sesamum orientale* Linn.).

Vegetables

Okra (*Abelmoschus esculentus* Linn.), Spinach (*Spinacea oleracea* Linn.), Cabbage (*Brassica oleracea* vaL *capitata* Linn.), Elephant ear yam/Kachalu/Arbi (*Colocasia esculenta* Linn.), Cucumber (*Cucumis sativus* Linn.), Pumpkin (*Cucurbita moschata* Duch. ex PoiL), Bitter gourd (*Momordica charantia* Linn.), Tomato (*Lycopersicon esculentum* Miller), Radish (*Raphanus sativus* Linn.), Brinjal (*Solanum melongena* Linn.), Potato (*Solamun tuberosum* Linn.), Broad bean (*Vicia faba* Linn.), and Bell pepper (*Capsicum annuum* var. *aviculare* Dierb.), Pipli/mirch (*Capsicum annum),* Kakhari/kheera (*Cucumis melo),*

Spices

Wild Allium spp., Onion/Pyaj(*Allium cepa)* Garlic/lahsun(*Alleum sativum),* Coriander (*Coriandrum Sativum* Linn.), Turmeric (*Curcuma longa* Linn.), Fenugreek (*Trigonella foenllln-graecllln* Linn.), Ginger (*Zinziber officinale* Rose.).

Fruits

Papaya (*Carica papaya* Linn.), Orange [*Citrus sinensis* (Linn.) Osbeck), Lemon [*CItrus limon* (Linn.) Burm. f.], Loquat [*Eriobotrya japonica* (Thunb.)Lindl.], Walnut (*Juglans regia* Linn.), Mango (*Mangifera indica* Linn.), Pear/Nakh/Nashpati (*Pyrus communis* Linn.), Peach/Aroo [*Prunus persica* (Linn.) Batsch.],), Banana (*Musa bauensis* Hakkinen & Meekion), Guava (*Psidium guajava* Linn.), Pomegranate (*Punica granatum* Linn.), Grape (*Vitis vinifera* Linn.) and Apricot/Chir (*Prunus armeniaca* Linn.)

Wild Edible Plant Species

Apart from the cultivated crop plant species, there are a large number of wild plant species identified by local inhabitants, which provide them vegetables and fruits round the year. Wild edible plant species are not only helpful in supporting the livelihood, but address the economic needs by selling them in the local market.

Wild Edible Fruits

Kaibel (*Berberis arislala* DC.), Kingora (*B. asiatica* Roxb ex DC.), Karaunj (*Carissa opaca* Stapf ex Haines), Kharik (*Celtis australis* Linn.), Jamir (*Citrus medica* Linn.), TusharI Tushiyari [*Debrigeasia longifolia* (Burm. f.) Wedd.], Anjir (*Ficus carica* Linn.), *Dudila* (*F. cunia* Buch.-Ham. ex Roxb.), Gular (*F. glomerata* Roxb.), Bedu (*F. palmata* Forssk.), Bhimal (*Grewia oplil'll* J.R. Drumm. ex Burret), Akhrot (*Juglalls regia* Linn.), ChiI'(*Pinus roxburghii* Sarg.), chir (*Prunus cerasoides* D. Don), Nakh (*Prunus napaulensis* Ser.), Dadu (*Punica granatum* Linn.), chir (*Pyrus pashia* Buch.-Ham. ex D. Don), Barah/chiu (*Rhododendron arboreum* Smith), Sirkuti (*Ribes alpestre* val'. *giganleum* Wall. ex Decne), Kareri (*Rosa macrophylla* Lindl.), Aakhre (*R. sericea* Lind.), Kala Aakhre [*Rubus niveus* (Hook f.) Kuntze], Aakhre (*Rubus ellipticus* Smith), Makoi/Makhou (*Solanum nigrwn* Linn.), Mat kakari [*Solemum amplexicaulis* (Lam.) Gandhi], Purain (*Vitis lanata* Roxb.), Ber (*Ziziphus mauritiana* Lam.)

Wild Edible Vegetables

Ficus carica Linn., *Bauhinia variegata* Linn., *Rhododendron arboretum* Sm, *Ficus benJamina* Linn, *Fagopyrum esculentum* Moench, *Diplazium escuien/l/Ill* (Retz.) Sw.], *Portulaca oleracea* Linn.), *Unicu parviflora* Roxb, Rambans (*Agave americana* Linn.), (*Berberis asiatica* DC.), Bathua (*Chenopodium album* Linn.), Timila/Timul (*Ficus auriculala* Lour.), Bedu (*Ficus palmata* Forssk), [*Morchella esculenta* (Linn.) Pers.]

Traditional Wild Vegetables

In addition to commonly used vegetables across northern India, there are other lesser known wild plants which are used as vegetables. A total of 12 vegetables including leafy vegetables were documented in the village (Table 10.1). These vegetables are very special cuisines, famous for their taste and nutritious values.

Phkudi/Bhruni

Phkudi /Bhruni is the dish made from tender leaves of fig (*Ficus carica* Linn.). For its preparation, tender leaves are boiled in an earthen pot for 10-15 minutes till soft and then ground well. Heat mustard oil in a pan. Add coriander seeds, cumin seeds, red chilies, asafoetida and turmeric powder, heat till brown and put boiled buds to it. Add salt and spices according to taste. Cook it on slow *fire* for 5 minutes and serve along with *chapati*

Karayaei/Kachnar

Boil the buds *of* Karayaei/Kachnar/(*Bauhinia variegata* Linn.) for *10-15* minutes till they become soft. Heat mustard oil in a pan. Add coriander seeds, cumin seeds, red chilies, asafoetida and turmeric powder, heat till brown and put boiled buds to it. Add salt and spices according to taste. Cook it on slow *fire* for 5 minutes and serve along with *chapati.*

Barah ki Chutney

Rhododendron (*Rhododendron arboretum* Sm.) locally known as *brah* is a flower present in the hilly areas of Himachal Pradesh. It is red to maroon in colour and slightly sour to taste. For making *chutney,* paste of fresh flowers of *barah,* onion, mint leaves, basil leaves, green chillies, salt and spices is prepared. It can accompany the main meal which is appetizing in nature.

Table 10.1: List of Plants Used in Local Recipes according to Seasonal Availability

Sl. No.	Name of Recipe	Plant Name/ Common Name/Family	Parts used	Time of Availability
1.	Fakudi	Fakuda/Fig/*Ficus carica* Linn./Moraceae	Buds	February-March
2.	Karayaei	Karayaei/Kachnar/ *Bauhinia variegata* Linn.Leguminosae	Buda & Flowers	March-April
3.	Chu ki chatni	Barah/Rhododendron/ *Rhododendron arboretum* Sm./Ericaceae	Flowers	March-April
4.	Aam ka Chhacha	Aam/mango/ *Mangifera indica* Linn./ Anacardiaceae	Fruit	May-June
5.	Chir ka Chhacha	Chir/Wild Apricot/ *Prunus armeniaca* L./Rosaceae	Fruit	April-May
6.	Phafru ka Sag	Phafru/Buckweat/ *Fagopyrum esculentum* Moench/Polygonceae	Leaves	May-June
7.	Sarson Ka Sag	Sarson/Mustard/ *Brassica compestris*/ Brassicaceae	Leaves	May-June
8.	Aynni ka Sag	Ayn/Bichchhu buti/ *Urtica dioica*/Urticaceae	Leaves	Nov-Fab
9.	Kasrood	Kasrood/Vegetable Fern/ *Diplazium esculentum* (Retz.) Sw	Stems	May-July
10.	Kachalu ke Patrodu	Kachalu/Colocassia/ *Colocassia antiquorum* Schott./Araceae	Leaves	August-September
11.	Seul ke Patrodu	Seul/Chenopodium/ *Chenopodium album L*	Leaves	May-July
12.	Kulfe ka Sag	Kulfa/Pigweed/ *Portulaca oleracea* Linn Portulacaceae	Leaves	Aug.-Oct.

Chhachha

Raw mangoes (*Mangifera indica* Linn.) are used for making *chhachha*. Onion and raw mangoes are taken in equal amount, peeled and grind together coarsely. Chillies, salt and sugar are added to taste.

Phafru ka sag

Buckwheat (*Fagopyrum esculentum* Moench.) leaves locally known as *Phafru* are available in the hilly areas. For making *sag*, buckwheat leaves are washed, cut into fine shreds and then boiled by adding salt till soft. After boiling make its paste. Mustard oil is heated in a pan; coriander seeds and red chillies are added to the heated oil and then paste of buckwheat leaves is added. Cook for some time and serve hut with rice or *chapattis;* ilt tastes a bit sour.

Kasrod ki sabji

Vegetable *fern/ Kasrod /Lungru [Diplazium esculentum* (Retz.) Sw.] available in hilly areas of Himachal Pradesh look like stems with curled top and with hairy growth over it. For its preparation, remove hair of *Kasrod /lungru* stems with the help of cotton cloth and then cut into small pieces after washing. It is fried in an open pan with slightly more amount of mustard oil. Add a pinch of asafetida also along with other spices. Curd can also be added at the time of frying.

Patrodu

Patrodu are prepared from healthy leaves of colocasia (*Colocasia antiquo rum* Schott). and Make the paste of black gram flour of pouring consistency. Now take few leaves of *bhavri* (*Ocimum basilus* Linn.), 2-3 medium sized onion, one piece of garlic, green chillies and salt according to taste. Ground all the ingredients and add these to the dough of Bengal gram flour. Take one leaf of colocasia keeping its lower side upwards; apply the dough over it properly. Cover the leaf with another leaf in reverse manner and again put paste over it' and repeat this process for 4-6 leaves. Fold sides of the leaves inside and then roll like bedding. Apply paste on all sides of bed while folding. For making it one piece, wrap it in a leaf of turmeric and tie with thread. Take a big pan and add small amount of water to it Put small sticks inside the pan to make rack over water. Place the folded leaves on the rack and let it stearn cook. It will take about 20-25 minutes to cook. Take out the leaves, let it cool and cut it into small pieces. Before serving, these pieces can be shallow fried or can be deep fried depending upon the requirement, occasion and availability of time. *Patrodu* are specifically prepared during rainy season.

Seul ke *Patrodu*

Patrodu are prepared from healthy leaves of Seul/Chenopodium/ *Chenopodium album L*/and Make the paste of black gram flour of pouring consistency. Now take 2-3 medium sized onion, one piece of garlic, green chillies and salt according to taste. Ground all the ingredients and add these to the dough of Bengal gram flour. Take one leaf of Seul keeping its lower side upwards; apply the dough over it properly. Cover the leaf with another leaf in reverse manner and again put paste over it' and repeat this process for 4-6 leaves. Fold sides of the leaves inside and then roll like bedding. Apply paste on all sides of bed while folding. For making it one piece, wrap it in a leaf of turmeric and tie with thread. Take a big pan or tavva and add small amount of Mustard oil it. Cook it on slow *fire* for 5-10 minutes and serve along with *chapati.*

Kulfa ka sag

Pigweed plant locally called, *kulfa* (*Portulaca oleracea* Linn.) is wildly grown near water channels. It is bit spongy and contains gum like substance. Pigweed leaves are washed, cut into fine shreds, boiled by adding salt till soft and ground into paste. Mustard oil is heated in a pan; COl'i:l11c1cr seeds and red chilies are added to the heated oi I and then add paste of pigweed leaves, cook for some time and serve hot *Kulfa ka sag* tastes bit sour and is served with rice or *chapati.*

Bicchu buti/Aynni ka saag

In whole district, leaves of *bicchu buti/* Ayn *(Unicu parviflora* Roxb.) are relished as vegetable. Boiled and mashed leaves (100 gm) are cooked in oil with spices like cumin seeds (½ tsp), coriander powder (Y2 tsp) and turmeric powder (lit tsp). It is locally called as *bicchu buti* ka *saag.*

Documentation of Ethnic Food Recipes

Diversity can be found in india's culture, geography as well as climate and same is true with its food also. In Himachal Pradesh various ethnic food recipes are famous not only for source of nutrition, but in larger part of rural area it constitutes stable food, while others are consumed during local festivals, marriages and special occasions. Earlier, when hilly state did not have well developed means of transport, people were more or less dependent on locally/naturally available food materials as well as seasonally for preparing ethnic food recipes. However, during last many decades' fruits, vegetables, herbs have been available round the year. But these ethnic food recipes are still in craze among local people and can be seen prepared in all the homes during the availability of plant material.

Table 10.2: Name of Some Ingredients Used in Indigenous Recipes

Plant Name	Family	Common Name	Local Name
Allium cepa	Alliaceae	Onion	Payaj
Allium sativam Linn.	Alliaceae	Garlic	Lahsun
Coriandum sativum Linn.	Umbelliferae	Coriander	Dhania
Mentha arvensis	Lamiaceae	Mint	Pudina
Tamarindus indica	Fabaceae	Tamarind	Imli
Brassica compestris	Brassicaceae	Mustard	Sarson
Cuminum cyminum	Umbelliferae	Cumim	Jeera
Curcuma longa	Zingiberaceae	Turmeric	Haldi
Ferula asafoetida	Apiaceae	Asafoetida	Heeng
Capsicum Frutescens	Solanaceae	Red chillies	Lal Mirch
Trachyspermum ammi	Umbelliferae	Omum	Ajwain
Trigonella foenumgraecum	Fabaceae	Fenugreek	Methi
Zingiber officinale	Zingiberaceae	Ginger	Adrak

Observations

Ethnic *food of* Himachal Pradesh is rich and varied, while relying heavily on local ingredients. It can be a healthy choice with a balanced diet *of* steamed rice or *roti,* lots *of* vegetables, *dal* (lentils), yogurt and saag (a spinach and/or mustard leaf based dish). Thus, the natives *of* the state consume a range of foods prepared from cereals, pulses, milk, fruits and vegetables. These foods have been described below (Table 10.3)

Table 10.3: List of Traditional/Ethnic Foods of Study Area

Item	Ingredients	Importance of food/ Time of Consumption	Method of Preparation
Pindari	Maize & Codra flour, green leaf, whey, gur	Baisakhi, occasion	Fermentation with butter milk and eaten with milk and gur
Babroo	Wheat flour	Snack food/Festive occasion	By deep frying after Fermentation
Chabru/ chele	Wheat flour/sugar	Snack food	Griddle (like *dosa*)
Rot	Wheat, jaggery, ghee	Religious ceremony.	Shallow frying on griddle (like parantha)
Terkeera	Wheat sugar, ghee	Snack food	Natural fermentation followed by frying in ghee
Madra	Rajmah, Curd, ghee	Social ceremony, Special dish in marriage feast	Boiled Rajmah followed by slow heat cooking in curd
Kadi	Buttennilk, spices, gram flour, ghee	Accompanimento the main diet, marriage feast	Boiling & slow cooking
Redu	Buttermilk, rice	the main diet-To relieve indigestion	Boiling & slow cooking
Chrori	Wheat flour	Special occasion	griddle (like *dosa*)
Ghadi roti	Wheat flour	Accompanimento the main diet	Fermentation and make like chapati
Kodre ki roti	Kodra flour	Special occasion	Simple making like chapatti
Liched	Chenopodium flour	Special occasion	Making like Haluwa
Alsi ke Ladoo	Crushed Alsi seed	Occasionally	Mixed with crushed seeds with wheat flour and dry fruits and make ladoo.
Kanak ke Ladoo	Wheat flour	Occasionally	Make ladoo and steamed
Maki ke Ladoo	Maize flour	Marriage feast	Make ladoo and steamed

ETHNOBOTANY

The history of plant exploration is concomitant with the evolution of human beings. Our ancestors have studied the plants around them to meet their basic requirements, which laid the foundation of civilization. Our knowledge of the intimate relationship between early man and plants has come to us mainly through surviving traditions. This relationship which forms the core of inter-disciplinary science known as Ethnobotany has attracted much attention. The enquiry of early man into nearby plant wealth was primarily to cater for basic needs like food, clothing and shelter. Incidentally some of them might have proved to be curative against certain ailments, which took wider range and scope by the experimentation on human beings with different plant parts through trial and error (Pandey and Verma, 2005) A number of workers have explored the utility of Himalayan flora (Dutie, 1906; Osmaston, 1927; gupta, 1968; Rau, 1975). But, however, more emphasis was laid on their systematic rather than their ethnobotanical use.

An analysis of data in the present communication reveals the uses of 41 species belonging to 29 families for health care among the people of the area (Table 10.4). Dominant species are Fabaceae, Asteraceae, Lamiaceae, Solanaceae, Ranunculaceae, Labiatae and Euphorbiaceae etc. The plant species have been arranged alphabetically according to botanical names with their family, local names, and parts used.

Although, due to increase in urbanization and regularly increased literacy rate are leading the district towards the new heights of development. But, these developments are migrating the youths of the area towards mainstreams, leading to the disappearance of the indigenous knowledge day by day. Younger generation is ignorant about the vast medicinal resources available in their surroundings and is more inclined towards market resources. It is interesting to know that, males are involved in this vast important knowledge comparatively more than females. The main reason is that the female of these age group mostly household workers and could have been a little hesitant. *Ficus religiosa* and *Ficus benghalensis* are considered as sacred plants and no one can cut them for their individual interest. Villager's uses the flowers of *Bauhinia variegata* as a vegetable by removing its stigma because they know it is poisonous. This clearly indicates their deep knowledge towards the importance of natural resources. Several types of studies from time to time in different areas of Himachal Pradesh have been carried out for the documentation and inventorization of biodiversity in the form of Medicinal and aromatic plants study, floral diversity, ethno botanical investigation and indigenous / traditional knowledge of Himachal Pradesh. Although, this chapter provides a information of several plants, which have been used as traditionally as well as edible purposes by the local people in the study area.

Table 10.4: List of Ethnobotanical Plants in Study Area

Sl. No.	Botanical Name	Family	Part(s) Used	Uses
1	2	3	4	5
1.	*Agave americana*	Agavaceae	Leaves	Leaves are used to increase the menstrual discharge in ladies.
2.	*Allium carolinianum*	Liliaceae	Leaves and psudo-bulbs	Leaves and bulbs are used in indigestion, cold and also as apices and condiments.
3.	*Aloe barbadensis*	Liliaceae	Whole plant	The mucilaginous inner portion is warmed and applied on boils to induce puss formation.
4.	*Asparagus adscendeus*	Liliaceae	Roots	Roots are used as tonic, demulcent and in dysentery with milk. In headache, the paste of root is applied on forehead.
5.	*Bauhinia vahlii*	Poaceae	Roots, eeds	Root juice with curd is used in dysentery. Roasted seeds are eaten as tonic.
6.	*Berberis spp.*	Berberidaceae	Ripen fruits	Ripen fruits are edible and are given as a mild laxative to children.
7.	*Betula utilis*	Betulaceae	The fungal growth	The fungal growth on bark is used against muscular pain and swellings.
8.	*Bombax ceiba*	Bombaceae	Throns	Thorns are crushed in cow milk and paste is applied on pimples. Paste of roots is also taken with unboiled cow milk to regulate the menstruation and with black pepper it is used to control the white discharge.
9.	*Cannabis sativa*	Cannabinaceae	Leaves and flower heads	The leaves are rubbed with hands to make bhang. This bhang is applied on the boils. Bhang is made into a paste with water, mixed with milk and sugar is taken as intoxicating on Shivratri. Bhang is used as an appetizer.
10.	*Carissa carandus*	Apocynaceae	Fruits, roots and leaves	Fruits are used in cough. Leaves are given at the commencement of remittent fever. The leaf juice with honey is used in whooping cough.
11.	*Cedrus deodara*	Pinaceae	Wood, bark	The decoction of bark is used in diarrhoea and dysentery. Wood oil is extracted which is used in skin diseases.

(Contd…)

1	2	3	4	5
12.	*Celtis australis*	Urticaceae	Fruits	Fruits are edible and used in stomachache.
13.	*Chenopodium album*	Chenopodaceae	Leaves	Leaves are used as laxative and used in the form of vegetable in piles.
14.	*Cynodon dactylon*	Poaceae	Entire Plant	The juice of plant is put in nose to check the bleeding. This juice is used to reduce the acidity, constipation. Also used in Puja.
15.	*Dalbergia sissoo*	Leguminosae	Bark, Leaves and Wood	Bark is used as abortificient. Leaves are used as fodder. Wood is strong, used in building construction, for furniture and legs of beds.
16.	*Datura stramonium*	Solanaceae	Leaves	Leaves of datura, opium poppy and dried ginger are ground and applied on swellings. The smoking of leaves is good for asthma patients.
17.	*Dioscorea deltoidea*	Dioscoraceae	Dried rhizomes	Used in rheumatic diseases, certain ophthalmic disorders. Rhizomes are used for washing silk, wool, hair and also in dyeing.
18.	*Dioscorea sativa*	Dioscoraceae	Roots, Seeds	Seeds are crushed and applied on the boils. Roots are used as vegetable.
19.	*Dodonea viscosa*	Sapindaceae	Leaves, Barks	Leaves are boiled in water and this water applied on stiff areas. The paste of leaves is also used on burns. Seeds are edible. Bark contains tannin. Decoction of leaves is taken once a day for two days to stop excess menstrual flow.
20.	*Emblica officinalis*	Euphorbiaceae	Fruits, Leaves	Powder of fruits mixed in rose water and applied on forehead. It relieves headache. Fruits powder used in indigestion. The poultice of fruits is used to stop bleeding from cuts.
21.	*Euphorbia hirta*	Euphorbiaceae	Entire plant	Juice of plant is given to stop bleeding in piles.
22.	*Ficus glomerata*	Moraceae	Fruits, Roots	The juice of roots, sugar and black zeera, are mixed together. This juice is given to treat the 'Sujak Rog' (gonorhoea). Green and dried fruits are ground in the water and mixed with Mishri.

(Contd...)

1	2	3	4	5
23.	*Ficus palmata*	Moraceae	Fruits, Latex	Dip two dry fruits in water for a night and eat them in the morning. Similarly, 2 dry fruits are dip in the water in the morning and eat them in evening. It removes pile in one week only. Latex is used for ringworms.
24.	*Ficus religiosa*	Moraceae	Bark, Fruits	In urinary trouble 10 gm of bark is boiled in half litre water and when it remains 1/4th it is filtered. This filtrate should be taken twice a day. If this decoction is taken with honey to purify the blood.
25.	*Juglans regia*	Juglandaceae	Fruits, Leaves, Bark	Nuts are edible and also used for extraction of oil. Oil is considered as digestive, carminative and stimulative. Bark and leaf is used as dye and also for cleaning teeth.
26.	*Justicia adhatoda*	Acanthaceae	Leaves, Roots	The juice of leaves provides relief in problems related to cough, nose, throat and urinary infections. Dried root powder is given in malarial fever.
27.	*Lantana camara*	Verbenaceae	Leaves	Crushed leaves are applied swellings. The paste of leaves is also used in snake bites to reduce the effect of poison.
28.	*Mallotus philippinensis*	Euphorbiaceae	Seeds	Seeds are dried in shade and then ground. Small tablets are made of the powder and are given with cold water in Jaundice.
29.	*Mengifera indica*	Anacardiaceae	Leaves	Powder of young leaves of mango is useful in diabetes. Decoction of the bark or the leaves used to wash the wounds to heal them soon.
30.	*Mentha longifolia*	Lamiaceae	Leaves	The aerial part is mainly used for making chutney and is considered as good remedies in cold, cough. Paste of the leaves is used on stiff and painful joints.
31.	*Nicotiana tabacum*	Solanaceae	Leaves, Seeds	The paste of leaves applied on scorpion stings and in skin disease. Plant is given in stomachache in cattle.
32.	*Ocimum canum*	Lamiaceae	Entire plant	Juice of the leaves is put in earache. Seeds are used in stomachache. Decoction of plant is used in cold.

(Contd…)

1	2	3	4	5
33.	*Ocimum sanctum*	Lamiaceae	Whole plant	Plant is used in cough and cold.
34.	*Oxalis corniculata*	Oxalidaceae	Entire plant	Juice of plant with salt is used in dysentery. Juice of the leaves is useful in cataract of the eyes.
35.	*Prinsepia utilis*	Rosaceae	Roots	The paste of roots is used on wounds for healing.
36.	*Prunus armeniaca*	Rosaceae	Kernels	The oil of kernels is warmed and applied on joints to get relief fro rheumatic pain.
37.	*Prunus cerasoides*	Rosaceae	Wood	The paste of inner wood with sugar is given in bone fracture.
38.	*Punica granatum*	Punicaceae	Seeds	The juice of seeds, ghee and syrup of sugar is given in vomiting and are good in jaundice.
39.	*Pyrus pashia*	Rosaceae	Young leaves	Young leaves are ground and applied on the head for cooling effect.
40.	*Rhododendron arboreum*	Ericaceae	Leaves, Flowers	Crushed leaves applied on forehead to cure headache. Sherbat is prepared from flowers. The dried flowers are fried in ghee and used to check the bloody dysentery.
41.	*Ricinus communis*	Euphorbiaceae	Leaves, Seeds	Leaves are heated and tied over aching joints and swellings caused by Vat Rog. The paste of the seeds is used on ulcers to cure it soon.
42.	*Rosa moschata*	Rosaceae	Flowers	Flowers are dried and powered in mustard oil. The paste of flower is used on skin burning.
43.	*Rubia cordifolia*	Rubiaceae	Entire plant	The decoction of roots with sugar is given to women to cure irregular menstruation. Infusion of plant with mustard oil is used in eyes and ear disease. The paste of stem is applied on pimples and blemishes.
44.	*Urtica dioica L.* (Bichhu Buti.)	Urticaceae	Leaves, roots, flowers and seeds.	The leaves of the plant are crushed to pulp and then it is applied to reduce swelling.
45.	*Vitex negundo*	Verbenaceae	Leaves	Leaves are smoked in headache. Flowering tips are chewed in mouth ulcers. Twigs used as 'Datun'. The leaves are used in gastric problems and also in leprosy.
46.	*Woodfordia fruticosa*	Lythraceae	Flowers, Leaves	Powder of the flowers is given in dysentery and cough. Oil is used in uterus pain. The paste of leaves used in skin diseases. The juice of leaves is applied three times a day for one week in conjunctivitis.
47.	*Xanthoxyllum armatum*	Rutaceae	Fruits, Leaves, Twigs	Fruits are used in toothache. The leaves and fruits are used as tooth brush and mouth purifiers.

Rapidly growing urbanization of this area unfortunately posing a threat to its biodiversity, traditional knowledge and cultural practices of the rural peoples. Therefore, our continuing work on documentation of plant biodiversity and their multifarious uses will not only provide recognition to this knowledge but will also help in its conservation for the betterment of human society and to the coming generation.

REFERENCES

Anju Kapoor, Promila Kanwar & Radhna Gupta (2010) Traditional Recipes of District Kangra of Himachal Pradesh Indian Journal of Traditional Knowledge Vol. 9 (2), pp. 282-288.

Arora RK and Pandey Anjula (1996) Wild Edible Plants of India. Diversity Conservation and Use, NBPGR (ICAR), New Delhi, India.

Aswal, B.S. and Mehrotra, B.N. 1994. *Flora of Lahaul-Spiti (A Cold Desert in North West Himalaya)*. Bishen Singh Mahendra Pal Singh, Debradun.

Atkinson ET, (1882) Economic Botany of the Himalayan Region, Cosmo Publication, New Delhi, India.

Chauhan, N.S. 1999. *Medicinal and Aromatic Plants of Himachal Pradesh*. Indus Publishing Company, New Delhi.

Chowdhery, H.J. and Wadhwa, B.M. 1984. *Flora of Himachal Pradesh*. Vol. 1-3. Botanical Survey of India, Culcutta.

Collet, H. 1908. Flora Simlensis, Thacker Spink. & *fo*. Calcutta and Shimla, Reprinted 1971. Bishen Singh Mahendra Paif Dehradun.

Gupta, R. (1964) Survey Record of Medicinal and Aromatic Plants of Chamba Forest Division, Himachal Pradesh. *Ind. For.* 90(7): 454-468.

Gupta, R. (1967) Cultivation of *Digitalis lanata* Ehrh. in Chamba hills, Himachal Pradesh. *Ind. For.* 93: 33-40.

Gupta, R. (1971) Medicinal and Aromatic Plants of Bhandal Range, Churah Forest Division, Chamba District, Himachal Pradesh. *J. Bombay Nat. Hist. Soc.* 68: 791-803.

Kanwar S S, Gupta M K, Katoch C, Kumar R & Kanwar P, (2007) Traditional Fermented Foods of Lahaul and Spiti Area of Himachal Pradesh. Indian Journal of Traditional Knowledge, 6 (I) 42-45.

Kaur, H. and Sharma, M. 2004. *Flora of Sirmour (Himachal Pradesh)*. Bishen Singh Mahendra Pal Singh, Dehradun.

Mehta PS, Kumar Dinesh and Bhatt KC,(2006) Wild Edible Plant Species for Subsistence in Kumaun Himalaya and Associated Traditional Knowledge, *J Econ. Taxon Bot.*, 30, 340-352.

Negi KS and Gaur RD, (1994) Principal Wild Food Plants of Western Himalaya, Uttar Pradesh, India, In: Higher Plants of India Sub-Continent, Additional Series of Indian Forester No. IV Published by Bishen Singh &. Mahendera Pal Singh. Dehradun, Gupta BK (ed), 1994, pp. 1-178.

Negi, S.S. 1993. *Biodiversity and its Conservation in India*. Indus Publishing Co., New Delhi, pp. 343.

Pennell, W.F. 1997. *The Scrophulariaceae of the Himalayas*. First Printed at Philadelphia, 1943. Indian Reprint. Bishen Singh Mahendra Pal Singh, Dehradun.

Sharma Neetu & Singh Anand 2012) An Insight into Traditional Foods of North-western Area of Himachal Pradesh Indian Journal of Traditional Knowledge Vol. 11 (1), pp. 58-65.

Sharma, M. and Singh, H. 1990. Observations on the Floristic Composition of Chamba District, Himachal Pradesh. *New Botanist*, 17: 273-281.

Sharma, M. and Singh, H. 1996. Phytogeographic Observations on the Flora of Chamba District (Himachal Pradesh) Part II. *New Botanist*, 23: 103-112.

Singh, N.B. 1990. Medicinal Wealth of Kinnaur. *Van Vigyan*, 28: 174-181.

Singh, N.B. 1990b. Some Important Trees of Kinnaur. *Van Vigyan*, 28: 55-60.

Singh, S.K. and Rawat, G.S. 2000. *Flora of Great Himalayan National Park, Himachal Pradesh.* Bishen Singh Mahendra Pal Singh, Dehradun.

Thakur N, Kumar D S & Bhalla T C, (2003) Traditional Fermented Foods and Beverages of Himachal Pradesh, *Invention Intelligence*,38, 173-178.

Analysis of Vegetational Diversity Across Different Sites in Garhwal Himalaya

Jagdish Chandra[1]; Vardan Singh Rawat[2*]

ABSTRACT

Four forest sites varying in different vegetation were studied along an altitudinal range of 2200 and 2500 m called high elevation forests. Maximum tree species were recorded on moist site (17) and minimum on ridge site (12). Maximum shrub species were present on stream bank site (18). Maximum herb species were present on moist site (35). Climber species richness was maximum on dry and moist site (6 each site). The tree density was high on Ridge site (1187 ind/ha) and low on dry site (808 ind/ha). The Total tree basal area ranged between 35.64±5.66 and 70.02±12.56 m²/ha. The herb density ranged between 67290 (winter season) to 215250 ind/ha (rainy season) on stream bank, 63630 (winter) to 253230 ind/ha (rainy season) on dry site, 66630 (winter) to 241460 ind/ha (rainy season) on ridge site and 105940 (winter) to 352900 ind/ha (rainy season) on moist site. The distribution and species richness pattern in this elevational range largely depend on the altitude and climatic variables like rainfall, temperature etc.

Key words: Himalaya, Species diversity, Canopy cover percent.

1. Department of Botany, D.S.B. Campus, Kumaun University, Nainital, Uttarakhand, (India).
2. Govt. Inter College Bagwadi, P.O. Bagwadi, Block Thalisain, Pauri Garhwal, 246285, Uttarakhand, (India).

INTRODUCTION

Garhwal Himalaya has been a source of knowledge for their unique vegetational wealth since time immemorial. The oak and oak mixed forest comprises the major forest types of Garhwal Himalaya and distributed at an elevations between 500 - 2000 and 1700 - 2800 m, respectively (Chandra et, al., 2010). There is a great diversity in the floristic pattern due to altitudinal, latitudinal variation and rainfall (Arora, 1995). Pearman and Peter (2002) reported that both local and regional habitat characteristics influence species richness and community structure. The distribution of communities varies in relation to the physical as well as a biotic feature. A decrease in species diversity was noticed from lower to higher altitude on a mountain in on a mountain in terrestrial environment (Chandra, et. al., 2010). The phytosociological study incorporates mainly the description of the vegetation of the terrain because it provides detailed information about composition of trees, shrubs, herbs and climbers communities and also the functional aspect. It is assumed that the dominating plant species actually determine the structure of a community and not another characteristic (Odum, 1971). The structure of a vegetational unit depends upon the species composition and their relative number. Diversity has been said to increase in a successional sequence, leading to climax stage. There is growing awareness that biodiversity is closely linked with long term health and vigour of the biosphere, as an indicator of global environment and also as a regulator of ecosystem functioning (Solbrig, 1991). The present study deals with quantitative analysis of vegetation on elevations ranging from 2200 to 2500 m in the Garhwal Himalaya.

METHODS

The selected sites are located in the western Pindar region in Chamoli district of Uttarakhand (30°2′43″ N and 30°3′27″ N latitude and 79°24′43″ and 79°26′46″, Rawat and Chandra, 2013). The vegetation of four sites (Stream bank, Dry, Ridge and Moist site) at higher elevation was analyzed. Within each site trees were analyzed by placing randomly 10, 100m^2 circular quadrats. Saplings, seedlings, shrubs and climbers were studied in 5×5 m^2 quadrats placed randomly. The vegetational data were calculated for density, frequency, abundance (Curtis and McIntosh, 1950). The distribution pattern of different species was studied following Whitford (1949). Importance Value Index was determined following Curtis (1959). Herbs were studied in 30, 1×1 m^2 quadrats placed randomly on each site during winter, summer and rainy seasons. The herb cover was determined by using a line transect method. Climber percent cover of was determined by line transect method (Bauer 1943). Species diversity was computed following Shannon-Wiener's Index (Shannon-Weaver, 1963) and Concentration of dominance was calculated following Simpson (1949). T-test was determined follwing Snedecor and Cochran (1967). Least significant difference (LSD) was also determined to differentiate richness between the elevations.

RESULTS

Stream Bank Site

Tree Layer

A total of 16 species were present on this site. *Rhododendron arboreum* was the most dominant species in terms of IVI (51.4%). Total tree density on this site was 987 ind/ha. The individual density ranged from 3 ind/ha (*Litsea umbrosa*) to 200 ind/ha (*Rhododendron arboreum*). Total basal area recorded was 70.01±12.56 m^2/ha (Table 11.1).

Sapling Layer

Saplings were represented by 13 species on this site. *Quercus leucotrichophora* was the most dominant species in terms of IVI (58.8%).Total sapling density was 1340 ind/ha. The individual sapling density ranged from 12 ind/ha (*Litsea umbrosa*) and 280 ind/ha (*Quercus leucotrichophora*). Total basal area was 4.75±0.12 m^2/ha (Table 11.1).

Seedling Layer

Seedlings were represented by 8 species. Total seedling density was 699 ind/ha. Density of individual species varied from 33 ind/ha (*Cedrus deodara, Cornus capitata, Machilus duthiei* and *Quercus semecarpifolia* each) to 255 ind/ha (*Cinnamomum tamala,* Table 11.1).

Shrub Layer

A total of 18 shrub species were recorded on this site. *Daphne cannabina* was the most dominant species in terms of IVI (37%). Total shrub density was 7354 ind/ha. Individual density ranged between 26 ind/ha (*Lonicera quinquelocularis*) and 2653 ind/ha (*Daphne cannabina*). Total crown cover percent was 35.69±5.50% (Table 11.1).

Climber Layer

A total of 3 climber species were recorded on this site. *Parthenocissus himalyana* was the prevailing climber (IVI=131.7%). Total climber density was 1798 ind/ha. Total percent crown cover was 16.60±3.95%. It was maximum for *Parthenocissus himalayana* (9.34±2.7%) and minimum for *Smilex aspara* (3.59±0.73%, Table 11.1).

Herb Layer

A total of 28 species of herbs were recorded on this site. Total herbs density varied from 6729 ind/ha (winter season) to 215250 ind/ha (rainy season) and total ground cover ranged from 26.4±0.6 to 43.00±3.4%.

Table 11.1: Vegetational Parameters of Different Vegetation Layers on Stream Bank Site

Sl. No.	Name of Species	Density (Ind/ha)	Total Basal Area (m^2/ha)/ Canopy Cover (%)	IVI (%)
1	2	3	4	5
	Tree			
1.	*Alnus nepalensis*	10	5.78±4.49	11.61
2.	*Carpinus viminea*	6	0.10±0.00	2.30
3.	*Cedrus deodara*	20	1.23±1.13	7.68
4.	*Engens*	6	0.24±0.16	2.51
5.	*Ilex dipyrena*	16	0.84±0.68	5.93
6.	*Litsea umbrosa*	3	0.04±0.00	1.14
7.	*Lyonia ovalifolia*	193	8.53±4.43	48.16
8.	*Machilus duthiei*	50	0.57±0.51	10.56
9.	*Myrica esculenta*	136	7.71±5.90	29.48
10.	*Pyrus pashia*	26	0.77±0.38	9.19
11.	*Quercus floribunda*	16	3.27±3.16	8.63
12.	*Quercus leucotrichophora*	163	9.70±3.75	47.48
13.	*Quercus semecarpifolia*	33	13.23±12.52	27.71
14.	*Rhododendron arboreum*	200	10.32±1.43	51.41
15.	*Symplocos chinensis*	63	1.18±0.66	15.88
16.	*Symplocos crataegoides*	46	6.51±6.04	20.21
	Total	**987**	**70.02±12.56**	
	Sapling			
1.	*Cedrus deodara*	40	0.08±0.00	9.30
2.	*Cinnamomum tamala*	240	0.71±0.46	45.17
3.	*Cupressus torulosa*	24	0.03±0.00	5.54
4.	*Litsea umbrosa*	12	0.09±0.00	4.32
5.	*Lyonia ovalifolia*	200	0.80±0.52	42.68
6.	*Machilus duthiei*	24	0.12±0.08	7.44
7.	*Myrica esculenta*	80	0.42±0.29	24.16
8.	*Pyrus pashia*	20	0.05±0.03	5.62
9.	*Quercus floribunda*	52	0.11±0.00	10.92
10.	*Quercus leucotrichophora*	280	0.98±0.81	58.80
11.	*Quercus semecarpifolia*	40	0.16±0.09	11.01
12.	*Rhododendron arboreum*	144	0.63±0.33	34.93
13.	*Symplocos chinensis*	184	0.58±0.10	40.08
	Total	**1340**	**4.76±0.12**	

(Contd…)

1	2	3	4	5
		Seedling		
1.	*Cedrus deodara*	33	0.01±0.00	15.07
2.	*Cinnamomum tamala*	255	0.06±0.04	84.72
3.	*Cornus capitata*	33	0.01±0.00	14.78
4.	*Lyonia ovalifolia*	67	0.01±0.00	28.84
5.	*Machilus duthiei*	33	0.02±0.00	19.92
6.	*Quercus leucotrichophora*	178	0.06±0.03	82.69
7.	*Quercus semecarpifolia*	33	0.03±0.00	23.67
8.	*Symplocos chinensis*	67	0.02±0.01	30.28
	Total	**699**	**0.22±0.03**	
		Shrub		
1.	*Berberis asiatica*	520	2.78±0.37	26.62
2.	*Berberis chitria*	213	2.91±0.66	13.27
3.	*Daphne cannabina*	2653	5.69±1.33	77.20
4.	*Desmodium elegans*	280	0.84±0.64	13.48
5.	*Desmodium gangenticum*	973	6.49±4.28	37.01
6.	*Eupatorium adenophorum*	40	0.15±0.00	2.90
7.	*Eurya acuminata*	40	0.78±0.00	4.47
8.	*Hypericum lysimachioides*	453	1.51±0.00	14.64
9.	*Indigofera dosua*	906	2.83±1.48	34.96
10.	*Lonicera quinquelocularis*	26	0.24±0.00	1.73
11.	*Plectranthus japonicus*	240	1.39±0.89	11.98
12.	*Rhamnus virgatus*	146	1.95±0.97	10.54
13.	*Rubus ellipticus*	66	0.47±0.00	4.70
14.	*Rubus lasiocarpus*	53	0.81±0.00	3.57
15.	*Rubus paniculatus*	200	3.41±1.82	11.57
16.	*Sarcococca hookeriana*	146	0.40±0.00	5.67
17.	*Viburnum coriaceum*	266	1.44±0.00	14.05
18	*Viburnum cotinifolium*	133	1.60±0.91	11.55
	Total	**7354**	**35.69±5.50**	
		Climber		
1.	*Parthenocissus himalyana*	786	9.34±2.73	131.77
2.	*Smilex aspara*	906	3.59±0.73	126.55
3.	*Trachelospermum frgranes*	106	3.67±0.00	41.68
	Total	**1798**	**16.60±3.95**	

Individual herb density varied from 660 ind/ha (*Cyperus niveus*) to 25330 ind/ha (*Carex condensata*) during winter, 330 ind/ha (*Anaphalis contorta*) to 25000 ind/ha (*Pilia scripta*) during summer and 660 ind/ha (*Ocimum tenuiflorus*) to 32000 ind/ha (*Oplismenus compositus*) during rainy season. The ground cover percent of herbs was maximum for *Senecio rufinervis* (7.0±2.3%) during winter, for *Gerbera macrophylla* (4.8±1.8%) during summer and for *Aechmanthera gossypina* (5.3±1.0%) during rainy season (Table 11.5).

Dry Site

Tree Layer

A total of 16 tree species were recorded on this site. *Quercus leucotrichophora* was the most dominant species in terms of IVI (70.7%). Total tree density was 808 ind/ha. Individual density ranged from 3 ind/ha (*Cornus macrophylla* and *Quercus floribunda*) to 210 ind/ha (*Quercus leucotrichophora*). Total basal area was 46.99±5.6 m^2/ha (Table 11.2).

Sapling Layer

A total of 12, sapling species showed their presence in this site. *Cinnamomum tamala* was the dominant species in terms *of* IVI (68.6%). Total sapling density was 1988 ind/ha. Individual density ranged between 24 ind/ha (*Abies pindrow* and *Quercus semecarpifolia*) and 520 ind/ha (*Cinnamomum tamala*). The total basal area recorded was 7.12±0.14 m^2/ha (Table 11.2).

Seedling Layer

Out of 16 tree species, seedlings were present for only 8 species. Total seedling density was 844 ind/ha. Individual density varied from 33 ind/ha (*Abies pindrow* and *Symplocos chinensis*) to 255 ind/ha (*Quercus leucotrichophora*). The total basal area recorded was 0.23±0.08 cm^2/ha. Total basal area varied from 0.01±0.0 cm^2/ha (*Abies pindrow*) to 0.08± 0.05 cm^2/ha (*Quercus leucotrichophora*, Table 11.2).

Shrub Layer

A total of 15 shrub species were recorded on this site. *Daphne cannabina* was the most dominant species in terms of IVI (68.4%). The total shrub density was 10035 ind/ha. Individual density ranged from 26 ind/ha (*Berberis asiatica*) to 2853 ind/ha (*Daphne cannabina*). Total crown cover percent was 45.07±5.6% (Table 11.2).

Climber Layer

A total of 6 climber species were recorded on this site. *Parthenocissus himalayana* was the most dominant climber (IVI=109.2%). Total climbers density was 1064 ind/ha. It was maximum for *Parthenocissus himalayana* (453 ind/ha.). Total crown cover percent was 11.20±1.8% while individual cover percent varied from 0.16±0.0% (*Smiles parvifolia*) to 3.58±1.8% (*Parthenocissus himalyana*, (Table 11.2).

Table 11.2: Vegetational Parameters of Different Vegetation Layers on Dry Site

Sl. No	Name of Species	Density (Ind/ha)	Total Basal Area (m²/ha)/ Canopy Cover (%)	IVI (%)
1	2	3	4	5
		Tree		
1.	*Abies pindrow*	6	0.21±0.14	2.80
2.	*Alnus nepalensis*	20	2.19±1.11	12.01
3.	*Cedrus deodara*	16	4.13±4.05	14.83
4.	*Cornus capitata*	50	0.99±0.84	13.17
5.	*Cornus macrophylla*	3	0.12±0.00	1.44
6.	*Ilex dipyrena*	13	0.30±0.00	3.87
7.	*Litsea umbrosa*	6	0.06±0.00	2.48
8.	*Lyonia ovalifolia*	176	10.66±5.40	60.73
9.	*Machilus duthiei*	20	0.81±0.77	11.52
10.	*Myrica esculenta*	13	1.65±0.00	14.05
11.	*Quercus floribunda*	3	0.12±0.00	1.43
12.	*Quercus leucotrichophora*	210	13.03±6.81	70.79
13.	*Quercus semecarpifolia*	53	3.67±3.45	20.05
14.	*Rhododendron arboreum*	130	7.50±5.16	43.42
15.	*Symplocos chinensis*	63	1.10±0.23	18.25
16.	*Symplocos crataegoides*	26	0.47±0.19	9.09
	Total	808	47.01±5.60	
		Sapling		
1.	*Abies pindrow*	24	0.15±0.08	5.61
2.	*Cedrus deodara*	64	0.22±0.11	10.91
3.	*Cinnamomum tamala*	520	1.54±0.55	68.61
4.	*Litsea umbrosa*	200	0.78±0.41	34.86
5.	*Lyonia ovalifolia*	80	0.35±0.00	14.76
6.	*Machilus duthiei*	40	0.13±0.07	7.28
7.	*Myrica esculenta*	172	0.60±0.45	25.19
8.	*Quercus floribunda*	40	0.21±0.00	7.27
9.	*Quercus leucotrichophora*	412	1.57±0.71	60.19
10.	*Quercus semecarpifolia*	24	0.08±0.00	3.50
11.	*Rhododendron arboreum*	92	0.35±0.28	15.83
12.	*Symplocos chinensis*	320	1.14±0.40	45.94
	Total	**1988**	**7.12±0.14**	

1	2	3	4	5
		Seedling		
1.	*Abies pindrow*	33	0.01±0.00	10.73
2.	*Cinnamomum tamala*	67	0.02±0.01	26.97
3.	*Machilus duthiei*	67	0.02±0.00	27.62
4.	*Myrica esculenta*	144	0.04±0.02	47.12
5.	*Quercus leucotrichophora*	255	0.09±0.05	89.12
6.	*Quercus semecarpifolia*	67	0.03±0.00	29.33
7.	*Rhododendron arboreum*	178	0.04±0.00	52.80
8.	*Symplocos chinensis*	33	0.02±0.00	16.30
	Total	**844**	**0.23±0.08**	
		Shrub		
1.	*Achne cordifolia*	280	0.69±0.00	7.51
2.	*Berberis asiatica*	26	0.54±0.00	2.31
3.	*Berberis chitria*	760	6.29±1.15	34.29
4.	*Daphne cannabina*	2853	7.99±1.32	68.44
5.	*Desmodium elegans*	426	2.93±1.47	15.49
6.	*Desmodium gangenticum*	893	2.93±0.23	24.27
7.	*Hypericum lysimachioides*	426	2.69±1.44	18.06
8.	*Indigofera dosua*	1000	2.93±1.92	23.55
9.	*Lonicera quinquelocularis*	66	0.77±0.00	3.14
10.	*Plectranthus japonicus*	1973	7.55±1.53	52.55
11.	*Rubus paniculatus*	160	2.53±0.00	7.73
12.	*Sarcococca hookeriana*	586	2.05±1.67	14.42
13.	*Strobilanthes alatus*	66	0.24±0.00	1.72
14.	*Viburnum coriaceum*	240	2.83±1.29	13.30
15.	*Viburnum cotinifolium*	280	2.11±0.00	13.16
	Total	**10035**	**45.07±5.60**	
		Climber		
1.	*Clematis buchananiana*	120	2.63±0.00	43.43
2.	*Hedrera nepalensis*	26	1.07±0.00	16.40
3.	*Parthenocissus himalyana*	453	3.58±1.87	109.22
4.	*Rubia cordifolia*	213	2.21±0.00	65.79
5.	*Smilex aspera*	186	1.55±0.86	48.74
6.	*Smiles parvifolia*	66	0.16±0.00	16.39
	Total	**1064**	**11.20±1.86**	

Herb Layer

A total of 31 herb species were recorded on this site. Total herb density ranged from 63630 ind/ha (winter season) to 253230 ind/ha (rainy season) and total ground cover from 28.1±12.8 (summer season) to 50.9±8.8% (rainy season). Individual herb density varied from 330 ind/ha (*Ajuga parviflora* and *Polentilla fulgens*) to 15660 ind/ha (*Viola canescens*) during winter season, 660 ind/ha (*Conyza japonica*) 25330 ind/ha (*Viola canescens*) during summer season and 330 ind/ha (*Anaphalis cinnamomea* and *Hedychium spicatum*) 46830 ind/ha (*Ainsliaea aptera*) during rainy season. The percent ground cover was maximum for *Senecio rufinervis* (6.7±1.1%) during rainy season followed by *Carex condensata* (5.3±0.6%) during winter and summer (Table 11.5).

Ridge Site

Tree Layer

A total of 12 species were recorded on ridge site. *Quercus leucotrichophora* was the most dominant species (IVI=67.13%). Total tree density was 1187 ind/ha. Individual density ranged between 3 ind/ha (*Quercus floribunda*) to 283 ind/ha (*Quercus leucotrichophora*). Total basal area recorded was 40.02±10.7m^2/ha (Table 11.3).

Sapling Layer

Saplings of 09 tree species were present on this site. Total sapling density was 2809 ind/ha. Individual density ranged between 12 ind/ha (*Alnus nepalensis*) and 746 ind/ha (*Rhododendron arboreum*). Total basal area of saplings was 7.43±0.01 m^2/ha (Table 11.3).

Seedling Layer

Seedlings of 08 tree species were present on this site. Total seedling density was 1933 ind/ha. It was maximum for *Lyonia ovalifolia* and *Myrica esculenta* (367 ind/ha) and minimum for *Carpinus viminea* (111 ind/ha). The individual seedling cover varied from 0.06±0.03 (*Carpinus viminea*) to 0.82±0.65 cm^2/ha (*Lyonia ovalifolia*, Table 11.3).

Shrub Layer

A total of 13 shrub species were recorded on this site. *Desmodium gangenticum* was most dominant species (IVI=53.5%). Total shrub density was 6728 ind/ha. Individual density ranged from 53 ind/ha (*Rubus lasiocarpus*) to 1600 ind/ha (*Desmodium gangenticum*). Total crown cover percent was 30.46±1.06% and ranged from 0.39±0.00% (*Eupatorium adenophorum*) to 6.37±3.61% (*Viburnum coriaceum*, Table 11.3).

Table 11.3: Vegetational Parameters of Different Vegetation Layers on Ridge Site

Sl. No.	Name of Species	Density (Ind/ha)	Total Basal Area (m²/ha)/ Canopy Cover (%)	IVI (%)
1	2	3	4	5
		Tree		
1.	*Alnus nepalensis*	13	0.46±0.00	3.67
2.	*Carpinus viminea*	06	0.08±0.00	2.15
3.	*Cornus capitata*	50	0.65±0.43	12.31
4.	*Lyonia ovalifolia*	250	8.85±4.39	61.19
5.	*Myrica esculenta*	170	4.80±2.40	39.28
6.	*Pinus roxburghii*	53	6.72±5.03	27.73
7.	*Pyrus pashia*	20	0.32±0.12	6.80
8.	*Quercus floribunda*	03	0.03±0.00	1.05
9.	*Quercus leucotrichophora*	283	10.70±5.79	67.13
10.	*Rhododendron arboreum*	223	5.69±1.79	49.43
11	*Rhus wallichii*	20	0.22±0.00	5.82
12	*Symplocos crataegoides*	96	1.50±0.43	23.35
	Total	**1187**	**40.02±10.75**	
		Sapling		
1.	*Alnus nepalensis*	12	0.08±0.04	2.43
2.	*Carpinus viminea*	146	0.21±0.12	14.44
3.	*Lyonia ovalifolia*	573	1.49±0.66	58.77
4.	*Myrica esculenta*	266	0.90±0.32	32.54
5.	*Pinus roxburghii*	120	0.23±0.16	12.82
6.	*Quercus floribunda*	93	0.28±0.15	11.70
7.	*Quercus leucotrichophora*	613	1.91±0.47	66.81
8.	*Rhododendron arboreum*	746	1.55±0.21	69.46
9.	*Symplocos crataegoides*	240	0.78±0.31	30.97
	Total	**2809**	**7.43±0.01**	
		Seedling		
1.	*Carpinus viminea*	111	0.06±0.03	16.66
2.	*Lyonia ovalifolia*	367	0.82±0.65	70.60
3.	*Myrica esculenta*	367	0.69±0.19	64.76
4.	*Pinus roxburghii*	289	0.16±0.16	33.23
5.	*Pyrus pashia*	144	0.15±0.00	22.38

(Contd...)

1	2	3	4	5
6.	*Quercus leucotrichophora*	178	0.17±0.15	27.89
7.	*Rhododendron arboreum*	255	0.21±0.05	36.32
8.	*Symplocos chinensis*	222	0.13±0.01	28.15
	Total	**1933**	**2.39±0.07**	
		Shrub		
1.	*Berberis asiatica*	426	2.71±1.37	24.48
2.	*Berberis chitria*	346	3.44±1.75	21.48
3.	*Cotoneaster acuminata*	160	0.95±0.56	9.60
4.	*Daphne cannabina*	853	2.84±0.83	32.30
5.	*Desmodium gangenticum*	1600	3.55±1.22	53.51
6.	*Eupatorium adenophorum*	66	0.39±0.00	4.52
7.	*Indigofera dosua*	1213	2.89±1.01	48.52
8.	*Leptodermis lanceolata*	333	1.77±0.00	14.68
9.	*Myrsine Africana*	146	0.67±0.00	6.61
10.	*Plectranthus japonicus*	706	2.57±1.64	26.11
11.	*Rubus ellipticus*	173	1.04±0.00	9.20
12.	*Rubus lasiocarpus*	53	1.27±0.00	4.77
13.	*Viburnum coriaceum*	653	6.37±3.61	44.17
	Total	**6728**	**30.46±1.06**	
		Climber		
1.	*Parthenocissus himalayana*	906	6.76±3.64	187.50
2.	*Rubia cordifolia*	200	1.41±0.91	54.41
3.	*Smilex aspera*	160	0.59±0.00	38.03
4.	*Vallaris solanaces*	66	1.03±0.00	20.52
	Total	**1332**	**9.79±1.86**	

Climber Layer

A total of 4 climber species were recorded on this site. *Parthenocissus himalyana* was the most dominant climber (IVI=187%). Total climber density was 1332 ind/ha. It was maximum for *Parthenocissus himalayana* (906 ind/ha).Total crown cover percent was 9.79±1.86%. Individual crown cover varied from 0.59±0.0% (*Smilex aspera*) to 6.76±3.6% (*Parthenocissus himalayana*, Table 11.3).

Herb Layer

A total of 25 herbs were recorded on this site. Total herb density ranged from 60300 ind/ha (summer season) to 241460 ind/ha (rainy season) and total ground cover varied from 23.8±5.4% (winter season) to 38.4±12.4% (rainy season). Individual herb density varied from 330 ind/ha (*Galium rotundifolium*) to 16660 ind/ha (*Carex condensata*) during winter, 3330 ind/ha (*Conyza japonica* and *Potentilla nepalense*) to 19330 ind/ha (*Ocimum tenuiflorus*) during summer and 1000 ind/ha (*Aster pedeiculris*) to 31000 ind/ha (*Ainsliaea aptera*) during rainy season. Percent ground cover varied from 0.2% (*Galium rotundifolium*) to 5.0±1% (*Carex condensata*) during winter, 0.8% (*Viola canescens*) to 5.3±3% (*Potentilla nepalense*) during summer and 0.5±0.05% (*Geranium nepalense* and *Oplismenus compositus*) to 3.8±0.9% (*Carum anathifolium* and *Desmodium polycarpum*) during rainy season (Table 11.5).

Moist Site

Tree Layer

A total of 17 tree species were recorded on this site. *Quercus leucotrichophora* was the most dominant species in terms of IVI (57.26%). Total tree density was 1089 ind/ha. The individual density ranged between 3 ind/ha (*Cinnamomum tamala*) and 230 ind/ha (*Rhododendron arboreum*). The total basal area was 46.98±8.03 m^2/ha (Table 11.4).

Sapling Layer

A total of 18 sapling species were recorded on this site. *Quercus leucotrichophora* was the most dominant species in terms of IVI (40.29%). Total density of saplings was 2028 ind/ha. Individual density ranged between 12 ind/ha (*Aesculus indica*) and 252 ind/ha (*Quercus leucotrichophora*). Total basal area recorded was 6.83±0.03 m^2/ha (Table 11.4).

Seedling Layer

A total of 8 seedling species were recorded on this site. On the basis of IVI values *Quercus leucotrichophora* was the most dominant species (IVI=79.29%). Total seedling density was 886 ind/ha. Individual density ranged between 33 ind/ha (*Betula alnoides*) and 222 ind/ha (*Quercus leucotrichophora*). Total seedling cover for the site was 0.91±0.04 m^2/ha (Table 11.4).

Shrub Layer

A total of 17 shrub species were recorded on this site. *Desmodium elegans* was the most dominant species (IVI=55.2%). Total shrubs density was 7113 ind/ha, while individual shrub density ranged from 26 ind/ha (*Rosa brunorii*) to 1493 ind/ha (*Desmodium elegans*). Total crown cover percent was 34.26±1.76% and ranged from 0.35±0.00 (*Rosa brunorii*) to 6.21±5.3% (*Rubus paniculatus*, Table 11.4).

Table 11.4: Vegetational Parameters of Different Vegetation Layers on Moist Site

Sl. No.	Name of Species	Density (Ind/ha)	Total Basal Area (m²/ha)/ Canopy Cover (%)	IVI (%)
1	2	3	4	5
		Tree		
1.	*Aesculus indica*	26	2.80±0.00	11.26
2.	*Betula alnoides*	6	0.09±0.00	1.91
3.	*Carpinus viminea*	50	3.63±2.89	18.12
4.	*Cinnamomum tamala*	3	0.03±0.00	0.91
5.	*Cornus capitata*	63	1.65±1.34	16.27
6.	*Cornus macrophylla*	36	0.74±0.38	8.95
7.	*Lyonia ovalifolia*	200	5.61±3.78	43.08
8.	*Machilus duthiei*	33	1.42±0.00	7.79
9.	*Meliosma pungens*	6	0.06±0.00	1.83
10.	*Myrica esculenta*	103	3.29±1.91	25.18
11.	*Osmanthus Fragens*	40	1.52±1.08	12.71
12.	*Pyrus pashia*	20	0.45±0.25	6.28
13.	*Quercus glauca*	20	4.33±3.20	16.86
14.	*Quercus leucctrichophora*	190	11.61±5.13	57.26
15.	*Rhododendron arboreum*	230	8.78±2.69	54.33
16.	*Rhus wallichii*	50	0.78±0.32	13.22
17.	*Symplocos crataegoides*	13	0.19±0.04	3.91
	Total	**1089**	**46.98±8.03**	
		Sapling		
1.	*Aesculus indica*	12	0.08±0.00	2.71
2.	*Betula alnoides*	40	0.15±0.00	6.79
3.	*Carpinus viminea*	144	0.23±0.17	16.76
4.	*Cinnamomum tamala*	184	0.48±0.39	22.47
5.	*Cornus capitata*	92	0.26±0.17	14.71
6.	*Cornus macrophylla*	80	0.43±0.24	14.75
7.	*Ficus nemoralis*	24	0.07±0.00	3.93
8.	*Lyonia ovalifolia*	144	0.62±0.31	25.21
9.	*Machilus duthiei*	144	0.42±0.28	20.48
10.	*Meliosma pungens*	132	0.36±0.00	16.27
11.	*Myrica esculenta*	52	0.16±0.12	7.53

(Contd...)

1	2	3	4	5
12.	*Osmanthus fragens*	120	0.56±0.28	19.53
13.	*Prunus cerasoides*	40	0.10±0.00	6.18
14.	*Quercus glauca*	92	0.28±0.15	14.90
15.	*Quercus leucotrichophora*	252	1.04±0.45	40.29
16.	*Rhododendron arboreum*	240	0.93±0.58	36.27
17.	*Rhus wallichii*	184	0.52±0.19	23.84
18.	*Symplocos crataegoides*	52	0.14±0.11	7.29
	Total	**2028**	**6.83±0.03**	
	Seedling			
1.	*Betula alnoides*	33	0.03±0.00	12.10
2.	*Lyonia ovalifolia*	66	0.05±0.00	18.20
3.	*Machilus duthiei*	111	0.07±0.05	29.78
4.	*Myrica esculenta*	66	0.06±0.00	19.31
5.	*Osmanthus fragens*	144	0.16±0.00	48.49
6.	*Quercus glauca*	178	0.26±0.23	68.27
7.	*Quercus leucotrichophora*	222	0.22±0.04	79.29
8.	*Rhus wallichii*	66	0.06±0.00	
	Total	**886**	**0.91±0.04**	
	Shrub			
1.	*Arundinaria falcata*	746	2.50±1.36	34.11
2.	*Berberis asiatica*	133	1.24±0.95	7.76
3.	*Daphne cannabina*	640	2.43±0.78	26.94
4.	*Desmodium elegans*	1493	4.88±1.09	55.25
5.	*Desmodium gangenticum*	453	1.05±0.54	18.31
6.	*Eupatorium adenophorum*	386	1.80±0.91	15.11
7.	*Hypericum lysimachioides*	653	2.04±1.23	24.33
8.	*Indigofera dosua*	386	1.61±0.84	14.66
9.	*Leptodermis lanceolata*	93	1.52±0.90	4.94
10.	*Maesa indica*	266	0.79±0.51	16.70
11.	*Myrsine africana*	506	2.25±1.38	18.31
12.	*Plectranthus japonicus*	160	0.99±0.49	8.31
13.	*Rosa brunorii*	26	0.35±0.00	2.54
14.	*Rubus ellipticus*	40	0.63±0.00	2.07
15.	*Rubus paniculatus*	266	6.21±5.28	15.89
16.	*Sarcococca hookeriana*	520	1.09±0.55	14.67
17.	*Viburnum coriaceum*	346	2.88±1.47	19.97
	Total	**7113**	**34.26±1.76**	

(Contd...)

1	2	3	4	5
		Climber		
1.	*Hedrera napalensis*	80	0.69±0.00	12.36
2.	*Parthenocissus himalyana*	533	10.17±1.49	125.29
3.	*Smilex aspera*	493	2.67±1.74	69.84
4.	*Smilex parvifolia*	120	0.73±0.00	21.64
5.	*Vallaris solanaces*	52	0.69±0.00	10.63
6.	*Vitis capreolata*	266	2.42±1.25	60.22
	Total	**1544**	**17.37±2.78**	

Climber Layer

A total of 6 climber species were recorded on this site. *Parthenocissus himalayana* was the most dominant species (IVI=125.2%). Total climber density was 1544 ind/ha. Individual climber density ranged from 52 ind/ha (*Vallaris solanaces*) to 533 ind/ha (*Parthenocissus himalyana*). Total percent crown cover was 17.37±4.48%. Individual cover varied from 0.69±0.00% (*Hedrera napalensis* and *Vallaris solanaces*) to 10.17±1.49% (*Parthenocissus himalyana*, Table 11.4).

Herb Layer

A total of 35 herb species were recorded on this site. Total herb density ranged from 105940 ind/ha (winter season) to 352900 ind/ha (rainy season) and total ground cover from 27.5±8.0% (winter season) to 53.74±18.3% (rainy season). Individual herb density varied from 330 ind/ha (*Micromeria biflora*) to 13330 ind/ha (*Ocimum tenuiflorus*) during winter season, 660 ind/ha (*Desmodium polycarpum*) to 28660 ind/ha (*Oplismenus compositus*) during summer season and 330 ind/ha (*Galium aparine*) to 47660 ind/ha (*Viola canescens*) during rainy season. The percent of herb ground cover was maximum for *Carex codensata* (5.8±0.7%) during winter season followed by *Geum elatum* (5.6±2.3%) during summer season and 4.8±2.4% for *Desmodium polycarpum* during rainy season (Table 11.5).

Species Diversity and Concentration of Dominance

The species diversity in different sites ranged from 2.9 to 3.5 for tree and sapling, 2.3-3.07 for seedlings, 3.16 to 3.6 for shrub, 2.7 to 4.48 for herb and 1.37 to 2.17 for climber. In contrast, concentration of dominance varied from 0.120 to 0.177 for trees, 0.093 to 0.161 for sapling, 0.138 to 0.234 for seedling, 0.098 to 0.178 for shrub and 0.098 to 0.178 for herbs.

Dominance Diversity Curve

The dominance diversity curves were drawn for tree, shrub, herb and climber layers across all sites. The curves of tree layer on stream bank, dry site, ridge site and moist sites showed a geometric progression. The curves of shrubs, herbs and climber layer showed the log normal sequence (Fig. 11.1).

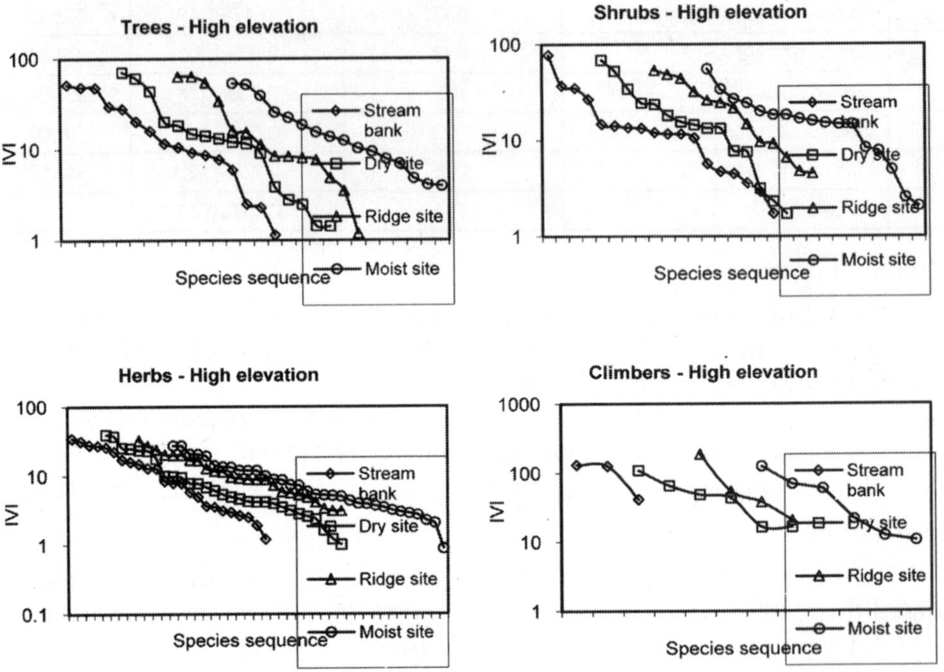

Fig. 11.1: **Dominance Diversity Curve of Different Vegetation and Sites**

DISCUSSION

Species richness, relative abundance, heterogeneity, spatial or temporal distribution in an area are the central subjects of community ecology (He and Legendre, 2002). The tree density was maximum on ridge site (1187 ind/ha) and low on dry site in the present study (808 ind/ha). The sapling density was high in dry site and low in moist site. The individual seedling density was low in stream bank habitat. These values lies within the range 350-2460 ind/ha reported earlier for different Himalayan forest of Garhwal and Kumaun region (Singh and Singh, 1987; Giri *et al.*, 2008; Rawat, 2012; Rawat and Chandra, 2013). All these studied forests are situated between 1700-3000 m elevational transect in the Central Himalaya.

Generally *Quercus leucotrichophora, Q. floribunda* and *Q. semecarpifolia* with other co-dominant evergreen and broadleaf deciduous species are predominant forests at this elevation. The total tree species richness in the present study was high in all the habitats, except at moist habitat, because of low disturbance, which provides time for germination and growth of many species. Maximum seedlings were present on ridge habitat because chir-pine mixed forest had high regeneration potential compared to oak dominated forest. In the present study density value of herbs was reported between 63630- 149620 ind/ha during winter season, 60300-161600 ind/ha during summer season and 100390-378200 ind/ha during rainy season.

Kumar (2000) reported total density of herbs from 1,19,000 ind/ha to 1,94,500 ind/ ha during winter, 2,27,000 ind/ha to 3,62,000 ind/ha during summer and 2,27,000 ind/ha to 3,62,000 ind/ha during rainy season. Similarly, Singh *and Singh* (1992) reported total herb density ranging from 75,000-25,800 ind/ha during winter, 27,000-153,000 ind/ha during summer and 96,000-3,62,000 ind/ha during rainy season. These values are almost similar as reported in the present study. The seedling cover was high in both dry and ridge habitats.

The Total tree basal area was reported between 35.64±5.66 and 70.02±12.56 m^2/ha. It was higher on stream bank habitat in the present study. The values of basal area reported for the present study are within the range reported earlier by different workers (Singh *et al.* 1994; Ram *et al.* 2004; Kumar 2005). Both density and total basal area declined abruptly at high elevations, above 2400 m and 3000 m elevations. Tree density and basal area values varied in the middle elevational transects. From 1800 to 2800 m elevation, the mean basal area per tree varied widely. Low to moderate number of trees were encountered in stands located above 3000 m. However, at mid-elevation stands, tree size and density varied both within and among forest types. Several forest stands located between 2400 and 2800 m elevation had low density but high mean basal area.

This was largely observed for stands of *Q. semecarpifolia* where *R. arboreum* trees formed dense under canopy layer. Low value of diversity in dry habitat and high in moist habitat were observed at high elevation. The sapling diversity was low in dry habitat and high in moist site. Seedling diversity was high in moist habitat and low diversity value was recorded in ridge habitat in the present study. The diversity values for the tree layer in the present study were within the range (0.88-3) reported for other Central Himalayan forests located at similar elevational range (Rawat and Chandra, 2013 ; Ram *et al.* 2004; Giri *et al.* 2008; Saxena and singh, 1982; Sriwastawa et. al., 2008;). The herb species diversity was high in moist habitat and low in stream bank habitat.

This revealed that the herb species diversity was low towards high elevations. The diversity of climber was low in ridge habitat and high in moist habitat. This indicates that the climber species diversity was high towards high elevations. The distribution and species richness pattern in this elevational range largely depend on the altitude and climatic variables like rainfall, temperature etc.

Table 11.5:

Sl. No.	Species	Winter Density (ind/ha)	A/F	Ground Cover (%)	IVI	Summer Density (ind/ha)	A/F	Ground Cover (%)	IVI	Rainy Density (ind/ha)	A/F	Ground Cover (%)	IVI (%)
	Stream Bank Site												
1.	*Aechmanthera gossypiana*	–	–	–	–	–	–	–		16330	0.13	5.3±1.0	27.24
2.	*Ainsliaea aptera*	8660	0.05	3.0±1.5	36.73	5660	0.14	2.3±0.4	17.54	27000	0.12	4.4±1.9	34.77
3.	*Anaphalis busua*	1000	0.10	0.2±0.0	3.80	10330	0.56	2.3±0.9	18.88	1330	0.13	0.3±0.0	2.65
4.	*Anaphalis cinnamomea*	–	–	–	–	–	–	–	–	11660	0.05	1.8±0.0	12.94
5.	*Anaphalis contorta*	3330	0.02	0.3±0.0	12.34	330	0.03	0.3±0.0	2.22	2000	0.07	0.1±0.0	2.49
6.	*Capollipedium assimile*	–	–	–	–	–	–	–	–	8660	0.05	0.5±0.0	7.85
7.	*Carex filiana*	–	–	–	–	–	–	–	–	14660	0.05	1.1±0.0	12.70
8.	*Carex condensata*	25330	0.08	5.5±1.1	85.03	3000	0.13	3.4±1.8	14.68	18000	0.07	2.6±1.5	22.41
9.	*Carpesium cernuum*	1330	0.13	1.7±1.0	11.54	–	–	–	–	1000	0.03	0.8±0.0	3.65
10.	*Carum anathifolium*	–	–	–	–	12330	0.10	4.4±2.2	29.42	3330	0.04	2.1±0.0	8.43
11.	*Conyza japonica*	2660	0.03	2.5±0.0	18.11	9000	0.13	2.0±0.6	21.81	1330	0.02	0.4±0.0	3.55
12.	*Cyperus niveus*	660	0.07	0.2±0.0	3.30	1330	0.13	1.3±0.7	9.15	16660	0.23	1.8±1.1	15.93
13.	*Desmodium polycarpum*	–	–	–	–	6000	0.08	4.2±2.1	22.69	11660	0.07	5.1±0.7	25.95
14.	*Fragaria indica*	1660	0.02	1.7±0.0	13.60	–	–	–	–	–	–	–	–
15.	*Galium rotundifolium*	–	–	–	–	–	–	–	–	3000	0.02	0.4±0.0	4.99
16.	*Gentiana capitata*	1000	0.10	0.8±0.0	6.08	–	–	–	–	–	–	–	–
17.	*Gerbera macrophylla*	–	–	–	–	18000	0.13	4.8±1.8	39.73	2330	0.11	0.9±0.5	5.84
18.	*Geum elatum*	1000	0.10	2.3±0.0	11.76	13330	0.15	2.3±1.3	23.65	4660	0.05	1.6±0.0	7.88
19.	*Hyperium elodeoides*	–	–	–	–	2330	0.12	1.9±1.1	11.48	–	–	–	–

(Contd…)

		Winter				Summer				Rainy			
Sl. No.	Species	Density (ind/ha)	A/F	Ground Cover (%)	IVI	Density (ind/ha)	A/F	Ground Cover (%)	IVI	Density (ind/ha)	A/F	Ground Cover (%)	IVI (%)
20.	*Ocimum tenuiflorus*	–	–	–	–	7000	0.34	2.9±0.6	20.14	660	0.07	0.1±0.0	1.21
21.	*Oplismenus compositus*	–	–	–	–	–	–	–	–	32000	0.12	2.6±0.6	31.59
22.	*Pilia scripta*	–	–	–	–	25000	0.29	3.9±2.5	37.04	19330	0.36	2.1±1.0	17.19
23.	*Pimpinella diversifolia*	–	–	–	–	2660	0.04	0.8±0.5	10.12	2000	0.05	0.3±0.0	2.96
24.	*Pouzolzia hirta*	–	–	–	–	–	–	–	–	660	0.07	0.4±0.0	1.91
25.	*Ranunculus diffusus*	–	–	–	–	5000	0.13	1.2±0.0	9.44	–	–	–	–
26.	*Scutellaria angulosa*	12330	0.08	1.2±0.4	41.61	4330	0.02	1.0±0.0	11.96	1330	0.03	0.5±0.0	3.11
27.	*Sencio rufinervis*	8330	0.06	7.0±2.3	56.08	–	–	–	–	10660	0.03	5.0±0.8	27.91
28.	*Stellaria paniculata*	–	–	–	–	–	–	–	–	5000	0.03	2.8±1.5	14.83
	Total	**67290**		**26.4±0.62**		**125630**		**39.0±2.11**		**215250**		**43.00±3.44**	
						Dry site							
1.	*Ainsliaea aptera*	8330	0.07	2.8±0.7	41.00	7000	0.14	0.6±0.3	14.61	46330	0.10	5.6±0.4	39.54
2.	*Anaphalis busua*	–	–	–	–	11330	0.04	1.9±1.2	25.60	–	–	–	–
3.	*Anaphalis cinnamomea*	–	–	–	–	13660	0.24	2.0±0.9	30.54	330	0.03	0.2±0.0	1.01
4.	*Ajuga parviflora*	330	0.03	0.5±0.0	4.05	–	–	–	–	3000	0.03	0.8±0.0	4.21
5.	*Carex condensate*	13330	0.09	5.3±0.6	60.95	11660	0.22	2.9±0.9	28.20	18660	0.04	2.8±0.4	23.11
6.	*Carex nubigena*	–	–	–	–	–	–	–	–	5000	0.13	0.3±0.0	3.53
7.	*Corpesium cernum*	–	–	–	–	–	–	–	–	4000	0.04	1.0±0.0	5.00
8.	*Conyza japonica*	–	–	–	–	660	0.07	1.0±0.0	5.40	1330	0.13	0.1±0.0	1.21
9.	*Cyperus niveus*	1660	0.02	1.9±0.0	14.55	1660	0.04	0.3±0.0	5.05	14330	0.10	2.9±0.2	17.70
10.	*Desmodium polycarpum*	–	–	–	–	4330	0.06	3.6±2.1	22.92	18000	0.04	4.4±0.8	25.51

(Contd...)

		Winter				Summer				Rainy			
Sl. No.	Species	Density (ind/ha)	A/F	Ground Cover (%)	IVI	Density (ind/ha)	A/F	Ground Cover (%)	IVI	Density (ind/ha)	A/F	Ground Cover (%)	IVI (%)
11.	*Erigeron karvinskianus*	–	–	–	–	–	–	–	–	3660	0.02	0.3±0.0	3.98
12.	*Galium aparine*	–	–	–	–	–	–	–	–	660	0.07	0.2±0.0	1.62
13.	*Galium rotundifolium*	–	–	–	–	–	–	–	–	2000	0.05	0.3±0.0	2.35
14.	*Geranium grandiflorum*	–	–	–	–	2660	0.02	0.8±0.0	10.22	5000	0.09	0.9±0.6	6.18
15.	*Geranium nepalense*	–	–	–	–	–	–	–	–	6000	0.02	0.8±0.0	6.87
16.	*Gerbera macrophylla*	–	–	–	–	–	–	–	–	21660	0.09	4.6±0.4	24.91
17.	*Geum elatum*	6000	0.07	1.7±0.0	20.69	8330	0.05	3.8±2.1	30.94	17660	0.06	4.7±0.4	23.52
18.	*Hedychium spicatum*	–	–	–	–	2000	0.05	0.5±0.0	6.06	330	0.03	1.0±0.0	2.58
19.	*Ocimum tenuiflorus*	11330	0.31	5.2±2.7	44.52	14330	0.25	1.2±0.6	24.53	–	–	–	–
20.	*Ophiopogon intermedius*	–	–	–	–	–	–	–	–	8330	0.02	0.8±0.0	7.79
21.	*Oplismenus compositus*	2000	0.20	3.5±1.8	18.58	3330	0.33	2.2±1.5	13.30	2330	0.02	0.4±0.0	3.17
22.	*Polygonum amplexicaule*	–	–	–	–	–	–	–	–	4660	0.24	0.7±0.6	4.67
23.	*Polentilla fulgens*	330	0.03	0.3±0.0	3.38	4330	0.13	1.3±0.7	12.24	3660	0.01	0.2±0.0	4.27
24.	*Pouzolzia hirta*	–	–	–	–	660	0.02	0.2±0.0	3.80	1660	0.04	0.6±0.0	2.80
25.	*Ranunculus diffuses*	–	–	–	–	–	–	–	–	5330	0.02	1.7±0.0	7.88
26.	*Satyrium nepalense*	–	–	–	–	–	–	–	–	3000	0.13	0.8±0.5	4.21
27.	*Scutellaria angulosa*	4660	0.08	4.2±2.6	34.03	–	–	–	–	8660	0.02	1.9±0.0	10.08
28.	*Sencio kunthianus*	–	–	–	–	–	–	–	–	7660	0.07	1.6±0.9	9.57
29.	*Sencio rufinervis*	–	–	–	–	–	–	–	–	34000	0.05	6.7±1.1	37.32
30.	*Verbascum thapsus*	–	–	–	–	1000	0.05	4.5±2.4	20.65	1660	0.04	3.7±1.9	9.87
31.	*Viola canescens*	15660	0.12	3.4±1.2	58.24	25330	0.11	1.3±0.1	45.94	4330	0.08	0.9±0.6	5.43
	Total	**63630**		**29.8±4.72**		**112270**		**28.1±1.30**		**253230**		**50.9±4.97**	

(Contd…)

Sl. No.	Species	Winter				Summer				Rainy			
		Density (ind/ha)	A/F	Ground Cover (%)	IVI	Density (ind/ha)	A/F	Ground Cover (%)	IVI	Density (ind/ha)	A/F	Ground Cover (%)	IVI (%)
						Ridge site							
1.	*Ainsliaea aptera*	7330	0.06	2.1±1.1	31.49	–	–	–	–	31000	0.10	2.9±1.5	27.22
2.	*Anaphalis cinnamomea*	1000	0.03	0.6±0.0	7.35	–	–	–	–	17660	0.06	2.3±1.1	17.03
3.	*Anaphalis contorta*	4000	0.10	1.3±0.0	14.79	7330	0.32	3.4±0.9	41.37	3330	0.08	0.6±0.0	4.18
4.	*Aster pedeiculris*	–	–	–	–	–	–	–	–	1000	0.10	0.8±0.0	3.11
5.	*Carex condensata*	16660	0.07	5.0±1.2	71.00	3660	0.37	2.0±1.7	19.32	15000	0.04	1.2±0.6	16.79
6.	*Carum anathifolium*	–	–	–	–	–	–	–	–	17660	0.13	3.8±0.3	24.04
7.	*Conyza japonica*	11660	0.11	3.4±1.0	50.12	3330	0.20	2.3±1.0	25.13	5550	0.09	1.1±0.6	8.89
8.	*Desmodium polycarpum*	–	–	–	–	–	–	–	–	8000	0.10	3.8±0.9	20.04
9.	*Erigeron karvinskianus*	–	–	–	–	6000	0.15	5.1±3.2	40.94	6660	0.09	1.3±0.7	9.24
10.	*Galium rotundifolium*	330	0.03	0.2±0.0	2.99	–	–	–	–	7660	0.08	1.4±0.7	11.78
11.	*Geranium nepalense*	–	–	–	–	–	–	–	–	1330	0.13	0.5±0.3	3.09
12.	*Gerbera macrophylla*	–	–	–	–	–	–	–	–	28000	0.07	3.5±0.7	32.51
13.	*Lespedeza gerardiana*	–	–		–	–	–	–	–	16660	0.10	1.6±0.9	16.66
14.	*Ocimum tenuiflorus*	13330	0.28	4.3±0.9	49.74	19330	0.16	2.1±0.6	66.24	19660	0.24	2.3±0.8	20.34
15.	*Oplismenus compositus*	–	–	–	–	11660	0.20	1.5±0.8	38.26	11000	0.03	0.5±0.0	9.58
16.	*Pedicularis pectinata*	–	–	–	–	–	–	–	–	2660	0.03	0.9±0.0	5.30
17.	*Pennisetum flaccidum*	–	–	–	–	–	–	–	–	8660	0.09	0.9±0.5	9.66
18.	*Potentilla nepalense*	1000	0.10	2.0±0.0	11.56	3330	0.13	5.3±3.1	34.75	2000	0.01	0.6±0.0	4.87
19.	*Polentilla fulgens*	–	–	–	–	–	–	–	–	9000	0.10	1.3±0.0	8.97
20.	*Pouzolzia hirta*	–	–	–	–	–	–	–	–	5660	0.34	1.2±0.6	7.33

(Contd...)

		Winter				Summer				Rainy			
Sl. No.	Species	Density (ind/ha)	A/F	Ground Cover (%)	IVI	Density (ind/ha)	A/F	Ground Cover (%)	IVI	Density (ind/ha)	A/F	Ground Cover (%)	IVI (%)
21.	*Ranunculus diffuses*	–	–	–	–	–	–	–	–	1330	0.13	0.6±0.3	3.35
22.	*Scutellaria angulosa*	3660	0.11	1.1±0.5	20.11	–	–	–	–	1660	0.09	1.2±0.9	5.68
23.	*Sencio nedicaulis*	1660	0.04	2.5±0.0	16.32	–	–	–	–	8000	0.10	2.0±1.1	12.87
24.	*Verbascum thapsus*	–	–	–	–	1660	0.17	2.1±1.1	16.41	2660	0.02	0.9±0.0	5.92
25.	*Viola canescens*	6000	0.07	1.3±0.7	24.46	4000	0.04	0.8±0.0	17.57	9660	0.19	1.2±0.4	11.48
	Total	**66630**		**23.8±0.24**		**60300**		**24.6±5.03**		**241460**		**38.4±0.55**	
	Moist site												
1.	*Ainsliaea aptera*	8000	0.09	2.6±1.1	27.98	5660	0.22	0.8±0.4	10.47	26660	0.06	3.9±1.9	20.74
2.	*Ajuga parviflora*	5660	0.25	1.2±0.6	14.58	–	–	–	–	6660	0.05	1.9±0.0	8.82
3.	*Anaphalis busua*	4330	0.03	0.8±0.0	11.88	1330	0.03	0.5±0.0	5.14	1660	0.04	0.4±0.0	2.06
4.	*Anaphalis contorta*	1660	0.12	2.0±1.4	12.50	–	–	–	–	8330	0.14	1.6±0.8	7.46
5.	*Apluda mutica*	–	–	–	–	–	–	–	–	20330	0.08	0.9±0.5	12.10
6.	*Carex filicina*	–	–	–	–	–	–	–	–	18330	0.04	1.9±1.0	14.24
7.	*Carex condensata*	12660	0.28	5.8±0.7	44.02	22330	0.10	2.4±1.7	35.22	34000	0.06	3.9±0.8	27.48
8.	*Carum anthifolium*	–	–	–	–	–	–	–	–	5000	0.02	0.9±0.0	5.21
9.	*Conyza japonica*	8330	0.05	1.4±0.7	21.49	1330	0.03	0.6±0.0	5.44	3330	0.04	0.8±0.0	3.70
10.	*Cyananthus microphyllus*	–	–	–	–	–	–	–	–	3000	0.08	1.2±0.0	3.93
11.	*Cyperus niveus*	–	–	–	–	1330	0.13	0.8±0.6	6.06	11330	0.05	1.4±0.9	10.06
12.	*Desmodium polycarpum*	–	–	–	–	660	0.07	4.0±2.0	15.36	19660	0.05	4.8±2.4	19.59
13.	*Elsholtzia strobilifera*	–	–	–	–	–	–	–	–	3000	0.08	0.8±0.0	3.19
14.	*Erigeron karvinskianus*	–	–	–	–	–	–	–	–	7660	0.04	1.6±0.8	8.96

(Contd…)

		Winter				Summer				Rainy			
Sl. No.	Species	Density (ind/ha)	A/F	Ground Cover (%)	IVI	Density (ind/ha)	A/F	Ground Cover (%)	IVI	Density (ind/ha)	A/F	Ground Cover (%)	IVI (%)
15.	*Fragaria indica*	–	–	–	–	8000	0.20	1.4±0.0	12.63	–	–	–	–
16.	*Galium aparine*	5330	0.13	0.4±0.0	8.92	2000	0.20	0.2±0.0	3.36	330	0.03	0.2±0.0	0.88
17.	*Galium rotundifolium*	6660	0.04	1.0±0.0	14.81	–	–	–	–	16000	0.06	2.3±1.2	13.47
18.	*Gentiana capitata*	5000	0.08	1.0±0.5	15.68	–	–	–	–	9330	0.17	1.4±0.9	7.37
19.	*Geranium grandiflorum*	–	–	–	–	–	–	–		3330	0.08	0.5±0.0	2.72
20.	*Gerbera macrophylla*	–	–	–	–	–	–	–	–	16330	0.09	2.4±2.0	12.07
21.	*Geum elatum*	9330	0.09	2.7±1.4	25.95	6660	0.05	5.6±2.3	36.53	3660	0.02	0.9±0.0	4.40
22.	*Hedychium spicatum*					3330	0.13	4.1±3.5	18.91	6330	0.07	1.2±0.0	5.29
23.	*Micromeria biflora*	330	0.03	0.5±0.0	3.25	–	–	–	–	3660	0.04	0.9±0.0	3.98
24.	*Ocimum tenuiflorus*	13330	0.18	0.7±0.5	21.22	5660	0.22	1.6±0.7	12.91	4000	0.04	0.6±0.0	3.52
25.	*Oplismenus compositus*	–	–	–	–	28660	0.19	2.8±1.5	40.94	16000	0.05	1.3±0.9	12.03
26.	*Oxalis latifolia*	2660	0.07	0.6±0.0	7.13	5330	0.06	0.3±0.0	8.71	9660	0.24	0.8±0.0	5.08
27.	*Pimpinella diversifolia*	–	–	–	–	–	–	–	–	3660	0.08	1.3±0.3	6.00
28.	*Polygonum amplexicaule*	–	–	–	–	22000	0.27	1.8±1.0	26.48	–	–	–	–
29.	*Potentilla fulgens*	3330	0.03	0.2±0.0	5.09	1660	0.12	0.6±0.0	4.34	3660	0.09	0.6±0.0	3.01
30.	*Scutellaria angulosa*	9330	0.21	3.3±0.4	31.79	2660	0.02	1.2±0.0	10.89	20660	0.10	4.2±1.0	20.87
31.	*Senecio kunthianus*	–	–	–	–	1330	0.02	1.0±0.0	8.01	3000	0.03	0.4±0.0	2.86
32.	*Senecio rufinervis*	–	–	–	–	–	–	–	–	12000	0.13	3.0±0.6	13.64
33.	*Sonchus asper*	–	–	–	–	–	–	–	–	3660	0.06	1.2±0.7	5.39
34.	*Verbascum thapsus*	–	–	–	–	1330	0.02	0.5±0.0	6.48	1000	0.03	0.6±0.0	2.25
35.	*Viola canescens*	10000	0.08	3.3±0.7	33.63	19330	0.22	2.5±0.5	32.06	47660	0.19	3.9±1.6	27.54
	Total	**105940**		**27.5±8.55**		**140590**		**32.7±7.77**		**352900**		**53.7±1.67**	

REFERENCES

1. Arora, R.K. (1993). Himalayan Resources, Diversity and Conservation, In: U. Dhar (ed.) Himalayan Biodiversity. Gyanodaya Prakashan, Nainital. 2: 39-55.
2. Bauer, H.L. (1943). The Statistical Analysis of Chaparral and Other Plant Communities by means of Transect Samples. Ecology 24: 45-60.
3. Chandra, J, Rawat, V. S, Rawat, Y.S. and Ram, J. (2010). Vegetational Diversity Along an Altitudinal Range in Garhwal Himalaya, *International Journal of Biodiversity and Conservation* 2(1): 14-18.
4. Curtis, J.T. (1959). The Vegetation of Wiscousin. An Ordination of Plant Community. University Wisconsin Press, Madison, Wisconsin. 657 pp.
5. Curtis, J.T. and McIntosh, R.P. (1950). The Interrelations of Certain Analytic and Synthetic Phytosociological Characters. Ecology, 31: 438-455.
6. Giri, D,. Tiwari, L.M. and Tamta, S. (2008). Quantitative Analysis of Tree Species in Oak Dominant Forests of Uttarakhand Central Himalaya, *Indian Journal of Botanical Research,* Vol. 4(2): 315-318.
7. He, Fangliang and Legendre, Pierre. (2002). Species Diversity Patterns Derived from Species-Area Models. *Ecology,* 83(5): 1185-1198.
8. Kumar, A. (2000). Plant Biodiversity in Forests of Middle Central Himalaya in Relation to Various Disturbances. Ph.D. Thesis, Kumaun University, Nainital.
9. Kumar, P, Bhatt, J. and Ram, J. (2005): Diversity of Herbaceous Plant in Mid-elevation Forests of Uttaranchal Himalaya. Van Vigyan a Journal of Forestry Science 39: 82-90.
10. Odum, E.P. (1971). Fundamentals of Ecology. W.B. Saunders Co., Philadelphia.
11. Pearman, B. Peter, (2002). The Scale of Community Structure: Habitat Variation and Avian Guilds in Tropical Forest Understory: Ecological Monographs 72(1), 19-39 pp.
12. Ram, J., Tewari, B. and Arya, N. (2004). Variation in Plant Biodiversity of Chir-pine and Banj-oak Forests of Uttaranchal Himalaya. In: Muthuchelian (ed.) Biodiversity Resources Management and Sustainable Use. Centre for Biodiversity and Forest Studies, Madurai, 54-56 pp.
13. Rawat, V.S. and Chandra, J. (2013). Human Impact on Diversity Gradient Around Govind Pashu Vihar National Park of Uttarakhand. *International Journal of Advanced Biosciences* 1(2): 10-16.
14. Rawat, V.S. and Chandra, J. (2012). Tree Layer Vegetational Analysis in Temperate Forest of Uttarakhand. *Nature and Science* 10(10):167-171.
15. Saxena, A.K. and Singh, J.S. (1982). A Phytosociological Analysis of Woody Species in Forest Communities of a Part of Kumaun Himalaya. Vegetatio, 50: 3-22.
16. Srivastava, A.K. Tewari, A. Shah, S. and Tewari, B. (2008). Species Composition an. Regeneration Pattern Along a Transect Perpendicular to a River Course in Foot Hill Deciduous Tropical Forest of Kumaun Indian Journal of Forestry 31(1) 7-12.
17. Shannon, C.E. and Weaver, W. (1963). The Mathematical Theory of Communication. University of Illinois Press, Urbana.
18. Singh, J.S. and Singh. S.P. (1987). Forest Vegetation of the Himalaya, Botanical Review, 52: 80-192.
19. Singh, J.S. and S.P. Singh, (1992). Forest of Himalaya: Structure, Functioning and Impact of Man, Gyanodaya Prakashan, Nainital, India.

20. Singh, S.P. Adhikari, B.S. and Zobel, D.B. (1994). Biomass Productivity, Leaf Longevity and Forest Structure in Central Himalaya, Eeo. Monog. 64: 401-421.
21. Simpson, E.H. (1949). Measurement of Diversity. Nature, 163: 688.
22. Snedecor, G.W. and Cochran, W.G. (1967). Statistical Methods, Oxford and IBM, New Delhi, 593 pp.
23. Solbrig, O.T. (eds.) (1991). From Genes to Ecosystems: A Research Agenda for Biodiversity. International Union of Biological Sciences, Paris, France.
24. Whittford, P.B. (1949). Distribution of Woodland Plants in Relation to Succession and Clonal Growth. Ecology, 30: 199-208.

Index